BY DUTY BOUND

★ ★ ★

BY DUTY BOUND

SURVIVAL AND REDEMPTION
IN A TIME OF WAR

★ ★ ★

BRIGADIER GENERAL
EZELL WARE, JR. (CA, RET.)

AND JOEL ENGEL

DUTTON

DUTTON
Published by Penguin Group (USA) Inc.
375 Hudson Street, New York, New York 10014, USA
Penguin Group (Canada), 10 Alcorn Avenue, Toronto,
Ontario M4V 3B2, Canada (a division of Pearson Penguin Canada Inc.)
Penguin Books Ltd., 80 Strand, London WC2R 0RL, England
Penguin Ireland, 25 St. Stephen's Green, Dublin 2,
Ireland (a division of Penguin Books Ltd.)
Penguin Group (Australia), 250 Camberwell Road, Camberwell, Victoria 3124,
Australia (a division of Pearson Australia Group Pty. Ltd.)
Penguin Books India Pvt. Ltd., 11 Community Centre, Panchsheel Park,
New Delhi - 110 017, India
Penguin Group (NZ), cnr Airborne and Rosedale Roads, Albany,
Auckland 1310, New Zealand (a division of Pearson New Zealand Ltd.)
Penguin Books (South Africa) (Pty.) Ltd., 24 Sturdee Avenue,
Rosebank, Johannesburg 2196, South Africa

Penguin Books Ltd., Registered Offices: 80 Strand, London WC2R 0RL, England

Published by Dutton, a member of Penguin Group (USA) Inc.

First printing, March 2005
10 9 8 7 6 5 4 3 2 1

 REGISTERED TRADEMARK—MARCA REGISTRADA

LIBRARY OF CONGRESS CATALOGING-IN-PUBLICATION DATA

Ware, Ezell.
   By duty bound : survival and redemption in a time of war / by Ezell Ware, Jr., and Joel Engel.
      p. cm.
   ISBN 0-525-94861-9 (hardcover : alk. paper)
   1. Vietnamese Conflict, 1961–1975—Personal narratives, American.   2. Racism—United States.
3. Ware, Ezell. I. Engel, Joel, 1952–   II. Title.
   DS559.5.W369 2005
   959.704'3'092—dc22   2004019857

Printed in the United States of America
Set in Sabon
Designed by Leonard Telesca

This book is printed on acid-free paper. ∞

This book is dedicated to Mr. Oscar Rothenberg, the man who was first to insist that this story be told, and who inspired and compelled me, through friends and relatives, to tell it. Because of him, I had to face past events that I'd long ago buried deep within the crevices of my subconscious. Though reluctant to face them, I was forever mindful of not wanting to let Oscar down. He deserved my best, which is what I have given here—and I am the better for it. Thank you, Oscar. I owe you much more than you will ever know and than I can ever repay.

AUTHOR'S NOTE

Since birth, it seems, I have kept my eyes focused on the future and my feet moving in that direction. As a friend once put it, "You keep going till you get there, then you keep going."

That attitude has served me well, but I know that there have also been downsides to my single-mindedness. One of them was that I too often paid too little attention to other people, as though they were simply marching by me in a parade. To some degree that's typical of a career military man, who knows up front that most service relationships come with a built-in expiration date and so doesn't extend himself the way civilians do. And yet, I'm sure that I was more guilty than most lifers. There were times in my life when I felt less afraid of wartime enemies than of human intimacy.

I admit this to you by way of an explanation for why, in this book, I've intentionally changed the names of everyone outside of family and childhood friends: I didn't want anyone wondering why I happened to remember one name but not another, and so decided that it was more polite to give everyone new names. (By the way, though I dislike political correctness, I tried to make the names ethnically accurate, at least to the degree that I remembered them.) Then, too, a number of soldiers and pilots I knew—many of them good friends—never came back at all or came back without either their wits or their limbs. I did not want to reopen past hurts for them and/or their surviving loved ones who might read this.

Never give in. Never give in. Never, never, never, never—in nothing, great or small, large or petty—never give in, except to convictions of honour and good sense. —Winston Churchill

BY DUTY BOUND

PREFACE

Since 1975, it has become an article of faith—conventional wisdom—that the Vietnam War was the wrong war at the wrong time in this country's history. I disagreed then, and I disagree now. Communism throughout the twentieth century was philosophically expansionist, which was why the domino theory won over so many believers and why there was, in fact, a cold war. "Who lost China?" was a topic debated everywhere, from kitchens to classrooms to water coolers to the White House, after Mao rose to power. Remember, America's entry into South Vietnam was only twenty years after the end of World War II, and it was clear by then that fifty million lives would've been saved if only Hitler had been stopped at the Rhineland—which wouldn't even have required a great military victory.

I don't consider it debatable that if Presidents Kennedy and Johnson had allowed another communist domino to fall in South Vietnam through inaction, the dominoes would have kept falling, because there would have been no reason for the imperial communist powers to stop knocking them over; they would've continued to grab countries, and millions more people would have been subjected to the kinds of unspeakable atrocities that the citizens of

South Vietnam and Cambodia endured after United States soldiers withdrew from Vietnam. At some point, the West was going to have to stop the monster from eating—and in the early 1960s it looked like Vietnam was the right place to confront it.

Now, you'll get no argument from me that the prosecution of the war was flawed and even bungled; that's what happens when politicians and bureaucrats, not field generals, make decisions. But to believe that the world would have turned out as it did— with democracy on the rise and communism on the descent— whether or not we spilled the blood of tens of thousands is a violation of logic; believing that requires believing that the outcome would've been the same even if everything else had been different. You can't extrapolate that way in science—pretend that the test group and control group are identical—and you certainly can't do that in history. It seems highly unlikely to me that the Soviet Union would have crumbled when it did or that China would have opened its doors to, first, President Nixon, and then to the West if not for our fight in Vietnam. Which is why I will go to my grave believing that every man and woman who served in our war there served for a good and noble cause, one that future historians will someday recognize and applaud.

1

There are wars and then there are wars, and within every war there are wars within wars.

In Vietnam, it's sometimes hard to tell which war I'm fighting. I know who the enemy is down there, in the jungle, and I know I'm supposed to be on the same side as Burdett, the man just behind me in the cockpit, but I also know he hates me as much as Charlie does. Probably more. Charlie doesn't really hate me; he just wants me dead so I can't kill him. But if he does hate me, it's because I'm an American, and Charlie hates all Americans the same—white, black, yellow, and brown. That's a rational hatred—a hatred for your wartime enemy, and it's nothing personal. Burdett's hatred is personal.

Burdett here, he doesn't think of me as American. He thinks of me as a Negro—something less than he is—and he tolerates me because those are his orders. He's stuck flying missions with me, the two of us sent way out in the jungle for hours, but he still can't figure out how the Army let a black man into the cockpit of a helicopter gunship and taught him to fly it into battle. Every time we get back to camp in Thailand, he runs out of there like a guy who's been holding his nose around a stink. That's all right; I'm in no hurry to share a laugh and a smoke with him, either. I'm here for me, and for those guys down there, not for him. I don't like flying with him any better than he likes being paired with me, but I can hide it better than he can; I've had a lifetime of practice.

I remember the day a few months ago when the eight of us from the two Cobra fire teams in our group met for the first time at a JUSMAG headquarters building in Wonju, Korea. It was strictly business from the beginning. Lieutenant Colonel Armstrong made the team pairings; what he based them on, I don't know. Burdett winced and whispered "Damn," when he learned which of us was Lieutenant Ware—*The only nigger in the group,* he must've been thinking—and when he opened his mouth, I knew why: that drawl in his voice.

It's not from Mississippi, that's for sure; I'd recognize a Mississippi or Alabama voice. So I don't know where exactly he's from—and won't ask—but if there's a lot more like him here, and there probably are, just keep me the hell away. That would be the only good reason to ask, so I can avoid the territory.

I make him for thirty-one or -two, but maybe that's just because of his weight. He's not quite fat, but he is the heaviest helicopter pilot I've ever flown with or seen. Tall and round-shouldered, like an offensive lineman, he has dark hair and a ruddy complexion, and he walks with a bully's ugly swagger. I can easily imagine him picking on smaller kids in school, just because he could. My guess is that he comes from a military family, with his great-grandfather probably fighting for the South in the Civil War—and that he's proud of old Grandpappy.

"You know how to fly, boy?" he teased when we met. "Or you just get this job 'cause the Army needs to show how open-minded it is?"

"Well," I said, "I guess you're gonna find out."

Why am I spending any time thinking about him—this pilot who I heard killed a woman and her ox one day just for target practice? Why aren't my eyes peeled on the jungle for the enemy?

Because it wouldn't make any difference anyway if we saw a platoon of friendlies being wiped out in an NVA ambush. A week ago we happened to fly over a line of American soldiers—and we knew they were Americans because they were black and white—being marched single file north, along the Vietnam–Cambodian border, to either their deaths or POW camps, which in most cases was the same thing. Instead of firing a few rockets that would've freed them all, we couldn't do a thing about it because our missions were bigger and more important, so we were told, than a single man or a dozen of them. I could imagine how these soldiers felt when they heard our chopper up there and thought they'd been delivered—and then when nothing happened.

Our number one task is to complete our mission and not be sidetracked by anything that might compromise it. Besides, what would happen to the war, let alone us, if the North Vietnamese Army or Vietcong shot down an unmarked Cobra helicopter flown by two pilots wearing jeans and T-shirts and vests? They would know that we're flying top-secret missions, and would use some of their excruciatingly creative ways of extracting information from human beings who prefer to keep secrets. No matter that each of us knows only what we know; we're not privy to the whole picture, so all the torture would be for naught anyway—unless you count the pleasure they take from it.

I look at my watch and make some quick mental calculations. I say, "We better burn some time, Captain. Cut it to eighty knots. We don't want to be there a minute early."

"There" was a rendezvous with a troop transport helicopter (called a slick because of its unadorned exterior) that was either picking up or dropping off Special Operations troops deep in the jungle of the Central Highlands. We don't know which, because we're not supposed to know which.

Burdett checks his watch and the gauges; obviously, he's making his own calculations to confirm mine. Satisfied, he cuts his airspeed without a word.

"Stinger two-three," I say to the other gunship crew trailing us by a hundred yards, "reduce your airspeed to eighty knots."

"Wilco," Lieutenant Roeper says.

We soon near the coordinates. I radio the slick pilot: "Playmaker three-five, this is Stinger one-niner, approaching position. Please advise your location."

"Stinger one-niner," he says, "we are half a mile from checkpoint—at your three o'clock."

"Roger that," I say, and now I can see the slick approaching. I alert my other gunship.

Burdett guides our Cobra about thirty meters wide of the slick as it descends toward a small clearing. We come in at about sixty knots, keeping to just above the tree level, and swoop down to give the slick cover in case of enemy attack, then come back up and clear the trees. Right behind us is Roeper's Cobra, covering both us and the slick from any bad guys. It's called a daisy chain attack, and if there really were bad guys down there shooting, we'd both be firing a torrent of rockets and mini-guns. These Cobras are lethal flying machines, like an airborne destroyer.

But not only are we not firing, the slick isn't actually at its real rendezvous point yet. This is a feint, in case the enemy is in the area, watching and waiting to launch an ambush. It's the first of several feints, actually, with both gunships making two passes each before the slick moves to the location known only to the pilot. We follow him.

After the second pass at the fourth location comes word, "Stinger one-nine, this is Playmaker three-five. Mission completed."

"Roger that," I say, still not knowing whether we've helped pick up or drop off; foliage was in the way. "Headed home." Then to Roeper's chopper: "Stinger two-three, mission complete. Return to base. Do you copy?"

"Stinger one-niner, wilco. See you back home."

Burdett and I watch the other Cobra leave before falling in about a half mile behind.

"Another mission complete," I say.

"Yeah," Burdett says. "Let's get back and have a cold one." He means it facetiously, like saying, "I want to share my girlfriend, Raquel Welch, with you." "Oh, I forget, you don't drink," he says, which, short of "You don't know what the fuck you're doing," is about the worst insult there is between pilots.

I let it slide. "So what do you think the mission was?" I ask. "Drop off, pick up, what?"

He says, "I don't have a damn clue what this shit is all about," and I can hear evil in his grin when he adds, "and if I did, I wouldn't tell you."

It's so childish, I'd feel silly even having a comeback for that.

I check our altitude—about four hundred feet and climbing. We're planning to go between mountains in the range instead of over them. Suddenly there's a flash, like the sun off a moving mirror.

Wham!

Where the shot came from—or what hit us—neither of us could see. It feels like we've crashed into a tank.

"What the hell was that?" Burdett says.

I say, "We're hit."

The instruments are going redline. We're losing power fast.

"Mayday, mayday," I say into the radio. "Stinger two-three, this is Stinger one-niner. Mayday, mayday."

No response.

I try the other frequency, to contact the slick pilot. "Mayday, mayday. Playmaker three-five, this is Stinger one-niner. Mayday, mayday."

No response.

I keep trying, hoping that the radio can still transmit even if it can't receive—all the while looking for a possible landing zone.

I try the UHF emergency frequency: "This is Stinger one-niner, at coordinates three-six-eight, two-four-four. Mayday, mayday. Receiving enemy fire. Mayday, mayday." That lets any aircraft within hearing distance know that there's an emergency and the area is hot.

Burdett cuts the engine to idle, pushes down on the collective, and cuts the throttle—doing everything by the textbook to make an emergency landing. We're definitely going down.

Burdett has the descent under control, but for how much longer? We're moving at sixty knots, going down at the rate of five hundred feet a minute, making small turns left and right. There's no way to tell how long before all the transmission fluid leaks out. It could all go any second, so we have to find some sort of clearing where we can set down—and fast. But not too fast. We better not come down too near the point of impact or whoever shot at us will be able to quickly track us down. Given how fond the enemy is of captured pilots, that's not a good option. We have to stay just above the treetops, where the jungle canopy will keep them from seeing where we're heading.

Right now we're traversing wildly, searching for any sort of clearing.

"Nothing over here," I say.

"Nothing here," he says.

As the seconds tick on, we have to be less choosy. The treetops are suicide—but that's still better than what Charlie has in mind for us.

Even so, I'm not panicked or nervous, and I'm sure Burdett isn't, either. I've been in this situation before, and no doubt he has, too. Besides, we've been trained for this.

"There," I say, pointing to the right. "Right there."

"That?" he says. "That little thing?"

It *is* a little thing—a small patch of green that's only slightly obscured by low-hanging branches.

"I don't see anything else, Captain. We either take it or take our chances."

"All right."

Burdett brings the helicopter down to fifty feet, eases slightly back on the cyclic, and pops the collective to reduce the speed of the main rotor. The chopper's skids hit the tops of the trees and luckily don't catch. He then levels the aircraft. I call off the altitude from the dial. As we reach ten feet Burdett pulls smoothly up on the collective to increase the rotor pitch, hoping to halt the chopper's forward movement and set it down gently.

We hit, not too hard, but I feel a jolt in my back, like electricity.

I turn around to check on Burdett. My back spasms.

"You okay?" I ask.

"Yeah, you?"

"Yeah."

There's no chance any good guys saw us go down. Our only hope for a quick rescue is to reach someone on the radio. I try one last time, on all frequencies, to report our approximate coordinates.

"We better get out of here, Captain."

"Anyone ever tell you, Ware, you have a command of the obvious?"

I unstrap myself and start to climb out. The back doesn't hurt now. Adrenaline's the best painkiller there is.

"Shit," he says. "Shit, shit, shit."

Only now does Burdett become aware that whatever hit us went through the bottom of the chopper and whacked his left leg, just below the knee. It's ugly, and it looks like it hurts like a son of a bitch.

"Can you move it?"

"Just help me get the hell out of here."

He grabs my hand and I pull him up. He winces and whimpers as the leg straightens, and when he comes out of the chopper, I notice he lands only on the right leg—and then immediately sits on his bottom.

"Crap," he says.

"Captain, we have to get out of here before this thing blows." Fuel was leaking onto the ground.

I offer him my hand, he knocks it away, gets up onto both feet, and limps as fast as he can to the edge of the clearing. I follow him in.

"We'll wait here a minute," he says. "If it doesn't blow, we'll blow it ourselves."

A minute's a long time when the guys who shot down your helicopter are right now running through the jungle looking for you.

Twenty seconds, thirty, forty—I'm staring at my watch, tapping my toe, and looking over my shoulder. Burdett, he's hardly even in the moment, seemingly oblivious. I don't know if it's the shock of being shot down, or the pain in his leg, or the real possibility that we might die badly out here. He checks his arm holster with the six-round .38 revolver and twenty extra bullets. I do the same.

Ninety seconds now. "Captain, I'll go blow it, and then we beat it as fast as we can."

I run in a crouch to the helicopter and reach in for the first-aid bag and two thermite grenades. There's no point in checking what brought us down. We know the NVA has been using radar-guided .50-caliber rounds six inches long and an inch in diameter. But what's the difference what hit us? I don't care if it was an unlucky bird that did it. I'm here and I have to blow the chopper so the bad guys can't get their hands on our radios and figure out our frequencies. True, the radio's probably dead, and exploding this thing is like shining a movie-premiere spotlight on us; if the bad guys don't know where we are now, they soon will. But our survival isn't the mission. The mission is the mission, and the mission says that nothing is as important as the objective—which we're not privy to.

I pull the pins and am about to drop the grenades inside when I remember I forgot the canteens. I find mine right away, next to my seat; it doesn't have a strap or a belt clip like Burdett's, but I can't find his fast enough. I turn and sprint to the edge of the clearing—Jim Brown in *The Dirty Dozen*—reaching Burdett before the big moment. Now we have to wait, because if the thing doesn't blow I'll do it again. "One thousand one, one thousand two, one thousand three . . ."

It blows. Boy, does it blow.

We recoil at the burst and watch the colors and the flame. That was our helicopter, the one we're not going home in. So what *will* we go home in? And will we go home at all? I'd feel a lot safer if I could take the chopper's rockets and mini-guns with us.

✫✫✫ 2 ✫✫✫

My father was determined not to have an ordinary life. No wonder. For black men born in 1912 and living in the South, an ordinary life meant saying "yassuh" and "nosuh" and sweating over whatever menial jobs white people happened to be offering them on any particular day. Ezell Ware wasn't built for that. His dreams were of hitting behind Babe Ruth in Yankee Stadium or ahead of Dizzy Dean for the St. Louis Cardinals. Instead, he settled for playing first base with the Birmingham Black Barons at the same time that Josh Gibson was catching for the Pittsburgh Crawfords. The Negro Leagues weren't the Major Leagues, but they sure beat working.

When his baseball days were over, Dad still liked playing games better than a day's hard work. He had an uncanny feel for the next card in the deck and whether snake eyes were about to be thrown. Shooting dice in a Mobile alley, he could make ten bucks a week, a lot more than he would have as a human mule plowing someone's fields—and do it without breaking a sweat or dirtying his suit. Dad dressed every morning with a smile and practiced winking at the mirror on his way out. He liked looking fine for the ladies—ladies like Lorena Catchings.

Dad met Mom in 1938. My sister, Dorothy, was born in '39, they lost another baby in '40, and I came along in early '41. Six weeks later, some of Mobile's white citizens paid Dad a quick visit to explain how it had come to their attention that he was unacceptably making his living as a gambler on the streets of their fine city. They gave him two options. He took the second, moving that night to East St. Louis, Illinois.

Mom's wages as a maid weren't enough to feed and house two little mouths by herself, so she and a Trailways bus dropped me off in Magee, Mississippi, 140 miles northwest of Mobile (and forty miles south of Jackson), to live with her parents, Letha and John. Until I graduated high school, I saw her on average twice a year and called her "Auntie." My grandparents were "Ma" and "Pa," and they referred to me not as Ezell but as "Man"—as in, "Man, I'm gonna whop the black off you if you don't come here right now." "Man" was short for "Little Man," because they said that's how I walked around. Even so, I sometimes wondered whether they didn't call me Ezell because they didn't like being reminded of the gambler who'd abandoned their daughter—a "purty feller," my grandmother called him in a way that wasn't admiring. But if they were mad about having me dropped on their doorstep, they never showed it in the eighteen years I lived there. Just the opposite. "Don't you cry, baby," Ma said whenever kids teased me about not having a mother. "I'm yo momma, and yo Aint 'Reen is yo momma, too. So, see, you got two times more momma than dem kids who picking at you."

Magee was a rural town of about twelve hundred, half white, half black. Whites lived within the city limits in pleasant but mostly modest homes. Blacks lived in the "colored quarters"—three separate enclaves on the outskirts—in less appealing houses with cinder-block porches along roads that quickly became muddy marshes when it rained hard, which it did every summer afternoon, the rain as terribly hot as the air and as loud as hail on the tin roofs. On dry days passing cars kicked enough road dust onto the porch to cover you in red if you sat out there longer than an hour. And oh, the flies. They swarmed in the house so thickly that if you clapped your hands you could kill a dozen. "Man, son," Pa would say, "don't let dem flies eat up all dem biscuits." Ma sprayed DDT from one of those pump cans, and I'd sweep up the bodies with a straw broom into a two-foot-square pile six inches deep that was satisfying to hear crackling in the fireplace.

Our house was in what they called the Goodwater section. It had one road in and out. Pa and Ma slept in separate beds in a small bedroom that I shared with them until I was older. The third bedroom was unoccupied except for the days when my mother and Dorothy came for short visits, or when a family member like one of Ma's daughters didn't feel like making the long walk back home after their nightly visit. My grandfather had been an only child, but Ma came from a large family and had had a large family herself, mostly girls. One of her two boys, John, Jr., sharecropped some land not far away. Aunt Leola, married to John McKinnis, lived about five miles from Magee when I was small, and then moved into Magee's colored quarters when I was a teenager. I called her "Aunt Lee" and thought of her as my third mother. "Come 'ere, baby, and get up in my lap," she'd say. "You too little to play with dem other childun." Virginia, Ma's youngest, married Ezra Tatum, and lived a hundred yards down the road. Their son Bo became my good buddy and later my roommate when his parents moved to Chicago. The only person who seemed to have it in for me was Aunt Dora. She never missed an opportunity to say something mean, like, "You ain't gwoin' amount to nuthin'—jes like yer daddy. Ma should send you back to yo momma, but yo momma don't wancha neither. Look atcha, suckin' that nasty thumb. Make me sick."

In winter we huddled around the living room fireplace and then sprinted into bed through the frigid air, sometimes waking with frost in our hair. Till I hit sixteen or so, there was no radio or TV, but we didn't need anything. We had Pa. The old man was a natural storyteller who'd cheer up the night with tales about the family stretching back to the eighteenth century, during slavery. He had a sense of humor, too. "Hey, you hear that rat?" he'd say, cocking an ear and getting my attention before cutting a loud fart that always made me laugh; Ma, too—against her better judgment. And if Pa's mood was right, and maybe the alcohol, too, he'd tell ghost stories—making banshee noises with his voice as punctuation, his fingers drawing monsters in the air that I can still see.

"John," Ma said, "stop scarin' dem chillen wit dem lying haint stories."

Too late. Those were the nights when I'd shake my legs for six hours, if I had to, instead of getting up and running thirty yards in the dark to the privy—a hole in the ground that was scary enough because of the smell and spiders and snakes (whenever it filled up we covered the mound with dirt and dug a new one; toilet paper was either corn cobs or the Sears catalogue). For toothbrushes we stuck wet index fingers in baking soda. Water trickled from a hand-pumped well that I pumped, and electricity—well, the colored quarters hadn't yet been wired. That was just fine, I suppose, because few of us had enough money to pay for electricity or anything that needed it.

The most prosperous man around was the trash collector who lived across the road. Laundry was a two-day chore on clothes that hadn't been new when they were new, and we bathed once a week in water drawn from the well and heated in a pot on the woodstove. I wouldn't have known a shower if you'd told me what it was, and in fact the first one I saw was in Magee's white high school locker room the day I began helping the janitor clean it for a dime when I was ten. He explained how the showers worked—knowledge that came in handy a few years later. I didn't have to embarrass myself taking that first shower in front of people who'd been showering all their lives.

I remember watching Ma and my aunts and some other ladies shelling peas and canning fruit for the winter. Half the time air ended up sneaking through the bent, worn seals on the old mason jars, and by the time we opened them in December and January, the peaches and apples would be ruined. Some winter nights, dinner was only a sweet potato, fresh from the potato bed, baked in the fireplace—and collard greens, always collard greens. I still can't stand them.

As a baby I cried nonstop unless someone held me, so Ma held me. Nothing stayed in my stomach except for goat's milk, so every few days, with me on her hip, Ma walked five miles round-trip to buy some. I'd double up in spasms that looked like I was an epileptic, which is what everyone who knew anything about these things said I was until worms began crawling out of my mouth and other orifices. Then they said I'd surely die before the age of three. Too puny and weak to walk, I'd sit in bed and have visions, talking to ghostlike figures as though they were in the room with me—and reporting their words to my grandmother. She was convinced they were spirits sent to escort me across the river of death. No matter. Ma wasn't going to give me up without a fight. "Ain't gonna let dem worms eat you here, so dey can't eat you down there," she said.

In those days there were no black doctors around, and white doctors either refused to treat blacks or provided them shabby treatment, even when we had the money to pay. It was an old woman, once upon a time a midwife, who gave Ma a thick syrup to feed me as medicine. The sweet syrup tasted good, and in time the worms got smaller and fewer and then disappeared. But it would be a long time before I was healthy enough for Ma to let me out of the house.

"Baby," she said, "I'm gonna learn you to cook, sew, and iron so you won't ever just have to have a woman."

The first time I helped her cook meat—something we ate rarely—she said, "When dat meat begin to boil, dem worms gonna come to de top of da pot. You take dis cup and dip 'em out."

I thought she was kidding. She wasn't.

The guys in white sheets would crowd onto the back of a flatbed truck, light their torches, and barrel through the colored quarters making all the ruckus they could—screaming and hollering and shooting rifles in the air. They needed to get our attention, and they always got it. We kept off the street and watched through the curtains until the crosses stopped burning. I never recognized any of their shoes or their voices, so as far as I knew every white man I saw could've belonged to the Klan—which I suppose was the point.

The first time I happened on a body lying in a ditch, I was walking home from school. I was about eight and had never seen a dead man, but there wasn't really any learning curve needed. The guy had a hole in his forehead the size of a quarter from which stuff had oozed out that the bugs found delicious.

I ran to tell Ma and Pa. "You hush up about that, boy," my grandmother said. "Ain't none of our business."

There was talk of what the man might've done to deserve a bullet in the head. It could've been anything or nothing—and it wouldn't have mattered anyway. Who were we going to complain to? God? Well, as we'd learned in church, God was waiting to reward us for our suffering *after* we got to the other side. The sheriff? No, not in those parts. In those parts, the sheriff didn't answer to black people or take their complaints. So the lesson here was the same as always: to mind your manners and stay out of trouble, even when it's looking for you. If you heard a man screaming and his bones breaking, you learned to keep going and not see what you were seeing and not hear what you were hearing—and to be careful not to trip over his body the next day. That's the way things were. Even so, Ma taught me, "All white people ain't bad, and all colored people ain't good." I never doubted her.

★★★ **3** ★★★

Our operational map is thinly laminated to keep it from crumbling in the humidity. But our survival map, I discover, is written in Vietnamese—and as far as I can tell isn't of recent vintage. At least three of the villages plotted just in our area don't exist anymore and haven't for a while.

Damn, we were only about half an hour from the air base—which at the speed we were going is almost fifty miles. Which puts us right . . . here. I point to it on the map. Yeah, the jungle of the Central Highlands—the middle of nowhere. This is Kontum Province, a hundred miles west of the South China Sea, twenty miles east of the Laotian border, and a mile or so east of a tributary of the Ho Chi Minh Trail.

We were flying east-southeast when they shot us down. The bad guys could see that. Protocol says that we keep going that way and then turn north later. But you don't always do what protocol says. So now it's a game of scissors-paper-rock, guessing what the enemy's going to guess we'll do. Do we keep going the way they know we were before, or do we circle back around them? And is that what they'll predict we'll do?

"I say we keep going east-southeast. At least it's heading some-where we want to be."

Burdett nods. "Can't argue with that."

We go east-southeast. Slowly.

Burdett is limping, and you don't need a medical degree to tell you that this isn't the kind of wound that can heal itself. It's going to get a lot worse, especially in the jungle's wet heat if we're here for any length of time. I keep an ear tuned to the sky, hoping to hear a rescue chopper. The other helicopter crew in my fire team, Roeper's, knows by now that something's happened to us, because we would've checked in with each other at least once in all this time. So that's good.

It's hard enough walking in these black leather and canvas steel-toed boots. I walk a little in front of Burdett, but at his pace. It takes two hands to make way and move through the thick brush, and I'm trying to run interference as much as I can.

Burdett's not making any noise but the pain of moving shows on his face. I hope a branch doesn't snap back on his leg.

We go for forty-five minutes and aren't more than half a mile from the site. We have to get much farther before stopping.

"Let's take a break," Burdett says. He drops down on his butt and straightens his leg with a stifled grunt.

"I'll be right back," I say.

I hand Burdett the first-aid kit and my canteen, and go at my pace now, scouting ahead. It feels good to move fast and I'm tempted for a second to keep going, but only for a second. I can't even think about leaving him, jackass or not. There'd be no honor in it, and I couldn't live with myself for another fifty or sixty years, even if he ended up surviving on his own.

The good news is that I haven't run across an NVA recon team, advance party, or some Vietcong fighters.

I look up at the small patch of blue sky that peeks through the jungle canopy and close my eyes, listening hard for a helicopter's rotor blades. Both Burdett and I have a small emergency transmitter in a vest pocket. There's no point in pressing the ETR's button unless we can actually hear a chopper; its battery doesn't have power to put out farther than that, and anyway the enemy may be listening for our signal on that frequency and use it to home in on us.

It occurs to me to check what's in my other vest pockets besides the ETR. I don't even know, it's been so long since I filled them; you see, I don't snack in the helicopter the way Burdett does. He usually has something in his mouth, even if it's just a cigarette. I'd like a cigarette now, too, but American cigarettes have a unique scent and I don't want to risk some bad guy being downwind. I check my cigarette pocket. A full pack of Marlboros. Good; I'll reward myself later. In the other pockets are three sticks of beef jerky, a small bag of dried peaches, a Payday, and a Baby Ruth—less, I'm sure, than what Burdett's got.

I freeze at a distant sound and cock my head to hear better. Voices. Men's voice's. Coming from just ahead—and getting closer.

Speaking Vietnamese.

I pull my .38 from its holster.

Yes, they're nearer, but they don't sound like they're searching; they sound like they're going somewhere else. How many voices? I can't tell.

I crouch between two leafy bushes. They're close on me now, just on the other side of a thick clump of foliage. But they're walking easily. Must be on a trail. I put one ear to the ground and peer under a cluster of vines. I can see their feet—marching. They all have on the same boots. NVA soldiers. They're not looking for us, but that doesn't mean they won't find us by accident.

I lose count at a dozen soldiers and wait three minutes after the last one to start back. I'm not so sure they won't find Burdett, and I won't be surprised to hear guns and shouting.

Thank God, I hear nothing.

He's still there when I get back, and my boots on the jungle floor hardly get his attention.

He looks relaxed—resigned, actually. He's finished putting a gauze bandage on his leg, and muttering to himself. I don't want to know, not yet anyway, what his leg looks like under the gauze. His injury is obviously the weak link in our survival, and I don't feel like knowing how weak we are until I have to.

"You hear that NVA squad?" I ask.

"Yeah, I heard 'em."

"Captain, we're in bad-guy country. There's a trail just up there, and it looks pretty worn-in. A lot of single-file feet. We have to move farther south, down in here, before we go back east-southeast. Okay?"

He looks up at me, points to my canteen on the ground. "Where's my canteen?"

"Couldn't find it in time."

"Couldn't find it, or didn't want to?"

I'm not in the mood. "Listen, Burdett, we're lucky to have one canteen. You want yours, go back and get it."

He didn't expect that. I didn't expect this: "You drink from that one yet?"

"You mean, have my lips been around the mouth of that canteen? You mean, is my nigger spit still on it? Is that what you mean?"

"You know what I mean," he says.

"Well, to tell you the truth, Captain, I don't remember if I drank from it or not. But I'm sure as hell thirsty now." I hold out my hand for the canteen. "You mind?"

He can't decide whether to take a swig first. In another circumstance, I'd find this funny. Not in this circumstance.

He hands me the canteen and I take a big swallow, then pour some water over my face before offering it back.

It humiliates him, I know, but he needs the water. He takes the canteen—and pours it on his face, not down his throat. He hands it back to me.

"Suit yourself," I say. "Let's go."

I carry the canteen and first-aid kit. We head farther south, and I keep listening for three things in this order: the enemy's voices, the enemy's footsteps, and a rescue helicopter.

All I can hear is us.

I turn around two or three times a minute, to make sure I'm not getting too far ahead of Burdett. His eyes are on the ground ahead, concentrating.

We don't talk. There is nothing either of us knows that the other doesn't.

★★★ **4** ★★★

My uncles worked in the sawmill, Pa was a cotton sharecropper, my grandmother was a housewife, and my aunts were maids—all of them either walking miles to work or hitching rides. They pooled their wages. I'd watch Ma put money in a small tobacco sack that was tied around her neck and see by her reaction that it was never going to be enough.

"Ain't nothing wrong with a good day's work," Pa said. "But boy, if you don't go get some schooling, you gonna end up just like me."

"We want you to have it bette'n us," Ma said, "so get some book-learnin'."

When I was still bedridden, I'm not sure how old I was, she and my aunts asked the white ladies they worked for if they could bring home old books and *Life* magazines. The ladies were delighted that some little colored boy might be interested in and learn more about the big world, and when they heard how I'd hungrily devoured every word and picture, they sometimes set the magazines aside for me even before they got stale.

"Man, you gonna be a smart man someday," Aunt Lee said. "You learn everything you can. Dem books gonna take you away from here. C'mere, baby, bert you some books to read."

Still hanging on a wall in my memory is a *Life* photograph of a Marine returning from the South Pacific after World War II. It was a close-up of his face—happy, sad, proud, angry, weary, and prematurely wise; the face of a man who'd left home a boy; the face of a warrior coming back victorious. He'd obviously seen and done things that I wanted to see and do. For some reason, I ached to be that Marine. That he was white and I was black wasn't a thought that occurred to me, not even in passing. Such a thing didn't seem to matter. As far as I was concerned, we were both Americans, and that gave us more in common than we had differences.

Sharecropping was a hell of a way to earn a living. You didn't make any money until you delivered the cotton at the end of the season and it had been weighed by the man who owned the land and was supposed to pay you what you deserved. Pa would stand under a big fig tree by the side of the road, waiting for Mr. Rankin to drive up with his cash.

Pa worked sunup to sundown, clearing Mr. Rankin's fields, plowing them, planting them, hoeing them, then picking the crop, plowing them again. A mile or so away were the train tracks, and half the time I was with Pa out there and the freight train whistle blew, he'd glance up and say to the wind, "I wish I was on dat train, goin' wherever it goin'. I don't know where it goin', but it'll take me away from here, and dat's enough." He'd look as beaten as the hollow black men I'd seen all over Magee—human piñatas who'd had their dreams and laughter knocked out of them.

Mr. Rankin drove up in his truck and stepped out slowly. Pa watched his feet. He wasn't allowed to look directly at a white man's face and eyes, same as we kids weren't allowed to look directly at our elders. "We ain't never men to white folk," Pa had explained. "We get from being 'boy' to being 'uncle.'"

"Well," said Mr. Rankin, "you made yourself seventy-five dollars this year, Uncle."

"Yassuh," Pa said.

My grandfather hadn't kept an exact count of what he'd turned over—what was the point?—but he was a smart old man and knew that he'd picked maybe four times that much cotton.

Mr. Rankin held up the cash, then made a show of peeling a five spot off the top and stuffing it back in his shirt pocket. "Of course," he said, "that's before the money I loaned you for the seeds."

"Yassuh."

Mr. Rankin handed Pa the cash like he was donating a million dollars to charity—doing Pa a favor, which in a way he was by paying him at all, since there'd be no legal recourse if he got a notion to pay nothing. The most Pa ever made in a year was a hundred dollars.

"Thank you, suh," Pa said.

Mr. Rankin drove off, the tires spitting a cloud of dust.

Pa looked at the crumpled bills and shook his head. "Dammit," he said, "I coulda made more than seventy bucks by stirring shit." It was barely enough to settle his account at the general store for the year's worth of supplies he'd bought to grow the cotton.

And that was considered a good year.

In bad years there wasn't enough to cover the store debts, and if the day by which Pa had promised to pay back the money came and went—his X on the IOU instead of a signature—it wouldn't be long before the shopkeeper and some of his pals, maybe even the sheriff, showed up with pistols and shotguns. They didn't knock politely and inquire as to the whereabouts of Mr. John. They'd just bust down the door if it was locked, demanding to see him. As Ma and Aunt Lee screamed in fear, the men would turn over furniture and mattresses, searching for money or my grandfather. They never found either. We didn't have any hidden money to find, and Pa was up in the rafters with me.

When the men left, promising to be back soon, we'd begin emptying our pockets of pennies and nickels, and begging and borrowing the rest from friends and family until we had enough to cover the deficit.

The first time I was old enough to hide up there with Pa, tasting that shame and fear, was the last time I didn't have any money to throw in the pot.

With the dust kicked up by Mr. Rankin's truck still on his tongue, Pa pulled a bottle from his pocket and swigged some white lightning. He said, "Son, people may shit on you, but don't never let them rub it in." He took another swig, then: "C'mere, Man. Take a sip of dis. Den eat some dirt so yo ma won't smell it on yo breath."

I said no, thanks, Pa, remembering Ma's words every time we'd come home to see him passed out—again. "Son," she'd moaned, "I hope you never drink that whiskey like yo grandpa."

I never have, Ma.

☆　☆　☆

I sold candy for ten cents a bar, keeping two cents as profit. With that money I wrote away for mail-order vegetable seeds and walked with them door-to-door, selling them for a nickel more than I'd paid. Sometimes I'd have corn from the field Pa had planted behind the house, peaches and plums I'd picked from wild trees, and blackberries off bushes. Four out of five people said no, they didn't want to buy anything, but I knew it was more likely they didn't have the money, so I never felt rejected. That helped later, when I sent away for Buster Brown shoes, to sell on consignment (my own usually had cardboard in the bottom to cover holes); it would take a dozen folks saying no before selling one pair, but the profit was good. Even people who said no sometimes tried on a pair just for the pleasure of it—something they couldn't do at the shoe store in town. Blacks weren't even allowed inside. If they wanted to buy a pair, they knocked on the door, pointed in the window to the ones they liked, and told the clerk their size. Whether or not they fit, the deal had been consummated; these shoes belonged to them. Same with clothes. (I got something new so rarely that I can remember every time.)

If you were trying to sell something at a white's home, you had to go around to the back-door entrance and ask the housekeeper to ask the master or mistress. Even if they said no you might get a day's work out of chores that needed doing there—like sweeping up straw or digging foundations.

My sales income went up the year after I bought my first bicycle with money made from picking cotton. At harvest I'd stand on the corner every Saturday and wait for a white man's flatbed to pick up workers for fields that weren't sharecropped. Cotton in the field is full of brambles and thorns, and your fingers callus quickly. Being short then, I didn't have to bend over as far as the adults, so I wasn't fighting backaches. "You grab that cotton sack, baby," Aunt Lee would say, "and pick the row right next to me. We gonna make some of dese white folk money today. You wana try and beat me pickin' dis cotton?"

On a good day I could make one buck—more than Aunt Lee made working all week in a white lady's kitchen—because there was no way to be cheated. The bag weighed what it weighed, and I watched it on the scales. Wet cotton weighed more than dry cotton, so I'd pick as much as possible before the dew evaporated, and one time I even dropped a little water from the creek into my bag.

I gave all of what I made to Ma for our household expenses, and she'd give some of it back to me. My take went up when I told her I was saving to buy a bike because I'd be able to cover more houses faster with my wares instead of lugging them on foot. She made sure I had enough to buy that bike. "Man is smart," she said to Pa. I was earning more than he was, even just working after school and on weekends. I could see he was proud of me, but I could also see something else—like he'd had the manhood kicked out of him, same as those living ghosts all over town. I didn't want any of the money I earned to go for a jar of his corn likker, but that was his business. Even then I knew it was a terrible thing to lose your dreams or to believe that they could never come true.

"A fool and his money soon parted," Ma said. "Just ask yo pa."

★ ★ ★ **5** ★ ★ ★

We've gone far enough off the road now—about two hundred yards—and I'll be happy if we make it another half mile east before dark. We've got about an hour.

I don't think we make it half a mile before we can't see well enough in the jungle twilight to go on any farther. In this light, Burdett stands a chance of something poking his wound when he moves. Even just touching the leg makes him wince.

I get the impression he's too proud to admit that he needs to stop.

"We can't go any more till first light," I say.

Relieved, he collapses under control to his rear.

I squat next to him, both of us quiet. He's breathing hard.

I think back to survival school. What did they teach us to do? I take a swig of water and remember that if you're not dying of thirst yet but you have only a teaspoon of water, you're supposed to clean your feet with it. Your feet and then your crotch. That's because you need your feet to get out of there, and feet covered in blisters and rot make getting out that much harder. Meanwhile, rashes like to grow in dirty moist areas—and no area is dirtier or moister than your crotch in the incubating heat of the Vietnam jungle. A bad rash down there can make survival—actually, *wanting* to survive—almost moot.

First thing we learned in survival school was to assess the situation. All right. My assessment is: We don't have a lot going for us.

I've got a few things to eat, Burdett's probably got a little bit more. There's half a canteen of water, but there'll be streams where we can refill it. Helicopters will come looking for us in the daylight. All we have to do is make it through the night alive and then, in the morning, find someplace clear where they can land.

It sounds easy enough, but Burdett's leg complicates everything. The fact is, a pilot's chance of being rescued lessens with every hour he's down on the jungle floor.

"Captain, I think we best spend the night in that tree up there." I point behind him at the banyan standing out against the twilight. It has a wide trunk and a hundred tentacled roots and branch nooks we can lean against when we sleep—if we sleep. It'll be the easiest tree for him to climb.

He looks at the tree and says, "Yeah, I suppose so." I can see him gathering his strength.

"You might want to relieve yourself first," I say. That's what I start doing.

He looks like he hadn't thought of it, but he turns the other direction from me and in two seconds it sounds like a horse at the stable.

"Christ, I didn't even know I had to take a leak," he says.

When he's finished he faces the tree. Both of us size it up.

"I'll go first," he says.

I watch him try on one leg. The problems, besides the leg, are his big belly and ass. He can't get onto the first Y notch. He needs help.

I could bend down and make my back into a stool, but I don't think I can get past the symbolism, let alone the thought of two-hundred-something pounds on my back, which I know is going to start hurting for real as soon as we stop and rest.

"Here," I say. "A boost." I lean over and cup my hands for his leg. Which leg, though, the bad one or good one? He lifts the good one. I say, "I think you should use the other leg."

"No, this is better," he says.

I've already sized up the physics of the situation. I can see where he's going and where he made his mistake. "Captain, the other leg is going to have to bend and support all your weight going upward, so that's at least double the G force. If you're expecting me to lift you over my head so you can just step, forget it. I'm strong; I'm not *that* strong."

"My way's better."

He steps in with his good leg and I lift as high as I can lift him; the man feels like deadweight. I can get him chest-high. "That's it," I say. My arms quiver, and my back starts to spasm. He gets his bad leg on the tree and tries to push off and up so he can grab the branches and use his upper body strength. He can't. All that weight on the bad leg. Burdett swallows a scream, and I lower him as fast as I can. He turns his backside into the tree to break the final shock when the bad leg hits.

It's getting dark now, and what moon there is won't make it through the canopy. If we can get up there we should be pretty safe from the NVA. As for tigers and snakes and other unwanted visitors—well, first things first. Anyway, tigers and snakes and spiders don't shoot AK-47s.

We exchange eye contact what little we can in the fading light, and I take a deep breath before leaning down to boost him up. He puts his hand on my shoulder for balance and guts out the ride up. It must feel like a sword being rammed through from his sole to his hip, but he doesn't cry out.

As soon as he's chest-high, his good leg catches the tree just right and propels him into the crook. The bad leg never touches, and now he's sitting on a wide branch. He catches his breath and reaches for the first-aid kit and the canteen. I toss them both up, one at a time, and start climbing.

I manage it, and get there in time to see Burdett take a swig of water. Then a second swig. I don't say a thing.

I go the other way from the tree's crook, so we both have more room and a place to lean. He tosses me the water without my asking. I don't know if he wants to see whether I'll drink after him, but I don't care what he wants. I'm thirsty. I take two long swallows. About a third of the canteen is left.

"We ought to bathe your wound," I say, swishing the canteen. "That's all we got."

"I'll get more tomorrow." Then: "Better do it, Captain. Infection sets in fast around here." Silence. "Want me to do it?"

He says, "No," quietly, like a whisper.

I toss him the canteen. He pulls aside the gauze and pours the water on the wound.

"Here," I say, handing him the yellowish antiseptic sulfa powder—or at least I think that's what it is—from the first-aid kit. He sprinkles some on and hands it back. The gauze sags. I don't ask, I just hand him the roll, and he refreshes the wrapping, cutting it with the knife from the sheath at his belt.

Done.

Burdett reaches into his vest and I can hear a candy bar wrapper being opened. I'm not hungry, for some reason, so I'm just still. And I'm curious if or when he's going to ask me if I have any food with me. Not every pilot carries. Some feel superstitious about having something put away for a rainy day; they think it might invite rain. But Burdett didn't pack that stuff away in case of emergency. He did it because he couldn't go very long without eating.

He munches away and doesn't ask me if I want some—or anything else.

I think about that for a while and then decide not to think about it anymore. I light a cigarette and cup my hand over the glowing tip, so it doesn't look like a beacon in the dark. There's nothing I can do about the smoke, but in this dead air it shouldn't be a problem. I drag deeply. The tobacco fills my lungs and feels like life, maybe because it's the first deep breath I've taken since we were hit. My back starts to seize up.

$$\star\,\star\,\star\;\textbf{6}\;\star\,\star\,\star$$

A bunch of us worked as caddies at the golf course three miles up the road, in Sanatorium. I'd ride my bike there just after sunup on weekend mornings during school, and most mornings in the summer, waiting by the caddy shack to be called.

The golfers never asked our names or for our advice, even though we knew the course better than they did. Why would they?

Carrying those clubs that were bigger than me was the easiest dollar I made—easier even than the extra quarter tip for cleaning the clubs and shoes afterward. I'd be done by noon and have the rest of the day to make more money.

Some golf courses would set aside an hour or two once a week, usually around sunup on Sundays, for black caddies to play. But not in Sanatorium. So now and then, during full moons, we'd sneak on at night and play with clubs that golfers had thrown in disgust or bent in frustration. In the dark we might lose sight of the ball and come home with a knot in our foreheads from getting beaned. Some of the guys were pretty good and probably had the talent to give Sam Snead decent competition. Snead himself, after all, had been a caddie from humble beginnings.

When I got a little older I found I could make more money

catching chickens at one of the big chicken farms for fifty cents an hour, sometimes a dollar. That was night work, because in daylight chickens could see you and tried to get away; it was hard enough without that extra fuss. We'd start after dinner at about eight and finish at four or five a.m., usually three times a week. You'd want to bring as many chickens as you could each trip from the house to the truck, so you'd put their legs between your fingers and carry eight at a time in each hand. With the average chicken weighing three pounds, it got to be tiring. But just the same, you'd better stay awake in school the next morning or you'd get a memorable whacking from the teacher.

When someone slaughtered a hog, everyone else stopped by to help scrape off the hair in exchange for a portion of meat or small chunks of fat for making into lard. Then they helped the owner carry the meat to his smokehouse for salting and curing. "C'mon, baby," Aunt Lee would say. "Help me clean dese hog guts. Da hog don't need dem no more." I looked more forward to hog head-cheese, which you made by boiling the head until all the meat fell off, then mixing it with some other ingredients. Nothing went to waste. Our soap came from a process using the shortening after frying the hog fat.

Syrup-making from sugarcane got the same kind of community participation. In exchange for a portion, neighbors showed up to help strip the leaves, send them through the squeezer, and cook what came out. The lower parts of the cane were sweetest, but you couldn't let anything go to waste, so the syrup never had a uniform taste. Meanwhile, the sugar we made wasn't as sweet as the kind we buy today in boxes at the store, but compared to nothing, it was sweet enough. That was pretty much the standard for everything—you compared what you had to having nothing at all.

It didn't take long from when Ma broke me of sucking my thumb by saying, "John, go out there in that chicken house and get some chicken shit so I can wrap it and put it on this boy's thumb," to when she noticed my first pubic hairs on bath day and started singing, "Little boy, little boy, doncha wanna marry? Yes, by God, my nuts getting hairy."

In between I'd gotten old enough to know I'd better carry my work gloves in my back pocket every time I went near town. The custom was for black males of a certain age to carry the gloves in case a storekeeper had some boxes to be moved from here to there, or a landowner wanted brush trimmed, or a truck driver needed help off-loading—but the custom carried the weight of law. Not showing the gloves was grounds for a beating, maybe worse, even if the work you were being conscripted for didn't need gloves, or even if no one needed you to do anything but someone noticed they weren't there. Mostly, whites drove trucks through the colored quarters calling out for workers and stating the terms of work and pay for the day. But for some jobs they could wait for help to just walk by, as it always would. The town, after all, was their domain, and the gloves were a symbol—a way of acknowledging their superiority and our subservience. Boys as young as nine or ten could not only be conscripted, they could be punished. It didn't matter if you were on an errand or going to your real job. It only mattered that you were there and someone with white skin spotted you and shouted out, "C'mere, boy!" You kept your eyes aimed at the ground and said, "Yassuh" and "Thank you, suh"— whether or not he paid you for the work.

$\star\star\star$ **7** $\star\star\star$

Things don't look good. I know that, and I think Burdett must, too. As pilots, we have a standing order to scan for good guys wandering in the jungle and report their position when we get back to base. What happens after we do, I don't know.

The song "Secret Agent Man" keeps running through my head, especially the line that goes, "Odds are you won't live to see tomorrow."

No, I'll live to see tomorrow; that I'm sure of. But it's tomorrow I'm worried about. If we don't get picked up tomorrow, our odds drop way into the red. Every day that goes by means that the bad guys are that much more likely to find us than the good guys are. To tell the truth, I'm not even a hundred percent sure the good guys will send anybody at all. Some missions are like that; one set of lives is more important than another set. I suppose every war is based on such notions.

Anyway, for all we know there's an entire regiment of friendlies operating in the area, and if sending a brigade to look for two people might blow the whole operation, they're not going to do it. My opinion is that we should've heard at least one chopper before dark if they were going to look for us. Either that or Roeper's chopper didn't make it back, either. I don't mention what I think, even though I'm sure Burdett's thinking the same. What's the point?

I say, "Captain, you're in command here. It's up to you to decide what to do if the enemy finds us. Do we fight or give up?"

To me it's no contest. I'd been a Marine. And besides—I am who I am. Giving up or giving in is not in my nature. I start to wonder how I'll hold up under torture, if it comes to that. In training, they teach you to take as much as you can, and then give in. Some men, they taught us, have high pain thresholds. Most don't. We've all heard more than once that you'd gladly throw your own firstborn into the fire if that would make the pain stop. My biggest fear is of being captured and broken, and appearing on North Vietnamese television to denounce my country—a black man reading anti-American propaganda to a worldwide audience, because he can't stand the pain anymore.

"You don't want these people taking you alive," Burdett says. "Believe me."

I believe him. "They won't if I can help it."

★★★ 8 ★★★

A bus passed me as I was walking home from the store. On the side it said "Boy Scout Jamboree," and through the windows I could see two dozen white boys my age wearing freshly pressed khaki uniforms. I asked Pa what Boy Scouts were, and when he told me I decided I wanted to have the same fun.

Here's where black skin in Jim Crow America gave you some kind of ironic advantage—if you managed to take it. Being black was like playing catch with a medicine ball: Unless it killed you, the extra weight made you stronger.

My buddies and I—Downhead (he had a flat head with a high back and low front) and Sleepy (heavy eyelids) and the rest—didn't earn merit badges or board buses for weekend excursions and camps. But our day trips into the woods to catch frogs and fish and rabbits (sometimes using slingshots made from the Y branches of trees), and clean and cook what we'd caught, and eat it in teepees we'd erected, taught us most, if not more, of what Boy Scouts were supposed to learn. And their trips couldn't have been filled with more laughter and camaraderie than ours.

Six of us were still laughing on the way back home one sweaty summer evening, rolling an old flat tire we'd found and pretending it was a car while shooting each other with blowguns using little paper balls as bullets, when we passed a service station. I was thirsty and saw a spigot on the side of a wall. It didn't say "White Only" and anyway looked ratty enough to be a colored's fountain. I turned it on and leaned over. The water hadn't even reached my lips when two white men ran out from inside the station, one of them waving a shotgun at me. "Damn nigger," he said, stopping to take aim. I froze and looked down the barrel. If I'd have run, he'd surely have shot me in the back. My only chance was to not move. The moment lasted a long time but I remember not being afraid; I remember wondering whether they'd kill all my friends, too.

"Don't do it," the other guy said. "They're just little niggers. They don't know better."

The man with the shotgun kept it raised for another three-count—through about a hundred beats of my heart—and then looked genuinely disappointed when he lowered it. "Well, I reckon they do now," he said. "I catch you here again," he said to us, "I'll blow your little black heads off."

Sometime later my friend Monkey and I happened on Magee's tennis courts, where two women were hitting a white fuzzy ball back and forth to each other. We'd seen the courts before but there'd never been anyone on them, and we didn't know what tennis was. I was fascinated by the shape of the rackets and the sound the ball made when struck. We stopped to watch, not even touching the cyclone fence. I don't think the women realized we were there. But a deputy sheriff did. He'd driven by and spotted us.

"Whatchu doin' lookin' at white women?" White women, black women—we were eight and didn't know women from a duck.

"We were watchin' the game," I said.

"Um-hmm," he said. "Come on along."

He handcuffed us and drove us down to the station and put us in a cell on the "nigger" side crammed with a bunch of living ghosts—those men with hollow eyes. We started crying, telling each other they might execute us. The older men never said a thing; they didn't want to give us hope, because it might not be deserved.

After a couple of hours, the deputy came and let us out. I noticed either embarrassment or an apology on his face when he said, "Don't be lookin' at any mo' white women." It wasn't a threat; it was more like telling a child to keep his hands out of the fire. These were the laws of physics Jim Crow style, and they had to be obeyed.

"Doncha be lookin' at any white women," Ma scolded me. "You go down in dem woods and cut me a switch to whop you wit. And you betta not bring me back a little one, cuz if you do, I'm gonna whop you wit it and den make you go get the nother one."

I do believe we'd had God on our side that day. If another white man instead of the sheriff had seen us watching those women play tennis—well, there's no need to imagine the outcome. Five years later a Chicago boy named Emmett Till came to visit some Mississippi relatives in Money, only 160 miles from Magee. He was fourteen and, being from the North, didn't grasp the rules. One day on a street corner he showed his cousin a photo of a white girl who was a friend in Chicago. The other boy pointed to a white woman in a store and dared Emmett to talk to her. Emmett went inside, bought some candy, and on the way out said, " 'Bye, baby," to Carolyn Bryant, whose husband, Roy, owned the store.

A few nights later Roy Bryant and Carolyn's brother, J. W. Milam, showed up at the cabin owned by Mose Wright, Emmett's uncle, and drove off with Emmett. His unrecognizable body was found in the Tallahatchie River, one eye gouged out, his skull crushed, a bullet in his brain.

Emmett's mother insisted his body be shipped back to Chicago, and she left his casket open for all to see his unreconstructed face.

She cried, "Imagine sending a loved son on vacation and having him returned to you in a pine box, so horribly battered and waterlogged that someone needs to tell you this sickening sight is your son—lynched!"

The story made national news and for a week or two it seemed as though whites, even in the South, had joined blacks in agreeing that this was a horrible crime and that the young man hadn't deserved such a fate. Bryant and Milam were arrested and charged with kidnapping and murder. For the first time ever, it looked as though whites in the South were going to be punished for harming someone with black skin. No defense attorney wanted to take the case.

Ma said that would change.

Sure enough, the Mississippi whites who themselves had been outraged soon began resenting the outrage they were hearing from the North; to them it was a replay of the Civil War, with the North imposing itself on the South. This hadn't been a lynching, they insisted, and suddenly half a dozen prominent defense attorneys volunteered to take the case pro bono. John Whitten led the defense team. He played to the jurors, white men who'd been chosen from the voting rolls, which was another reason blacks were never on juries. Even if they'd had the money to pay the poll tax, they couldn't pass the "test" that went along with it—questions like, "How high is high?"

Under questioning by the prosecution, Mose Wright pointed to the two men who'd dragged his nephew away that night, and other blacks from the neighborhood who'd seen them put Emmett in the car did the same. But when Whitten told the jurors in his summation that "your fathers will turn over in their graves if you vote to convict these men, and I'm sure that every last Anglo-Saxon one of you has the courage to free these men in the face of this Northern pressure," there was no doubt how they would vote.

It took only an hour for the jury of their peers to find Bryant and Milam not guilty. That night, under cover of darkness, the NAACP hustled Emmett's uncle and the other prosecution witnesses out of the state for their own protection.

A year later in Alabama, Rosa Parks and Martin Luther King began turning the tide of history. But in my corner of Mississippi, at least, most black people I knew were as resistant to change as most white people were; integration was the devil they didn't know.

"Lord, we don't need no integration," Ma said. "Martin need to stop messing with these white folk." She stuck a finger in my face. "Boy, doncha dare go down there marchin' with dem people. You do, you gonna get yoself killed."

Until the time I left home in 1959, I never knew anyone who had a bank account; never met anyone who voted; never talked to someone who questioned why we had to stand cramped in the back of buses while there were plenty of seats on the other side of the curtain up front. Things were the way they were. This was the natural order.

The mosquitoes and other flying things are enjoying a feast. This may be the best eating they've ever had. I can hear Burdett slapping at his arms and face so fast, it sounds like bongo drums. Me, I don't pay attention to the bugs.

"Dammit," he says. "Goddamn bloodsuckers."

I say nothing.

"What's the deal, Ware? You got some repellent on you're not telling me about?"

"Wasn't any in the kit, Captain."

"So I guess skeeters don't like dark blood."

"Got the same color blood as you."

"Then they must not like dark skin."

"No, they like me fine."

I debate whether to say something sarcastic about how maybe the bugs are attracted to all those candy bars in his pocket—the ones he didn't offer me a bite of. But there's no gain in it. Instead, I tell him about Marine boot camp at Parris Island, where the drill instructors made entire platoons stand at attention for hours under the blistering sun on the hot sand, just so the sand fleas would attack. And boy, did they ever attack—vengefully. Some of us were covered like those beekeepers who let honeybees accumulate on their faces—but if any of us moved even a finger, everyone had to stand there that much longer. I haven't forgotten how to take that kind of punishment. The trick is to tell yourself you don't mind.

"Asshole Marines," Burdett says.

"It wasn't just punishment, Captain," I tell him. "It was to teach us not to give away our position when we're lying in the jungle. Remember, some of those DIs had fought in Okinawa."

There's a long silent moment. Burdett tries not to slap himself. He can't help it. But he doesn't hit quite as hard, and he does lower his voice.

He says, "I didn't know you were a Marine."

"Four years."

"Why'd you get out?"

"I wanted to fly."

"Oh, yeah. Marines used to not let niggers fly. I heard that."

"It's not that simple."

"What're you defending the Marines for?"

"I'm not." But I am.

"*Semper fi* and all that, huh?"

Yeah, all that.

★ ★ ★ **10** ★ ★ ★

My friend Bo and I were walking home along a road between the white part of town and the colored quarters, past a house that looked like an antebellum mansion. It had a large fenced yard with big pecan trees for cool shade. From one of them hung a homemade swing on which a little white girl my age—about nine—was swinging. Every time she went forward her dress lifted up and showed her panties. We made sure to keep our eyes on the ground as we passed, so we didn't accidentally see anything, and tried to hurry past. But the four or five men out front with her stopped us.

"Boy," one of them said, referring to both of us. "Hey, boy."

Uh-oh. That's your first thought—uh-oh. No good can come from a white man calling you over. Had he seen me looking at the little girl? That was a lynching offense.

"Give us a little buck dance and we'll toss you some money."

There was no arguing. We started jumping around, doing something that resembled a tap dance. The men laughed and clapped their hands to the rhythm they wanted us to dance to—"Come on, faster, faster," they said—and threw pennies at our feet. "Smile, boy, smile."

Smiling—that was the hard part. What if one of them turned around and saw the girl swinging the way she was? He'd have known we'd seen her underpants, or could've seen them—which was just the same.

They wouldn't let us stop dancing. "Keep goin', boy." Every once in a while I'd catch a glimpse of that little girl, just swinging and watching us as though something like this happened every day. We went on for more than half an hour until the leader said, "That's enough."

We scrambled for the pennies in the dirt, and I grabbed Bo before we'd gotten them all, worried the girl's father would turn around and see his daughter swinging.

"Hey, there's still more down there," Bo said as I dragged him off. That made the men laugh.

"Stupid little niggers," I heard one of them say, "don't know nothin' about money." They roared again with laughter.

We earned fifteen cents—enough for three twelve-inch Baby Ruths.

☆　☆　☆

School was a big barn. In the middle of it was a makeshift auditorium, with four rooms off to the side. First through fourth grades were in one class, fifth through eighth grades were in another. Between them was a potbelly stove on cinder blocks, which the older boys were in charge of filling with wood gathered from the surrounding field—where, a hundred yards away, two outhouses stood. Younger kids would dart from class to there and sometimes not make it before having an accident. Magee's white schools, of course, were solid brick structures that had modern classrooms with science labs and indoor plumbing and individual desks and hallways and lockers and showers and grass playing fields. They got new textbooks every year, and we got their old ones. In the fall, they started two or three weeks before us. Few black families could pass up the money we kids would make picking cotton, so there was no point in opening up the school for nearly empty classrooms. We'd work under the hot sun by the side of the road and see the white kids being driven to or from class. This was as natural as gravity; no one I knew ever complained about it.

Our teachers were black men and women, some of whom had actually attended college. Education, they insisted, was our only hope to live better than our parents—education and the discipline to use it well. And they relied on harsh punishment to instill discipline, whacking our hands with rulers and switches and our bottoms with something heavier when we acted up or hadn't studied properly. I noticed that the smarter you were, the harder they were on you.

Some of them had been raised in the South but studied up North, and some had been in the military and served overseas. Listening to their tales, I felt like a sixteenth-century European lucky enough to hear Magellan describe what he'd seen in the New World. Just as I couldn't imagine not having gotten immediately on a ship for the Americas, I couldn't imagine staying in Magee any longer than I had to. Of course, one of the reasons I wanted out of Magee so bad was that my ancestors had been forced onto ships bound for the Americas.

"Son," Ma said, "someday I wancha to teach me to write my name."

Too bad that day never came.

★　★　★

Mr. Smith drove his pickup into the colored quarters and asked if anyone wanted to work for twenty-five cents an hour pulling nails out of planks from a demolished house. Eight of us signed on and climbed onto the bed of the pickup for the ride across town. There were so many of us, the job took only five hours till we'd yanked every last nail out of the demolished woodpile, filling a zinc bucket with them. Mr. Smith wandered over, poked around, and declared that we "niggers" had done a right good job. Then he handed each of us a quarter. Not a quarter per hour; a quarter, period.

"All right, let's go, I'll ride you back to the colored side," he said, turning toward his truck.

Well, that was the way of things and there was nothing you could do about it. We started to fall in behind him—all of us, that is, except William Johnson. He was a couple of years older—maybe sixteen—old enough to know better than to do what he did, which was entirely out of character with the quiet and polite William Johnson I thought I knew. He said, "Excuse me, sir, I think you've made a mistake. The pay is supposed to be twenty-five cents an hour. You gave us just twenty-five cents total."

Mr. Smith pivoted in time to see which of us was doing the talking. He almost ran at William when he located him. It's a good thing he didn't have a shovel or a pick or a gun in his hand, or William would've been dead on the spot. William didn't even flinch.

"You say what I thought you said, nigger?"

"I said that you promised twenty-five cents *an hour*." William held out his hand, but still kept his eyes on the ground.

Mr. Smith's face flushed crimson with rage. He was trembling—for a lot of reasons, I imagine, including that he'd been called out by a black man in front of several other black men and there were no other whites around. It's not that he was afraid for his safety; it's that, by himself, he was a two-legged stool.

"Get out of here," he said, and turned away again. "You damn well walk home, too—ungrateful niggers."

"No, sir, we're not leaving till we get what's comin' to us." By saying "we" he'd made us a part of the fight. I don't know how many of us wanted any part of it, believing we could only lose for winning.

The yes-no went on for another couple of rounds. William just kept repeating what the man had promised and how he wasn't going to leave. Then I saw something in Mr. Smith's face that said we were all going to leave there with a buck and a quarter in our pockets.

"Damn," he said quietly, shaking his head.

He used his fingers to work out the total, and watching him struggle I began wondering if he hadn't originally settled on a quarter because that was easier for him. He could've multiplied eight workers times five hours, and then multiplied forty by twenty-five cents—but he didn't. William was smart to wait until the pile had reached ten dollars before saying, "That's right, ten dollars for all of us."

Mr. Smith tried to look contemptuous. "I know that, nigger," he said. "Don't you think I'm smarter than you, boy?" Now he was looking for a fight.

William said, "No, sir, of course I don't. Sorry, sir."

Mr. Smith said, "Good," not realizing he'd been insulted.

We were ecstatic when we left (though we didn't show it till we got farther on toward the colored quarters)—not because William had won some battle with a white man, but because we'd received the money we had worked for. Soon, though, then the silliness left and reality moved in, roosting in each of us down the line. There was a real possibility that we, or at least William, could be killed over what had happened; a group of men might show up that night and do whatever they pleased. None of us had ever seen a black man stand up successfully to a white man, and we doubted that any white man wanted to be known as the first. In that way we'd been fortunate: Only Mr. Smith had witnessed his own humiliation—which is ultimately how we made peace with the anxiety. Surely, we decided, he'd not admit to anyone how he'd been faced down by niggers.

As the days passed, our anxiety lessened and then disappeared. It wouldn't have, though—and I'm sure William would never have confronted Mr. Smith—if we'd been fully aware of the bus boycott in Montgomery, Alabama, that had begun when Rosa Parks refused to give up her seat to a white man. With only one radio station in town, news spread slowly. There'd been violence and people injured, but the reports we'd heard focused on the "troublemaker" named Martin Luther King, pastor of a Montgomery church; it was he, they said, who was inciting the coloreds to rebel. Maybe Mr. Smith had given in to William because he thought we were some of the rebels. If so, that's really funny. Almost everyone I knew who'd heard anything about King—Ma, for example—insisted on not giving whites any reason at all, even accidentally, to prove that Magee was no Montgomery. Even after the Supreme Court outlawed school segregation in 1954, no one even suggested integrating our schools. "No good can come of this," Ma told me. "You keep your head down."

My guess is that something like ninety percent of blacks in Mississippi were too scared of what might happen if they lifted their heads. Over and over, our church pastor preached that our reward awaited us on the other side. I never liked that notion. Why, I wondered, would God put us on this earth for the express purpose of making us miserable just so we can drive nice cars in heaven? Did it mean that all people who lived well and easily would be punished in the next life? It sounded like nonsense to me—and apparently Martin Luther King agreed. Hearing that got my attention, and made me want to learn more. I learned that he'd lived in the North and seen blacks and whites living together in relative harmony, a fact that sounded like fantasy until I read his words from a speech given to the folks he wanted to join him in the boycott; they could've only come from someone who'd seen the possibilities: "We have no alternative but to protest. For many years we have shown an amazing patience. We have sometimes given our white brothers the feeling that we liked the way we were being treated. But we come here tonight to be saved from that patience that makes us patient with anything less than freedom and justice."

I listen for anything and try to discern snakes and other animals from human footsteps. It's not easy. Every fluttering leaf might be an NVA soldier or Charlie guerrilla. The enemy's out there—and even right this minute they're looking for us. Of that, I have no doubt. They shot down a helicopter and didn't find the pilots, so they'll never stop looking till they do. Could be the bounty on the heads of pilots—as much as five hundred bucks. Could be for what we might fetch on the open market. Could be for any other reason, none of which were pleasant.

I haven't heard anything but breathing from Burdett for a while. He must be asleep. I try to settle in myself. Forget it.

"Hey, EZ," he whispers.

"Yeah?"

"You didn't bring a pillow, did you?"

"I think you got one permanently attached down there."

A long pause. He's thinking about it. Now comes a snorting laugh.

I'd ask about his leg, but I don't want to remind him, in case he's forgotten. Small chance. Still, what counts is how it feels tomorrow, not now.

"You think we'll make it?" he says.

"I can't think any other way. You can't be a pilot if you're not an optimist."

A pause. I can hear him fingering his .38 revolver. Then he says, "You know the only thing the Green Berets say these guns are good for?"

"Yeah, I know." Pause. "Listen, partner, if you're gonna have thoughts like that, you'd best keep them to yourself. I don't want that shit anywhere near me."

"You're a regular Boy Scout, aren't you?"

"Yeah."

"Well, you're not the one sittin' here with a bum leg."

"Actually, I am." I don't know if he got the message.

He holsters his gun and lets out a long sigh. "This is not where I want to die," he says.

★★★ **12** ★★★

South and east about forty miles from Magee was Laurel, the KKK capital of Mississippi. Thousands of Klansmen of all ranks—Exalted Cyclopses, Kleagles, Kligraphs, Kludds, Klexters, etc.—ran respected businesses and attended church on Sundays.

Before the presidential election of 1956, a white man from Laurel whose name has been lost to history let it be known that he would pay the poll tax for every black who wanted to vote. His house was firebombed but he and his family escaped with their lives. Where they went to, I don't know.

Ten years later, in 1966, a black man by the name of Vernon Dahmer announced that blacks could use his store to pay their poll taxes, and for that sin Sam Bowers, the imperial wizard of the White Knights of the KKK, led three cars full of Klansmen to Mr. Dahmer's house, which was next to his store in the nearby town of Hattiesburg. They broke in, planted a dozen cans of gasoline, and set them off. Mr. Dahmer's wife and two young children survived, but not before watching the burnt flesh drop from his body as he died. It would be more than thirty years until a jury of blacks, whites, and an Asian convicted Sam Bowers. With the exception of a couple of years in prison for helping to plan the killings of three civil rights workers (the infamous Mississippi Burning case), Bowers had continued to live all that time in Laurel, winning awards and respect for running his business—Sambo Amusements.

Five or six of us decided to join the Navy. The others were older than I was, but none of us was old enough to enlist on our own. That didn't seem important, though. All we had to do was lie. Hell, that wasn't even breaking the rules; not really. Boys had been lying about their ages to get into the service for as long as the services had had a minimum age. How were they going to prove I wasn't yet eighteen? We blacks didn't have driver's licenses, and sometimes not even birth certificates (though I did). And if I told them I was seventeen and about to graduate high school, how could they tell one of my own scribbled X's on the consent form from the one Ma or Pa would mark? I was fifteen.

We hitchhiked up to the recruiting office in Jackson. It's among the smallest state capitals of the lower forty-eight, but to me it always looked like the New York of my imagination. Most of what I knew about Jackson came from taking the bus there with a lot of other people once a year on the day the Mississippi state fair set aside for blacks.

The recruiter greeted us. "We want to join up," I said.

"How old are you, young man?" he said.

"Uh, seventeen, sir," I said, careful not to look directly into his eyes. "Graduating high school in June."

"And why do you want to join the Navy?"

"To see the world and serve my country." It was my first true statement. The reason I sometimes took jobs working for Mr. McCarty, a feed manufacturer, was that he had to make deliveries all over—from Vicksburg to Jackson—and I wanted to see all these places.

Frankly, I'm not sure why the others wanted to join, except maybe just to get out of Magee. As far as I knew, none of them had grand plans for their lives.

"Um-hmm. And you?" he asked Monkey. "How old are you?"
"Eighteen, sir."

He was sixteen.

My other friends, Snoot and Odell and the rest, lied, too, and soon the recruiter had us filling out a pile of forms with personal info, and after that we found ourselves in a room taking a general knowledge test. To pass, you needed a score of at least twenty-one, which should've been easy considering you got three points just for signing your name. That's how many Monkey ended up with. Odell and I were the only two to pass, and I had the highest score. Before we left, the recruiter told me that the Navy would be "very, very interested" in having me as a sailor; he said he'd mail the paperwork for my parents' signature. "I look forward to seeing you in uniform," he said, shaking my hand.

I went home excited and immediately began fretting over how to break the news to Ma and Pa that I wouldn't be finishing high school after all. "Man gonna be the first in the family to go all the way," Ma liked to say, meaning that I'd make it to college. This was going to break her heart. Where would I find the words to explain? I didn't know and didn't want to have to think about that yet, so I decided to say nothing until the forms arrived.

For two weeks I ran home from school, anticipating the packet and wondering if the day of reckoning had arrived. The empty mailbox always left me equally relieved and disappointed. Then came the envelope from the Department of the Navy. It was thinner than I'd expected. No wonder. Inside was a single sheet that said, without elaboration, that while the Navy appreciated my interest in serving my country, I was unfortunately too young for the job and should reapply on my eighteenth birthday, or after my high school graduation—whichever came first.

I don't know how they found out my real age, but I felt comforted by the fact that my government couldn't be so easily duped by a poor country boy.

✶ ✶ ✶

My mother remarried and moved to Oklahoma with her new husband. Ben J. May, whom we called Mr. Shorty, bore no resemblance to my father. He was maybe five-five and plain to the eye. The dissimilarities didn't end there, either. Mr. Shorty had no aversion to hard work. He actually worked several jobs, among them garbageman. But the most lucrative of his jobs was making moonshine for the local sheriff. Twice I went out there to visit, and twice he let me help him make it. To me, it was a science experiment, with tubes and pipes and heat turning this solution into something powerful that got poured into barrels and buried in the woods. Men—white men—would come by his place at night in pickups and give him money for a gallon. Most of the money he turned over to the sheriff, keeping only a bit for himself. When the feds busted him, old Mr. Shorty kept his mouth shut about the sheriff and, when he got out of prison two years later, picked up the arrangement where he left off. The sheriff didn't even increase his cut.

I remember a real Oklahoma twister kicking up one summer day. My mother's little shotgun shack didn't have a storm cellar, so she led me across Highway 66 (yes, *that* Route 66) to her neighbors', a white couple who lived in a beautiful white house. I froze. How could we go in there? But the lady was as sweet as Aunt Leola, insisting that we come in out of harm's way, then feeding us milk and cookies till the danger passed. She turned out to be one of a few white ladies who taught Sunday Bible school at the summer Bible school, where my mother made me go.

Mr. Shorty was a great hunter and fisherman, and tried teaching me what he knew. He pulled me out of a fifty-gallon moonshine barrel I'd fallen into, kept me from drowning when we were fishing for catfish, stopped me from blowing my leg off with a shotgun, introduced me to fresh turtle meat, and let me help him pick up garbage on his rounds. He called me "son" and I thought about staying there in the fall, but I missed Ma and thought she'd have missed me, too.

I rode the bus alone to Mississippi. In Texas, there was no curtain between the white front of the bus and the black section in back. At one stop an older white man got on, sat down next to me, and unzipped my pants. Black people all around me saw what he was doing to me but were too scared to say anything. So was I. But tears were running down my cheeks. Finally, a white lady noticed and told the bus driver, who shouted for him to move up front. At the next rest stop, the man didn't get back on. I never told anyone what happened.

☆　☆　☆

I was ten years old when the first traffic signal was installed in the colored quarters. For months, people gathered just to watch it change.

Some years later the Rural Electric Authority (REA) finally connected the black population to the rest of the city. For us that meant a bare lightbulb hanging from the ceiling. ("Mm, mm, mm," Ma said, staring at it. "Just like those nice, fancy houses." We took turns pulling it on and off.) But for Mr. Jones, the sweet old man up the street, electricity meant he'd at last be able to turn on the television he'd bought used from the family he worked for when they got a bigger one. Every night he'd let in several of us to watch with him and his wife. There were ten times more kids who wanted to watch than he had room for, so we'd stand out in front in the yard, waiting to be invited in. Whoever made it sat on the wood floor and didn't get up to pee or for anything else, for fear someone would take his place, until Mr. Jones said we had to leave. Most kids liked *Boston Blackie* or *Dragnet*—crime dramas. Me, I couldn't get enough of *Men of Annapolis,* the series about cadets of the Naval Academy. The first time I watched it, I felt something switch on inside me. Those upright young cadets in crisp uniforms who were training to serve the United States—their stories were what I wanted my stories to be.

And so I wrote to the Naval Academy and West Point. Annapolis wrote back first and enclosed an application and a sample entrance exam. It was loaded with math and science—my best subjects. I'd been taking math like calculus, algebra, geometry, and trigonometry—classes taught by Mr. Magee (who was not named after the town)—and sciences like biology and chemistry from Coach Pickett. Thank you, Mr. Magee and Mr. Pickett. Those men took their jobs seriously enough to stay after school for some specially advanced classes with their best students. In a way, they did the same thing Martin Luther King was doing; they were teaching us to be more than we'd been born to be. They believed our way out was through our brains, so where Martin wanted us to remove the shackles, Mr. Pickett and Mr. Magee thought we could fly. That's a difference without a distinction.

"Ezell," they'd say to me, "you can do it. You can make it. You can be someone. You can help people." I'd always believed in myself anyway, but Mr. Pickett's and Mr. Magee's faith blew away any doubts that might've still been lurking. They saw something in me I'd hoped was there, and that's how I knew it was. We didn't have fancy lab equipment—in fact, we didn't have a lab, period— but Mr. Pickett found a way to make it happen. At least he did for me, giving me a lopsided amount of attention and energy, compared to the other students. Some of that must've come from seeing me try to soak up whatever he was saying and doing. The best audiences always get the best performances.

Mr. Pickett liked how I'd always test myself against the smartest kid in the school, James Brown—Lollie, we called him, because he was shaped like a lollipop: fat in the middle and skinny at the bottom. Of course, part of the reason his legs were skinny was that he'd had polio as a kid and still had to drag one leg as he walked. Lollie lived just up the road, and didn't mind tutoring me even though he could see how much I wanted to beat him. It was obvious, but he didn't care. He knew he'd somehow be able to squeeze that extra point or two ahead—and he always did. At graduation, I was third in the class to his valedictorian. Many teachers thought I should have been salutatorian.

Between Lollie and Mr. Pickett and Mr. Magee, I figured there was nothing on the Naval Academy test I couldn't handle, which was pretty much confirmed by the sample test. I filled out the application and earned the money for postage. Six months later, just before my senior year, a Naval Academy cadet came down to interview me. He was white and from Michigan, and I don't think he expected to see what he was seeing. He'd probably visited a dozen white schools, maybe even the one in Magee, but I doubt he'd been to a school before like Magee Consolidated Colored High School; applying for the Naval Academy wasn't something blacks usually did. The cadet hid his shock at the conditions, but a little still leaked through his face and gestures.

We had a side room to ourselves. It seemed the whole school had a lot riding on this. The idea that one of us might really be accepted to the Naval Academy was like sending off our homecoming queen to the Miss America Pageant. Everyone was excited. For ten minutes the cadet talked about the Academy—what it was like and what was expected of the cadets. Then he asked if I had any questions. Questions? The truth was, I didn't even know enough to know what I didn't know. He said, "Well, then, good luck with the test, and I hope to see you in Annapolis."

I said, "Thank you," and we shook hands. I'd never done that with a white person before.

The test was given in Jackson. James drove me there in his truck, and the whole quarters turned out to wave good-bye. I found myself in a large room with a hundred guys. I was the only black. I noted the fact and put it away, not even wondering how many of the twelve thousand applicants taking this test this day across the country had the same skin color as I.

The question is why: Why did I want to serve my country? That didn't occur to me until years later, after I remembered how much ugliness I'd chosen to ignore—and by then I'd seen enough of the world to know that America was still the best place in it and that I'd been lucky to be born here; lucky, too, that my elders hadn't taught me to hate America, even if they didn't necessarily teach me to love it.

Not that it would have mattered if they had. The only way you can command men in battle is if you have an army or navy to command—and only countries have fighting forces like that. Oh, and charismatic rebels on fire with revolutionary passion, which let me out. Anyway, in my mind a military branch that would allow me to work myself up the ladder was a military worthy of my command, and I believed that the United States Navy was just such a place.

I would run to the mailbox, looking for my Naval Academy results. The envelope took a month to arrive. Out of the twelve thousand applicants, my test came in number 346. The school and some of the colored quarters erupted in joy. Ma and Pa said, "See, that's why we call you 'Man.' " I was as good as in, right? All I needed now was a recommendation from a member of Congress.

It crossed my mind to ask a black congressman, but I didn't know any black or white congressmen; in fact, I didn't know if there *were* any black congressmen (like Adam Clayton Powell). I sent off a letter, my photo, and some commendatory letters from my teachers and principal to Mississippi senator John Stennis. At the time I didn't know that you could ask more than one member of Congress—or all of them. Stennis never replied, not even to say sorry. A week after the deadline, a letter from Annapolis informed me that my application had been rejected for being incomplete.

For a week, I couldn't think clearly. The disappointment filled me like poison, as much for letting down everyone else as for not getting what I'd wanted. It didn't matter that there were good excuses available. The truth was that I hadn't succeeded because I hadn't done what it took to succeed—and I vowed never to make that mistake again.

★★★ 13 ★★★

It's a long, uncomfortable time till morning, though not as long as I expected, so I must've fallen asleep now and then without knowing it. Burdett probably feels the same. At first light we make eye contact. The night wasn't good to him, and it's not just the mosquito welts.

"How's the leg?"

"Number ten thousand, GI," he says, meaning in Army slang that it's ten thousand times worse than terrible.

"Let's get out of here."

I slide out of my crook and jump down, ignoring the feeling that somebody just whacked me on the back with a carpet beater. Burdett throws me the canteen and first-aid kit and then has to shimmy on his behind till he gets to the Y. A hand on each side branch, he lowers himself as far as he can, like a guy doing dips on the parallel bars, and drops onto his good leg. I keep him from falling over on impact.

It's good to be out of the tree. I check the map and figure out a destination. Psychologically, that's what keeps you going—having someplace to go. And as your mind goes, so goes your body. Anyway, that's how it's always been for me. "As a man thinketh, so is he," says the Bible.

"Can you walk?" I ask.

He takes a beat too long to answer. By the time he says yeah, I've already spotted the flared branch I'm going to cut for his crutch. I pull my bayonet from its belt sheath and try to carve the branch so the top won't slice his underarms. It's not going to feel like there's anything close to a rubber pad under there, but it's a trade-off. However much it rubs and chafes and even cuts under his arm should pay off on the leg times two or three.

He tests out the crutch. "Good enough, I guess," he says, and we start in the same direction—moving no faster than yesterday. Uphill. The map's markings are unclear. Experience tells me that there'll be some kind of opening a chopper might be able to set down in at the ridge—which we may never get to if we don't hurry.

After an hour, Burdett is exhausted. Looking at the leg, I can only imagine how painful each step is. He hasn't complained and whimpers only when something touches it.

He leans against a tree and I run off to find a stream. It's a quarter mile south. To fill the canteen I have to risk coming out of the deep foliage.

I do. I lie on my belly and splash water over my face, then re-move my boots and wet my feet in the gentle current. It feels cooler than it has a right to. I'd like another pair of socks, but oh, well; I'd love another canteen even more. Now I lower my pants and clean my groin. I fill the canteen and get back to Burdett.

Before giving it to him I take a malaria pill from the kit and drop it in. He drinks deep. I do, too. He pours the rest on his leg—right through the blood-soaked gauze—and hands me the canteen. I run off to fill it again, and when I come back the leg's been re-bandaged.

The old bandage and a Hershey wrapper are in a ball stuffed into the first-aid bag. The candy wrapper reminds me I'm hungry, but we haven't gone far enough yet for the day. Let breakfast be a reward for making progress—a dried peach and stick of beef jerky.

Of course, progress is made at Burdett's speed.

I hear it first, Burdett a second later—the thwacking slash of a helicopter's rotor blades. Nothing else sounds like that. And no one else but the friendlies are flying helicopters in Vietnam. These are the good guys.

We both stop, cocking our ears to the east. Yes, from the east. East to west. Coming our way. We're going home.

I take the ETR from my vest pocket and begin pushing in the S-O-S code—once, twice, three times; time after time. Burdett does the same with his.

There's no way to know whether they're receiving the signals.

"Dammit," he says. "They could've given us two-way radios—send and receive instead of just send. Only Air Force gets those."

I don't know if he's right, and I don't care. I keep pushing the button, and the chopper keeps coming right for us. But he's not going to be able to see us.

"Captain," I say, "we better make a break for some kind of clearing."

"I can't. You do it. Go. Run."

I run east, hoping to see the sky. I take my gun from the arm holster, because the way I'm running is the way I used to practice football by juking and jiving through the cornfields back home, and I may accidentally run into some bad guys. My left hand holds the gun, my right thumb pushes out S-O-S. But I'm not getting to a clearing. The helicopter is almost overhead. I can see it like a dream—there and gone—through a tiny opening in the canopy, at about a hundred feet. And now it's past me, still going. I stop and listen.

Wait, now it's turning. Turning north. That's no coincidence. The helicopter must've fixed our position and turned north. They're looking for us, they know we're alive, and they're telling us to go north.

I sprint back to Burdett. The joy is on his face, too. Both of us had been pretending not to worry whether they were coming for us. Well, they came, and now we know we're going home.

"They turned north," he says. "That's where we need to go."

I agree and look at the map. There's no way to tell whether the topography has changed. Some areas of the jungle have been defoliated with chemicals and napalm, and some that used to be nothing were taken back by nature. But if the map's right, we've got at least two miles to go before we get to a place that looks logical—a meadow of three or four square miles. Maybe that's where the chopper wants us.

Burdett's moving a little faster, like he took some kind of painkiller. He did. It's called hope.

$\star\,\star\,\star$ **14** $\star\,\star\,\star$

Annette's family lived six or seven miles out, on a huge spread of land in the country. Compared to the rest of us, even the trash man, they were prosperous. They had their own cotton field. They had a truck and a car. All of them either worked the family's own land or had good jobs. For instance, the principal of my high school was her brother.

In my mind Annette and I had been boyfriend and girlfriend since the ninth grade—but we never even held hands. She was a good girl who obeyed her parents, and they didn't want her mixed up with me. "That boy's not going to amount to anything because of his upbringing," her mom said. "His family's no good."

One day James rode me out to Annette's in his truck, promising he'd be back to pick me up at six. I was going to spend the day showing her parents what kind of character I had, but things didn't turn out as planned. All day she and I sat on the front porch talking, and every once in a while Annette would get up and go inside, pleading with her mother to invite me in. Then she'd come out and we'd sit and talk for a while longer, both of us pretending that I hadn't heard what I heard and didn't know what I knew.

Six o'clock came and went, and, as it was early spring and a moonless night, it was dark as pitch. Her mother said I had to run along, that my ride might never show up. Annette pointed out that it wasn't safe for a black man to walk alone at night in that part of the world, but the old lady wasn't swayed. I walked and jogged for over an hour along the road, diving into the bushes every time a car drove by—before anyone could see me. By the time I got home—and found out that James's truck had broken down—I was skinned and bruised.

So why did Annette's mother dislike me—a boy who her own son, the principal, believed had the tools to make good? The answer also explains everything else about their situation in comparison to ours: because my skin was black, and if you didn't know better, you'd think Annette was white. All of her family were light-complected; "high yaller," Ma used to call it. There were obviously as many white genes in them as black genes, but you could still tell they were black. With Annette, though—well, she could pass for white. So for her, hope had no ceiling.

I couldn't be angry at her mother. The poor woman was probably going to lose her daughter to the North and white society—and wanted to—for what she thought was the girl's sake.

* * *

Sometimes we played pickup basketball games with white high school kids on dirt courts that had netless rims. Actually, it wasn't *with* them; it was against them. I can't imagine that any of us, white or black, ever thought of mixing sides. Literally, that would have been unthinkable. We didn't say much to each other while we played, either, but what we did say was respectful enough. Not more than a few times did I hear any of us called "nigger."

Even so, the rules still applied—meaning, the coloreds better not win. We'd be ahead 70–25 and one of the white guys would moan, "Come on, let's go home."

"No, wait," I'd say, "just a little while more."

"Well . . ."

"Please."

At last they'd give in—and we'd give up: five guys, just like that, turned to marble statues.

On offense, they ran around us like we were bolted down, and on defense they were transformed into octopuses, blocking shots and passes and sucking up rebounds of shots we intentionally missed. In fifteen minutes they'd pick up sixty points and give up maybe six, and that was the game. The funny thing is, it always looked like they walked off happy at catching up and winning. As far as I could tell, none of them ever figured out what happened; they didn't get that my buddies and I were the Washington Generals—the team that plays the Globetrotters. The difference was that, for the Generals, it's about keeping a job. For us, it was life and death. We knew that because one time we did beat them. Two of their guys had to leave suddenly before we let them back in a game, and a few hours later their fathers barreled through the colored quarters in trucks, shooting and shouting how we'd better not be beating their kids anymore. They didn't need to add an "or else."

★★★ 15 ★★★

Hope as a narcotic soon wears off. Fighting through the relentless jungle in the heat and humidity is too much for Burdett, and we're back to moving at that morning's pace—slower, even. The air under that canopy feels like the inside of a car that's been out in a baking sun with the windows rolled up and a radiator shooting steam.

Hours later, there's no sign of the helicopter again. We have to stop often for Burdett to gather himself. He's suffering badly, but still says nothing. I now know that the battle is going to be one day at a time. One hour at a time. One minute at a time. The goal is to survive from one minute to the next enough minutes to make an hour, and enough hours to make a day until the day we go home. That day is not today. I doubt it's tomorrow, either.

At a break I glance down at Burdett's leg. The bandages are caked with blood. I'm not worried about his bleeding to death; I'm worried about the smell of blood in the air attracting an animal. I haven't seen them myself, but guys have told me they've run into tigers, and I read a report in *Stars and Stripes* about a couple of guys getting eaten by them. It has a keen nose for blood and a shark's appetite.

I reach into the bag and sprinkle some powder on the wound. We're out of water again, or I'd wash it.

I go off to find a stream, cutting through maddeningly thick foliage for half an hour—and find one about a half mile away. A half mile in half an hour, and that's on my own.

The stream's three feet wide and about eight inches deep. It's moving well enough so that I think I can get away with not putting the pills in; there aren't many left, and I'm thinking long-term. I kneel beside the water, cup my hands and drink, fill the canteen, and wash myself again.

There are about two hours of daylight remaining when I make it back to Burdett.

I sit down next to him and ask if he's all right. He doesn't answer.

"Captain. Hey!"

I pull out a stick of beef jerky and bite into it, chewing slowly. It tastes like filet mignon.

Burdett fixates on my mouth as I chew. He rubs under his arm where the wooden crutch hits and says, "How do we know it wasn't some coincidence that the helicopter turned north where it did? Doesn't mean it got our signals."

"If that was a coincidence," I say, "it would be a coincidence as big as this jungle."

He says, "I'm trying to remember where all the red pins were in the map on the ops officer's wall"—the ones marking known enemy sightings. "I think there were some right where we're heading."

"We keep inside this thicket, we'll be okay."

"Yeah? Then what? What happens when it ends? And what if it doesn't?"

Burdett's starting to doubt again. We don't have time for that.

"Listen, EZ—" he says.

I know where he's going with this and I can't let him finish. I don't feel like reassuring him in so many words that I'm not going to abandon him. I say, "Captain, let's just move on out. We'll go till it's twilight again. Then we'll stop for the night. Okay?" And when he doesn't answer: "Nothing good can come of staying right here."

He says, "Stop talking like a Marine."

We move on another quarter mile or so. It takes more than an hour. For me, it's not about the distance as much as feeling like we're progressing.

Neither of us has what it takes to climb the tree tonight, so we camp out between the emerged roots of a banyan, our backs to the trunk. Burdett's asleep inside of five minutes. Maybe asleep's not the word. Passed out is more like it. I'll let him stay that way. It's like anesthesia.

I recall my grandmother telling me that even the lion wakes up running every day. "If he don't," she said, "he ain't gonna catch somethin' to eat." The memory makes me smile, but the smile doesn't last long. Right behind it is fear and despair. It comes on as hard as whatever brought down our helicopter and pushes away my hunger, which is really something, because I'm hungrier than I've ever been. Not seeing that rescue chopper again today has me worried. No, this is just my imagination, playing tricks. I tell myself—and work to convince myself—that nothing I think about or feel right now is going to make sense. Nor is it going to make a difference to the plans. We have to do what we have to do to survive, and that means we have to keep going as fast and as far as we can—and treat fear and despair with contempt. They're the enemy in here, and they'll get us killed if we give in to them as surely as the enemy out there. I eat a Payday bar and a dried peach. That clears my head a little.

★★★ 16 ★★★

Every other year or so I boarded a Trailways bus in Magee and stepped off in East St. Louis to visit my father for a week or two. He lived in a small apartment that seemed impossibly luxurious, though if I saw it now it would probably look just ordinary. I remember him as a tall man with a soft, well-spoken voice and quick smile that showed some gold in his teeth—a sign of wealth in those days. He said that East St. Louis was a bad town. "You hit somebody on the head with a two-by-four, you just keep runnin'," he warned. "And don't look back; somebody may be gainin' on you." I found out later he took that from Satchel Paige, who'd been a buddy of his first in Mobile and then in the Negro Leagues.

For all I knew, Dad was still a professional gambler; he didn't say and I didn't ask. Whatever he did, though, it was a job that he dressed up for. The man woke every day in his pretty apartment and put on a suit, adjusted his tie and hat, and practiced his smile in the mirror—and when he liked what he saw, he'd turn and smile at me.

"See you tonight, son."

At night he'd walk through the door looking spiffy and whistling a happy tune.

Something in me just had to know how he earned his living. One day when I was older I followed him after he left, staying far enough behind so he wouldn't see me. For half an hour, through streets and alleys and then out past the railroad tracks, I trailed about a hundred yards behind, running to catch up when I thought I might lose him and dropping back every time I thought he sensed me.

What I saw was the last thing I expected.

He'd disappeared into a huge railroad warehouse, and while I was trying to figure out a way to slip inside without being seen, he came out wearing coveralls—and got busy as the human mule he'd always refused to be. The man had so wanted me to think of him as elegant and professional that he was willing to scrub the oil and dirt off his hands and fingernails with a wire brush before changing into his suit and leaving for home. The man had so needed me to think well and be proud of him—believing that that's what it took—I never let on. Of course, I didn't really know whether he did that for me or for his own pride on the long walk there and home. Either way, it wasn't my place to share a secret with a man trying to keep it. So I said nothing. Which means I never told him what a hero he was to me for doing that.

My best memory is of telling him I played baseball—center field. That's all I had to tell him, and in just those words. What a smile that was. He smiled in a way that—well, I didn't spend a son's full measure of time with his father, but I think I saw him enough to believe that that smile he smiled right then, with the light suddenly switched on in his eyes and the corners of his mouth almost tickling his ears, was in the running for best and happiest of his life.

He never saw me play, and I never told him that baseball wasn't my favorite sport. "Nobody could play first base better'n yer daddy," Aunt Lee once told me. "The man could hit dat ball a country mile, den run and catch it before it fall. He was one purty colored man."

⭐　⭐　⭐

At thirteen, we weren't sure if I'd ever not be short and puny—a present left by the worms when I was a kid and had too little good food. I was way too small to be out on the pocked gravel football field with strong teenage boys at least twice my size. But on the team's first day of practice I showed up unannounced and told Coach Pickett I wanted to play football—at quarterback. I can't explain why. I'd played catch with friends but had of course never seen a pro or college game. Maybe it had something to do with football being like a military battle and the quarterback being his teammates' general. Cowboys and Indians, Capture the Flag, Army—I loved every game that had anything to do with fighting and war. Even the grasshoppers we used to catch just to watch them pulling little sticks we tied with thread to their legs—for me, in my imagination, the grasshoppers were tanks that could go wherever they needed to. Playing and being the leader out there was just something I was intent on doing.

Mr. Pickett had studied science, earning his master's from Ohio State University in Columbus, Ohio, on the GI Bill. Those two disciplines, math and football, don't usually go together, and in fact, as I came to learn, there wasn't anything usual about Mr. Pickett. He would become one of the most significant men in my life, and this was our introduction to each other. I remember it well—his dark skin and muscular build, that fedora tilted just so, and most of all his attention-getting baritone.

He raised an eyebrow, gave me the once-over up and down, and started laughing. "Son," he said, "you're too small to play football."

"But I want to play," I said. "And I'm gonna grow."

"Maybe you should come back then."

"No, Coach," I said. "I want to play now. You'll see. I'm good."

He stared at me a long moment, coughed out a breath, said, "You ready to prove yourself?"

"Yes, sir, I am."

"All right." He shouted, "Butler." Butler heard his name and came running. He got there inside of five seconds—the biggest guy on the team.

"Yes, Coach."

"I'm playing quarterback, and your job is to protect me from this oncoming rusher."

"Who, Coach, this little thing?"

"That's right, son. You keep him away from me as best you can. Understand?"

"Yes, sir."

"Young man," Coach said to me, "you stand three yards away from Mr. Butler and when I say 'Now,' you try to get around him and to me any way you can. Got it?"

"Yes, Coach."

"All right, let's do it."

Coach Pickett stood just behind Butler, leaned over as if he were going to take the snap, and yelled, "Now." He dropped back into the pretend pocket and I charged Butler. Two seconds later, I was on my butt.

"You see," Coach said. "Too small."

"Let's try it again," I said.

"Suit yourself."

He set up, said the word, dropped back, and in less than two seconds I was on my butt.

I didn't wait for him to say the tryout was over. I shouted, "One more time," and jumped to position. He played along.

This time I faked left, doing a little juke-jive move before streaking right, past Butler and up to Coach. It wasn't anything I'd planned; it just happened.

Coach liked that. He put me on the team—sort of. I got to come to practice and during games sit on the bench wearing a little uniform his wife sewed for me that had the padding already in the shoulders. I'd run in for one play and everyone would start yelling and clapping for the little guy, and then I'd come out; once a game, one play. But Coach would stand nearby me on the bench and point out what the quarterback was doing right and wrong, and why. Most mascots don't get treated like that, so if I'd needed extra motivation to make myself great at football, that would've been more than enough. I didn't need anything else—not here, not in school. In school, I wanted to get nothing wrong ever.

At the end of the season Coach let me keep a football. He said to practice with it. He just didn't say how. Now and then I'd throw passes to friends, but mostly I'd spend hours whenever I could chucking it as far as possible. For accuracy, I threw at spots on a wall or a particular tree, and then through a swinging tire for a moving target.

The best thing I did was run through the cornfields behind the house. I'd tuck the ball under my arm and sprint full speed, juking and jiving, dodging the cornstalks like they were a thousand defenders.

Coach hadn't seen me in months, and on the first day of summer practice, he almost didn't recognize me. I'd grown to six feet, 185—and gotten good enough to be his first-string quarterback. For the next four years, I was never less. Better, I was almost that important in his math class, too.

My amazing growth spurt happened when it did that summer because I really needed it to. I believe that. I do. I may not have believed it back then, but back then I hadn't had so many things happen just when I really needed them to.

The toughest game of my sophomore year came early in the season. I hadn't been playing as well as I could and was frustrated. On offense, my passes were just a little off and when running I'd hit the hole a half step too late. On defense, playing safety, they'd already scored once on me. So I was in a bad mood when I tackled their halfback after a long gain and then kicked him when I stood up. The refs blew their whistles and marched off fifteen yards against us for the unsportsmanlike-conduct penalty. Coach pulled me from the game.

He stared at me like I'd really disappointed him. "That behavior is wrong," he scolded. "I will not deal with that kind of behavior. You sit down."

He was pulling me? *Me?* For the rest of the quarter I kept thinking that I'd be back in any moment. We were losing now, and he'd want his best guys out there. Wouldn't he? No. Apparently he had a hierarchy of values, and winning at any cost wasn't near the top. When I figured out he was sitting me the rest of the game, it didn't take more than ten seconds to get that message. After the game I apologized to the guy I'd kicked. He accepted it. Would Coach?

The disappointment wasn't on his face anymore, but the shame stayed on mine.

"Young man," he said, "you take that anger and instead of doing something stupid, do something positive. You understand?"

"Yes, Coach." And I did.

★ ★ ★ **17** ★ ★ ★

Something lands five feet away, almost scaring me off the branch. In the dark, I don't know what it is and reach for my gun and am about to squeeze the trigger when I realize it's a monkey. Good thing I didn't fire. That would be like sending up a flare. The monkey must've smelled the peanuts in the Payday and swung down from an upper branch. I toss him one. He wants another. I toss it to him. He wants a third. This time I throw it on the ground. He jumps off and finds it and is soon back.

Apparently, the monkey and I have a lot in common, but I'll just keep that to myself. No use giving Burdett any ammo.

Anyway, the monkey finally leaves when he can smell that there aren't any more peanuts. Me, I'm a lot harder to get rid of.

★　★　★

I don't know how much I sleep—a few minutes at a time, fitfully, my hand on the revolver. But it's first light now. I stand. Burdett startles awake at the sound and sees me grimacing, trying to work the spasms out of my back.

"Jesus Christ," he says in a groggy whisper, disappointed to be awake and back in pain. "I was dreaming. Goddamn good dream, too." He looks around and then at his leg. The sight disgusts and discourages him. "Fuck me. Look at this thing." He takes a cigarette from his vest and lights it.

I squat down next to the leg to take my first good look at it. It's getting worse.

"I don't know how it feels, but it looks like it's getting better," I say.

"Better?"

"Yeah. Not so angry-looking. Here."

I cut away the old bandages, pour some water on it, sprinkle the sulfa, and rewrap. "Good as new," I say.

"You know what?" he says.

"What?"

"If I'd let you fly command pilot, it would've been you getting hit instead of me."

"Yeah? And you know what else?" I say.

"What?"

"If I'd been command pilot the other day, we wouldn't have gotten hit."

I'm not in a particularly facetious mood, but if I don't give back to him as good as I get, he'll think I'm feeling sorry for him. That doesn't help either of us.

"How many missions we flown together?" he asks.

"Sixteen, I think."

"How come you never asked to fly CP?"

"You'd think I was asking a favor. I figured either you'd ask someday or you wouldn't. Besides, in Cobras, the copilot's got a better view."

"How many missions you fly last tour?"

I shrug. "I don't know. Hundreds. Probably same as you."

"So you don't like asking favors?"

"Of some people—no."

"Me?"

"You're some people."

He checks the leg again. I can tell he doesn't want to stand on it.

I say, "Here's the deal, Captain. You take the crutch under one arm and put your other arm around my shoulder. If you've got the strength, maybe you don't have to put any weight on it. I'll go sideways through the brush if I can, keep it off you."

"That sounds like a favor to me."

"It's a favor to both of us. I want out of here."

"Okay."

"You wanna eat first—breakfast?"

"Got any of that beef jerky left?"

I take my last one out of my pocket and give it to him. While he eats I study the map, hoping to see something I missed before. There's nothing else to see.

"Let's go," he says.

I offer my hand. He grabs it and I lean back to brace myself for his weight. He's up.

Too bad the scheme doesn't work. After eight or nine steps, it's obvious that we're not going anywhere with him holding on to my back. The jungle's too thick for that. I can't make it through to clear the way.

Burdett tries it on his own for a while, but I'm impatient to do better. I find another Y branch and try to carve it into a usable crutch, so he'll have two and can keep off the leg.

Burdett tries using both crutches and grumbles.

"Shit," he says, "now it's like *two* knives under my arms."

And there's more weight on each.

I take off my vest and my T-shirt.

Burdett says what the hell.

I put the vest back on and tear the T-shirt in two.

"Christ," he says, "I can't believe what you're doing for me."

"I told you, I'm not doing it for you. I'm doing it for me." Pause. "This is just a problem to be solved."

Burdett shakes his head. I wrap half the T-shirt on the top of one crutch, the other half on the other. Padding.

"It's not much," I say. "Better would've been a sweatshirt. There's more of it and it's thicker."

I try the crutches first and hand them over without comment. He takes two strides and stops. He says, "I think you just wasted a good T-shirt."

Now what? I look around and find a three-inch-diameter branch and hack two eight-inch lengths.

"Now what?" he asks.

"Now you take off your T-shirt—no, better. Here, gimme those crutches. Stand up straight. Put your arms at your side."

He complies. I measure the first crutch against him and mark a spot where his fist hits his side.

"Handles," he says, "you're making handles. Straight-arm crutches, like guys with polio use. God almighty, EZ."

He grins, an appreciative grin, as I start cutting a V-shaped notch at the spot.

"Ladies and gentlemen," Burdett says, "the hardest-working pilot in this man's army—Lieutenant Ezell Ware."

"Junior," I say. "Ezell Ware, *Junior*."

We both hear it at the same time. A helicopter. That low beating of the blades on the air like a broken speaker woofer through a wall.

I'm up and running as fast as the jungle lets me go, my finger pushing on the ETR button. The chopper's coming east to west again. If it turns north when it passes, I'll know that we're in someone's rescue plans.

I run wildly. I want to see it. I want to find that opening. I want to break through. I want to flag it down.

But I may not get everything I want, and I don't want to do anything stupid that'll get someone else shot down and get us all killed. I can't abandon sound judgment; there's no telling where the enemy is now.

No, I'm not going to get there in time, not today. The chopper's passing almost overhead. It found us again—and again I can only see a glimpse of it that lasts as long as a shutter click.

Let's see now if the pilot notices the signal getting weaker. But wait, it's not getting weaker, not if Burdett's pushing, too. The pilot might think we've been separated. I better run back.

I close my eyes and listen. He's still going west.

I'm pressing the ETR like crazy. Burdett's doing the same, I'm sure—and I'm sure his stomach drops farther every second the chopper doesn't turn and go north.

And then it does turn north. Definitely. That's worth a deep breath.

Such great news—fantastic news. Hopeful news. And strangely, I find myself wishing that Burdett and I had shared it at the same time, face-to-face.

✮ ✮ ✮ **18** ✮ ✮ ✮

Spring of 1959. It was time to line up all my dreams and decide which of them I wanted to come true. Obviously, they all couldn't; I had to be practical. So when Tougaloo Southern Christian College—as it was known at the time—offered me a free ride in academics and football, I decided to live with numbers two and three on my dream list, and give up number one—wearing a military uniform. At least for now.

My high school graduation was the proudest moment of Ma and Pa's lives. "I never thought I'd ever live to see kin of mine finish school," Ma said, her chin quivering as she studied me up and down in my gown and mortarboard. "Mm, mm, mm."

"Hell," Pa said, his chest out to here, "Man's goin' on to college. College!" All summer he turned around and announced to everyone he passed: "My boy's goin' on to college—and on a scholarship!" He even told some white people.

Ma and Pa wouldn't have been prouder of themselves or each other. My success was theirs, and I told them so. I said, "We did it together."

By car, Tougaloo was only a couple of hours northwest of Magee, but for Ma and Pa it might as well have been Tibet. Their place in the world was in a small radius around Magee, and nothing could change that. They'd been born too early and in the wrong place for anything more, so their expectation of how good it could get for them was sadly low—and absolutely correct. But for me, they'd always said, life could be different; the choice was mine. I wanted to prove them right.

My success meant everything to them. It meant I was taking them into the world—the only way they could get there. As much as I was in a hurry for the future to start, I knew that leaving was going to hurt me; but I also knew that as much as they were going to miss me, my staying would hurt them more.

Tougaloo had only about six hundred students. Some had grown up in the North and gone to mixed schools, so they took a while getting used to the idea, but Tougaloo's being all-black didn't get a second thought from me. I lived in a small dorm room with a roommate who also played football. Compared to high school, this was elementary school. We were being taught material I'd learned years before, and moved along in class at half the speed I was used to. I spent more time playing and practicing football than I did in class and studying. From the first day, I was the team's starting quarterback, and from the second day I knew this wasn't going to be much fun. No, this was serious business now, and much depended on winning. The coach built the offense around me, a left-handed quarterback. We'd take bus rides to places like Texas and New Orleans, which were unfortunately more interesting to me than the games we played there. The good thing was that I had a lot of success—I was a good passer and probably even a better runner—so the school newspaper wrote about me almost every week; I was a big man on campus, which I think scored some points with Annette.

Annette. Apparently there'd been some sort of hiccup in the grand plan for her to pass into white Connecticut or wherever.

That would have to wait till she finished her education, which was just fine with me. Her dorm was the fourth building over, and I spent most of my free minutes during visiting hours sitting in its lobby with her. We talked; that's all. I don't know if I was in love with her or with the idea of being in love with her, but something had me in its teeth. Seeing her, sitting next to her, holding her hand if she'd let me, smelling her perfume—they were the best part of my day.

Homecoming was the last game of the season. After we won I walked out of the locker room and from about twenty yards away saw Annette talking to a player on the other team, right by their bus. I stopped dead. First I recognized his team colors, then I recognized him—their halfback. He was handsome—and had light skin. I watched them for a long time, trying to read their lips and body language. In my imagination they were making plans to elope. In reality, they were just talking. My imagination was stronger than reality.

On Monday morning I rode the bus to the recruitment office of the French Foreign Legion. In those days, Americans loved the French and considered the Legion romantic—maybe because movies about it always featured guys who'd joined after getting their hearts broken. Anyway, that was the cliché, and it must've been for good reason: Recruiting offices were in every major city—more than one if the city was big enough. Jackson's office was downtown.

I got there at noon and tried the door. Locked. I sat down to wait and was glad for the time to make sure, to ask myself if I really wanted to give up school and football and everything I'd worked for just because some girl had broken my heart. The answer was yes; I was sure. It didn't matter that the other player had gotten on the bus and driven away with his team fifteen minutes later; didn't matter that I'd taken her to dinner that night. I'd seen all I needed to see to give me the excuse I think I'd been looking for since choosing football and school over the military. It wasn't rational, it was emotional.

A young man—white—wearing a U.S. Marine uniform came bounding up the steps. I stood up to get out of his way and kept my eyes on his spit-shined shoes. He unlocked the door and I noticed for the first time that not only the Legion but the four American military branches kept offices inside. He just happened to be the first one back from lunch. When I didn't follow him in, the Marine sergeant asked what I was waiting for. I said the Legion.

"Why? You thinking about joining?"

"Yes, sir," I said.

"Why you want to do that? You don't want to join the sissy French Foreign Legion. You want to be a tough guy. I can see you're a tough guy already. The Legion's not for you. The Marines are for you."

"They are?"

"Come on in," he said. "I'll show you."

The first picture he showed me reminded me of the *Life* magazine shot I'd seen years before, of the soldier coming home from World War II. That's all I needed to see. Actually, I'd already been sold by the sergeant's uniform. They couldn't hand it to me soon enough.

I signed my name, and that afternoon he gave four of us a test. The other three were white, and when he'd finished grading them he said, "Which one of you is Ware?" I raised my hand. He nodded and told the other three that they'd scored, respectively, thirty-six, forty-two, and forty-eight out of a hundred. "Congratulations," he said. "Y'all passed."

"How much you need to pass?" one of them asked.

"Twenty-one."

They whooped and hollered for beating minimum by so much. Then the second guy said, "So this nigger didn't even get twenty-one?" and they all laughed.

The sergeant waited while they laughed, and in the meantime winked at me in a way that said I'd passed, too, so I wouldn't worry. He didn't know I wasn't worried. In fact, I was fairly certain I hadn't missed a single question.

"He got a ninety-eight," the sergeant said, enjoying how fast the smiles dropped off their faces.

Ninety-eight? I'd have said, *Dammit!* if I'd been alone. Instead I just shook my head. To this day, I'm angry about missing those two points.

The four of us were taken that afternoon for physicals. We lined up in a military clinic, prospective Marines on one side, Army on the other—facing each other. I couldn't help noticing that I was the only black in the Marines line—and I couldn't help it because of the way everyone in both lines kept staring at me. For a while I thought I was in the wrong line. Judging by their faces, the black guys in the Army line didn't like my being in the Marines line any better than the white guys did. The guys in my line, I couldn't tell. Didn't matter anyway. No way was I going to be in the Army. Just standing there on my side, I already thought I was better than they were.

Not a day later, I swore allegiance to the United States Marines in defense of the United States Constitution and our commander in chief.

Ma and Pa took it hard. Here I was, the first person in the family ever to get to college. Ma tried to talk me out of it, and Coach did, too. They both wanted me to get an education first, before I did anything else.

"Are you sure?" Ma kept saying.

"Boy, I hope you know what you're doing," Pa said. "That's somethin' awfully good to pass up."

I should've said, *Right now, Pa, I hear that train whistle in the distance, like you do in the cotton fields—that train to anywhere but here.* What I really said was that this was something I'd set my mind on.

When Ma's son, John, Jr., had been drafted at the end of World War II, a couple of authentic Mississippi Delta bluesmen came to the house the night before he left and sang and played their guitars. My uncle wasn't even going to Germany or Japan. He was going to Arkansas.

Me, I was on my way to South Carolina, and after that—any-where. Ma hugged me like it was for the last time.

"You're our son," my grandfather said.

Before leaving, I promised them I'd get my college education someday.

"Remember, baby," Aunt Lee said, "if dem soldier peoples don't treat you right, you can always come home."

★ ★ ★ **19** ★ ★ ★

I cut the two notches in the crutches as deeply as I can without weakening the wood, then wedge the two handles in, wrap the T-shirt around them (it goes a lot farther on these), and lash them with as much excess shoelace as I can cut from both my boots.

"Here you go," I say.

Burdett tries them.

"Whaddya know?" he says.

They're good. They're not great, but good is good enough right now. We're moving better, and that's what I care about.

We make decent time for a mile or so in silence and take a break. It's a long mile, especially for Burdett. I give him a swig of water and pour the rest on his leg, then take off to find a stream. Forty yards out I hear something. Sounds like wailing or screeching. Louder and louder. I hurry back to Burdett. He's already backed up against a tree, revolver drawn. I lean up next to him.

"What the hell?" he says.

"I don't know." Then I recognize the sound. "Monkeys."

Dozens, hundreds—maybe more—of them are swinging through the trees and scurrying along the ground. Different breeds. A monkey stampede.

What a wonderful moment. But it lasts only a moment. Because that's when the wonder turns to terror. A growling tiger leaps out of the bushes and runs past the tree at full speed, disappearing again into the thicket.

There's only one thing to say, and after a while Burdett says it. "Get me the fuck out of here." Pause. "I think I pissed in my pants."

He did.

★ ★ ★ **20** ★ ★ ★

The four of us who'd taken the Marine test met at a bus depot in Jackson. Our recruiter greeted us and handed out vouchers for tickets and incidentals, like food. Turned out that the Marines' custom for something like this was that the recruit who scored the highest on the test held the tickets and vouchers for everybody, because they figured he was smartest. The white guys didn't like it, but they didn't say anything. The recruiter did it strictly by the book; you couldn't tell whether he gave a damn one way or another about a black guy being first. All he said to me was, "Make sure they eat."

This was 1959. JFK and Vietnam were still over the horizon, and I was in the back of the bus. The three white guys sat up front. I just watched the scenery anyway. Everything looked new, even when it looked just like home.

First meal stop was in Birmingham. We had an hour, which meant a choice between a white café that I couldn't eat in or a black one that they'd be uncomfortable in. We had to eat together, because I had the goods, so we went where I wanted; being uncomfortable for once wouldn't kill them. They sat by themselves, at their own table. The café owner wasn't sure whether to serve them and didn't until I explained. We all ate collard greens, fried chicken, turnip greens, and corn bread, with sweetened iced tea. They didn't have a please or thank-you in them but were otherwise polite enough.

The bus took us into Georgia, where we caught a train for Buford, South Carolina.

When we got off, Marines were waiting for us. We rode in a canvas-covered truck to Parris Island. I'd never seen the ocean before.

It was night when we got there, and just like that we were in hell. (Three years before, some Marines in training had been marched into quicksand and died.) Drill instructors screamed and bright lights shone on us. I didn't have the time or interest to notice how few black faces there were.

The DI wasn't bigger than five-eight and was on the other side of thirty, but you knew you didn't have a chance against him. He walked up and down the aisle, looking for the biggest, meanest-looking of us, and when he found him, the DI stood next to him for a count of three before suddenly slugging him in the belly hard enough to make the guy crumple to his knees and drool. And that was our lesson.

They shaved our heads and gave us olive drab uniforms with these things to put on our feet that weren't even boots; they were overshoes. We called them "boondoggles."

That first night, getting undressed with and going to the bathroom with and sleeping under the same roof as white men, I was as embarrassed as you get in those dreams about standing naked in front of a crowd.

This being October, the weather didn't quite reach jungle-hot, but there was still a summer's worth of sand fleas to fight off. If you smoked, and I didn't, they gave you smoking breaks. To take one, you put a bucket over your head before lighting up, and kept it there for the whole cigarette. For some reason—hmm—a lot of guys quit. At chow, you could take seconds, but if you did you'd better finish, because one way or another you were going to; the only trash receptacle was our mouths.

I'd thought I was in great shape from playing football, but I barely passed the tests they gave—running, jumping, calisthenics. About half the guys couldn't pass, and ended up in the fat man's platoon, where the DI worked their tails off—literally. You did not want to be in the fat man's platoon.

Just for the record, there were very few black faces. The Marines were the last of the armed services to really integrate. And yet, I can't remember feeling like the DIs—all of them white—or the sergeants and lieutenants and even colonels I saw ever went out of their way to get in my way. The only other black in my platoon was from Lynn, Massachusetts. Darrell and I eyed each other but didn't speak for a couple of weeks, I think because we were both conscious of not looking clannish, no pun intended. Anyway, when we did hook up, there wasn't much to share. I was a poor backward country boy, and he'd grown up in and around the big city. He was relatively sophisticated, I was a complete bumpkin.

During those twelve weeks of boot camp, there were days I was sure I'd made a mistake coming here. Mornings started at five when someone came in and started throwing trash cans against the concrete floor and hitting you with batons, yelling, "Get up, get up, get up!" We had five minutes to shower, brush our teeth, and shave; fifteen minutes to march into and out of chow; and then a full day of hell. When we weren't drilling and exercising to exhaustion and cleaning every cubic inch of the base, we were at parade rest in the barracks—one hand behind us, one hand in front holding the *Marine Corps Guide Book*. They insisted we know every period and semicolon, and tested us on everything—from how to wear our uniforms and shoot M-1 rifles, to where a bed gets tucked in.

Anything wrong, no matter how small, was a punishable offense. Guys would come out of the DI's punishment hut with bumps on their heads. Me, I got off lucky. Our DI once kicked me in the rear for walking a little too slow, and another time he socked me in the stomach for telling the Marine marching behind me in the drill line to "get with the program" and stop stepping on my heel.

But there was a method to the brutality. The harder we trained, the more we bonded to each other. We'd started as individuals, each to his own, and eventually became a solidified unit.

Here's one thing I remember learning; it's what Marines want the Marines' legacy to be: The Marines were founded in the days of great naval battles, when there was cause to have fierce warriors boarding boats for fierce battles. In order to distinguish the Marines from the sailors they were fighting, they put an X on their caps. To this day, there's a cross on Marine officer caps.

To test how tough you were mentally, the DIs liked to play with your mind. They'd tell you that, at most, sixty percent graduate boot camp; the rest wash out. That was true, but knowing the truth could also become a self-fulfilling prophecy, and they wanted to weed out those who took it as inspiration from those who took it as discouragement.

At night, you'd hear a lot of crying from young men who were sick of being called "maggot" by their DI, and homesick for mom's creature comforts. Some nights one guy whimpering into his pillow would jump-start a second guy, and then a third followed, and soon it'd sound like a hospital nursery. Me, I'd never had it so good. The food tasted fine and filled my plate. My clothes were washed and pressed and free. There was some activity all the time, the learning curve was enjoyably high, and I was getting paid. All I had to do was keep my mouth shut, pay attention, and do what they said. I'd had a lifetime of practice for that.

In my head I took notes, silently marking the guys I thought would make it and those who wouldn't. I knew only one thing for sure—I was going to be in the make-it group.

There's no better place to spread rumors than a military base.

Word was that we'd be getting a week's leave at Christmas—that General Shoup, the Parris Island commandant, would be giving us the good news when he addressed us five days before Christmas. All the platoons marched out onto the parade field, hundreds and hundreds of raw Marines, to listen to his speech. He talked about all the Christmases that fighting Marines missed in the service of their country—how keeping their posts in the Korean snows and the Japanese jungles had made us the richest, freest nation in the world, and that we owed them all a debt of gratitude we could never repay. Obviously, we weren't going home for Christmas, and by the time he finished speaking, I felt guilty for wanting to.

Darrell and I were the platoon's best athletes. He was a little bigger, I was a little faster. One day, during some platoon-against-platoon competition, we happened to get paired up on a two-man team carrying heavy logs on our shoulders. We beat the whole company. That night, before lights out, Darrell wandered over. He was smiling.

"My shoulder's killing me," he said.

I said, "Mine, too."

He said, "You want to see a picture of somebody?"

I said sure, and he opened his wallet. Inside was a twenty-five-cent photo-booth Polaroid of him with a girl who looked eighteen. She was pretty and had kind eyes. "That your girlfriend?" I asked.

"Someday. So far she's just a friend. But I like her a lot."

I could see he did.

He said, "The minute we graduate, I'm on a bus up to see her. Spend the whole two weeks' leave with her. Gonna make her mine."

"What's her name?"

"Gwen."

Over the next two weeks Darrell came by to say hi a couple of times, and I did the same. He always managed to work Gwen into the conversation.

I don't know that we would've anyway, but we didn't fasten on to each other because we were both still conscious of how it might look if the only two black guys buddied up. Anyway, there was no shortage of white guys to mix with and get to know. Most of them from the North were friendly enough and some were truly genuine. That took getting used to. A few kidded me about my polite manner, and I explained that that's how I was raised—that it had nothing to do with being black other than the fact that my grandparents who'd instilled humbleness in me were black.

Darrell got around to asking me about growing up black in Jim Crow country. He said, "I wrote Gwen about you—you being from Mississippi—and she wants to know what it's like to be a Negro in the South. I'm gonna tell her all about it."

Days later—three weeks before graduation—he was dead. We'd been out on nighttime field maneuvers in the boonies, standing waist-deep in a rain-swollen creek for about ten hours. Afterward Darrell said he didn't feel well. He kept getting worse and then he couldn't stand up. They ran him to the hospital right before he died. Spinal meningitis.

I took the liberty of writing Gwen a long letter about Darrell. I figured she'd hear about his death pretty fast, but she needed to know more than that.

It looks like it's going to be a hard climb for Burdett, but we don't have much choice. The tiger coming out of nowhere that afternoon was too busy chasing monkeys to stop for human meat, but for all we know he wanted them for lunch and us for dinner. So just before dark we choose this banyan tree with a wide limb spreading both ways fifteen feet above the jungle floor. We want to stay alive another night and maybe even catch a few hours' sleep.

Burdett and I stand at the base of the tree and plot the choreography without a word between us, each reading the other's thoughts. He leans the crutches against the tree trunk and takes a deep breath before putting the foot of his bad leg in my cupped hands. He groans, but the groan has an invisible cork in it, as I lift him chest-high. His good leg can't quite get into the crook, so he has to hoist himself by grabbing on to a limb and doing a kind of pull-up. His arms are tired from the crutches and for a second it looks like he might fall, which would be the end of his leg. He wiggles around and finally gets himself onto the broad limb.

"Okay," he says, grimacing.

"Looks like that tiger turned you into Tarzan."

"I didn't know they were that big," he says. "You?"

"Never thought about it before."

I toss the crutches and first-aid bag up to him, and then fight my back to get up the tree. Every movement hurts.

"Going kind of slowly, there," he says.

"Just let me know if you want to race."

He fingers the crutches, inspecting them in the fading twilight. "I don't know how much longer these are gonna last. Gettin' kinda loose." He cuts some excess lace off his right boot, then watches me wiggle into place.

He lets out a breath when I'm finally settled. I watch him work on the crutch and then inspect the other myself. He's right: They don't have long; the way I've lashed the laces means cutting them to retie. That was a mistake. Burdett doesn't have as much excess lace as I did, so his bolster job is only going to delay the inevitable. Oh, well, they'll last as long as they last.

Right now I can only concentrate on right now, and right now I'm famished and exhausted. I've got one melted Hershey Bar and a few slices of dried peach left.

"You got anything left to eat?" I ask, knowing he began with three times as much as I did—and hasn't offered me anything. I don't begrudge him that. He's the one with a bad leg and a pot-belly.

"Half a Baby Ruth."

"Here," I say, offering him a slice of dried peach. "A change of pace."

He takes it and thanks me and puts the whole thing in his mouth. I take a small bite of one remaining in my pocket and re-member to chew slowly, savoring it, making it last in my mouth. Umm. A peach is a wonderful thing.

"Hey," he says, "didn't your mama teach you to wash your hands before you eat?"

"When I was a kid," I say, "we didn't have running water—and I was *still* never this dirty."

"Where you from, EZ?" He sounds like he sincerely is interested.

"Mississippi." I wait. But he wants to be asked. "You?"

"West Virginia."

"That's one state I've never been to."

His hometown is near the Kentucky border. "It's so small, every time someone dies or a baby's born we go out and change the population on the sign."

The conversation starts to flow now. Neither of us has the energy to be on guard, and these three days have forced an intimacy on us. Burdett especially. It must be odd for him to have to rely on a black man for his well-being—and his needing me more than I need him has extracted most of the bugs he's had up his rear since we first started flying together.

I learn that Captain Ronald G. Burdett is indeed thirty years old and the great-grandson of a Civil War soldier (fighting for the Union; West Virginia, after all, was founded by Virginians in the western part of the state who wanted to remain loyal to Lincoln's side; obviously, not all of them shared Lincoln's progressive nature), as well as the grandson of a World War I soldier, and the son of a World War II and Korean War officer—or, as he puts it, "the son of a bitch." He says his father was bitter at the Army for not promoting him faster, and finally left the service after twenty-two years with all that bitterness intact. It's there, he says, to this day—in both of them. Burdett moved a lot as a kid, thanks to the Army's stationing his father here and there, but had settled into the family's West Virginia home by ninth grade, when his dad quit. He says he hardly remembers anything about moving around except the moving around itself—and proving himself every time as the new boy in town. He joined clubs, picked fights, and did reckless things—anything, he says, to be accepted.

It's a lot to take in, and I feel obliged to reciprocate in some way, so I relate a few memories about growing up in Magee with my grandparents.

"What about your parents?" he says.

I tell him about my father's getting run out of town and my mother having no choice but to leave me with Ma and Pa.

"That's a damn shame," he says.

"My attitude," I say, "is that everything happens for the best."

"You really are a Boy Scout," he says, and now the conversation has reached a plateau. It could go anywhere, or nowhere. Burdett seems not to like the silence. I think he wants to take his mind off the pain, or our circumstances.

He says, "You think we're safe up here?"

"From what?"

"Whaddya think? Tigers, man, tigers."

"Well, they can climb trees, but at least we'll have warning enough to shoot."

"Yeah, and every NVA guy in the sector will hear it and come lookin' for us."

"Hey, you only asked about the tiger." Pause. "Anyway, I'm more worried about snakes. Good thing the mongoose ate 'em all."

"Except for the cobra."

"Yeah, but they're mostly farther north than we are. Otherwise I'd be taking my chances down below with the tiger."

"Snakeophobia, huh?"

"Man, I've hated snakes since I was a kid. Use to work the cotton fields and had to keep one eye on the cotton and one out for copperheads. Just the thought of something slithering at me in the dark, up here where I can't do anything except fall—shit." I actually shiver with goose bumps, which isn't easy in this heat.

Burdett laughs and says, "You're not afraid of the mongoose?"

"No, why?"

"Christ, EZ, the thing carries rabies and leprosy. Me, I'd rather fight a cobra than end up a leper. You ever see *Ben-Hur*? You see what those people looked like down in the leper colony? Jesus ain't here to cure lepers anymore."

"It's a bacterial disease, Captain."

"The hell's that got to do with anything? And stop calling me 'captain.' My name's Ron."

"Antibiotics. Leprosy's curable now with antibiotics."

"Yeah? Well, how 'bout rabies? I don't see any hospitals around here with anyone holding up long needles to shove in your belly."

"No problem, Captain—uh, Ron. All the water around here, we'll be so foamy-mouthed we won't know what hit us anyway."

Burdett snorts a one-syllable laugh and then suppresses a groan, trying to get his leg comfortable. It's a losing proposition. Same with my back.

He says, "So I guess all we got to worry about is the tiger."

And the NVA and VC and starvation and dysentery and poisonous spiders—and about a dozen other threats, none of which I name. As hungry and tired and scared as we are, we've managed to find a laugh. That's as nourishing right now as food.

"Damn, Ezell," he says, pronouncing my name with the accent exaggerated on the first syllable—*eeee*—believing (wrongly) that that's how to make fun of me. Making fun is all he has now. He doesn't have the hate anymore, and he's just getting used to the idea. "It's black as shit pitch out here, but boy, look at you, grinning at me. All I can see is your teeth and eyes. Damn, I swear you look like little black Sambo."

"I got news for you, Captain Ron. Your lily skin ain't so lily white anymore, either. I'd say you're darker'n I am. Only reason your teeth aren't showing is 'cause they're so yellow."

Not exactly Richard Pryor quality, but Burdett laughs again.

And then he stops laughing and turns serious. He leans forward, his face now catching just enough light to look charcoal-gray against a black background. "Ezell," he whispers, "I, I, I want to tell you something. It's important."

I figure this is it, Burdett's giving up. He knows that even if the bad guys who shot us down aren't still pursuing us, someone's always out there looking. He understands that his leg is keeping us from making real progress and feels the injury worsening by the day. And he thinks he's going to die. So now come the deep dark secrets. I brace myself for things I'll be embarrassed to hear—because I know he'll regret telling me them if we survive.

"There's something you need to understand," he says, pausing to find the right words. Then: "Hell, boy, the mongoose didn't eat all the snakes. There's a shitload of 'em crawling all over this damn country. Poisonous, too."

I'm not sure what my face looks like, and I'm not sure Burdett can see it anyway in the dark. But he stares at me as if he can—and I'm about to ask if he's serious when the laugh he's been swallowing bursts out. He covers his face and laughs in silence, his body having to do the work.

"Damn, Captain," I say, "you are one sadistic bastard." And then I start laughing too. The man has gotten me good—and God, it feels great. Too bad we can't really let loose. But then we'd either fall out of the tree or get our heads cut off, which all of a sudden is why, I think, we laugh even harder—though quietly, of course.

Against my better judgment, I'm starting to like this man. I've taken a peek under that racist skin and decided that his skin is as deep as the racism goes. He was raised to be the way he is—the way generations of Southerners have been raised to be. Racism is a kind of heirloom that gets passed down through the generations, but maybe now, after this experience with me, he won't pass it on if he ever has kids. That's another good reason to survive.

I check through the first-aid bag and find just enough gauze remaining to dress Burdett's leg one more time. I'll do it in the morning, and hope that tomorrow's the day we go home.

$\star\star\star$ **22** $\star\star\star$

Everyone was milling around the center of the camp, mostly keeping to the guys in their own platoons, when my DI called everyone present to attention. Graduation was in five days. "Listen up, maggots," he said. "We've been looking at people for outstanding recruit." I didn't even know they had such a thing. Apparently the company DIs get together and vote on one guy from that whole graduating class who's impressed them the most. Criteria were, well, everything—academics, physical fitness, field performance, weapons-handling, demeanor, attitude, etc. It's a great honor to be outstanding grad, even if the only material payoff is a free Marine dress blue uniform, which everyone else has to pay for out of their checks.

"We've made our choice, and it's one of you. Private Ware, front and center."

I stepped to in front of him. Everyone else stayed at attention.

He stared at me and said, "You, maggot, you've been selected outstanding recruit. Report to the DI hut tomorrow morning, zero-six-hundred. That's all."

He walked away and I was suddenly in a swarm of guys—white guys—patting me on the back, telling me congratulations.

The next morning I was fitted for my dress blues, and a few days later someone came in to deliver them, so I had the honor of being the first recruit to don his uniform. It was almost embarrassing how much I loved the feeling. I didn't even have to look in the mirror, but when I did, it was even better. In my mind, I was somebody now—and I'd earned it. Honor, courage, and commitment.

The day before graduation is when you're assigned your military occupational skill—MOS—a three-word phrase that means job. Assignments are made by your superior officers, based on the needs of the Marine Corps, your test results, and personality. The best scores got the best jobs—or were supposed to.

"Private Ware," the man called out, "electronics communications."

What? I didn't want to do that.

I visited my DI. "Drill instructor," I said, "I'd really like to be considered for another MOS." I explained that I believed they'd shafted me with this electronics communications thing—whatever it was. In 1960, electronics communications wasn't a common pair of words.

"That's what you think?" he said. "You think we're giving it to you up the butt?"

I didn't say that I thought my being black might've had something to do with it. And the reason I didn't say it was that I couldn't really bring myself to. So far, every Marine superior had treated me exactly like every other man there. The message was that we were Marines, not colors. That's why I was surprised by the MOS assignment.

"Well, let's see," he said. "What do you think you're better suited for?"

"Engineering."

"Engineering. All right. And why is that?"

"Sir," I said, "my test scores show that I can handle difficult math and science computations. I'd like to be with the engineers."

He laughed, and the more he thought about it, the more he

laughed. "Listen, maggot," he managed. "You don't want to be an engineer. It's not what you think it is."

"It's not?"

"Not in the Marines."

In the Marines, the engineering units do grunt work. "You don't wanna end up out there digging ditches and driving trucks," he said. "Believe me, you'll love communications. It's right up your alley and they need people like you."

The way he said it and how he looked convinced me I was getting something choice.

That two-week leave suddenly got replaced by AIT—advanced individual training—which every Marine gets because, when you take everything else away, the Marines are infantry; war preparedness is the whole point. Most of the time they had you report to the AIT camp after coming back from leave following boot camp, but not us. We had to pack quickly for Camp Geiger, which is located on the grounds of Camp Lejeune, North Carolina.

The guys took it hard. We were all in a hurry to show off how we looked in our uniforms—and out of them, too. Every last one of us had a body by Michelangelo—sculpted to the last detail. In sixteen weeks I'd gained thirty-two pounds of muscle. My chest was forty-two, waist twenty-eight.

Camp Lejeune.

On the bus ride there I saw my first snow in the mountains of North Carolina.

On my first day there I heard the roar of a fighter jet directly overhead, and a moment later noticed a sharp-looking young man in a flight suit walking across the base as though he'd just stepped out of a cockpit. I wanted to be in that jet, and I wanted to be that pilot. Flying, I decided, was what I would go after. As outstanding recruit, I obviously had a head start.

They made me a platoon sergeant. The job meant getting up

earlier than the guys and making sure everything that was supposed to happen happened. Technically, platoon sergeants didn't have to work as hard as the regular grunts, but the genius of it was that a platoon sergeant who wanted to be more than that had to set an example for his men—and I wanted a lot more. That meant outworking the hardest-working of them. It's impossible to say what they might've been thinking, but if any of them were having trouble taking orders from a black man, I didn't see it. Apparently we'd been taught well—that our color was Marine, not white or black. I fast had to get over the discomfort of giving orders to young Southern white men for whom I used to step off the curb. Now it was my job to stare them down. To do that, I at first had to pretend to be somebody else—someone capable of looking defiant white men from the South in the eye—until at last the action had its own kind of muscle memory.

For thirty days we practiced firing an array of weapons, from mortars to machine guns, and learned Marine Corps tactics for land and sea. By the time they gave us our ten days' leave, we'd been away for twenty weeks. I'd written letters home, knowing someone would have to read them to Ma and Pa, and got letters back, knowing someone had taken their dictation. Their last letter said that all of Magee was proud of me and would turn out to see me get off the bus—"even the white folk. Just kidding."

As it turned out, I rode a bus most of the way there with a Marine from my platoon. Dale and I sat next to each other for fourteen hours, both of us feeling fine and fit and proud in our uniforms—and both of us thinking that other people, too, would see the uniform as more important than our skin color. We either laughed or talked for all but five minutes of the whole trip.

Then the bus pulled into Birmingham. Before we could get off to take a pee, two Alabama state troopers busted down the aisle and dragged us outside. They handcuffed us and rode us to jail. Integration was a crime. We were race-mixing. Suddenly I wasn't so homesick anymore.

Dale did most of the talking.

"No, sir," he said, "we weren't trying to break any laws. We were just going home."

The troopers called Camp Lejeune and confirmed our leave orders and ID numbers. This was serious, because we were in the South and people ended up dead for less than laughing at state troopers who suspected a black guy and a white guy might actually forge leave orders and go AWOL while wearing their uniforms, or choose to impersonate Marines just for the hell of it. But it was hard not to laugh. They kept us for six hours before riding us back to the bus station. By then our bus had left, and our duffel bags were lying on the floor of the station. We had to promise we'd take different buses. At least I didn't have to promise I'd ride in the back of mine.

The troopers sat in their car to watch.

Dale let me know I should get on the first one that came; he'd go later. He said, "Better for you to get out of here first."

I said, "I think you're in bigger trouble than I am around here."

We waved to each other through the window of his bus as it pulled away, and that was the last time I saw him.

I'm sorry to say that he was far from the first and wouldn't be nearly the last person who came into my life, left a lasting impression, and then disappeared.

Ma and Pa made a fuss over how good I looked in my uniform. Aunt Lee called me purty. " 'Next time, baby," she said, "don't stay 'way so long. 'Member, we gettin' old." Even Aunt Dora asked me to her house—nicely, for the first time—like I was some kind of celebrity. In fact, everywhere I went that week people followed me—only one of two black Marines to come out of Magee. I didn't take off the uniform the whole time there. I didn't want to and they wouldn't have let me.

I'd only been gone twenty weeks—less than half a year—but I

was surprised by how small everything looked. To me it suddenly seemed provincial, even quaint. Coach Pickett and Mr. Magee were glad to see me but admitted being disappointed I hadn't stayed in college. To them, being a Marine wasn't a positive for someone who had as many other options as I did. I think my family believed the same. That's what started me feeling a little distant from everyone there. Between us were the things I'd seen and done in the last twenty weeks that they couldn't have imagined and I couldn't have explained anyway. It scared me to think that if I'd gotten a good job offer from Mr. McCarty's feed mill I might've stayed and worked, delivering feed to the chicken houses and never seeing anything outside a hundred-mile radius; oh, and never experiencing equality—or what felt like it anyway.

On Saturday afternoon I walked to town for some exercise and, I suppose, also to show off the uniform. People were used to seeing guys wearing their Army uniforms, but Marines were known to be something special—so special that I couldn't remember whether I'd ever seen a Magee Marine. I'm not ashamed to say that this tall, fit, proud Marine enjoyed the stares from white people—and wasn't afraid of not having work gloves in his back pocket. My peripheral vision caught the lineup of men sitting on the six-inch perch built into the outside wall of Stephens Department Store. As one, their eight or nine faces turned to watch me pass. I kept from laughing. On the other side of the door was another perch, this one filled with blacks, who were also watching the passing parade. One of them called to me, a female. I stopped and turned and saw Doris Woods running to me. She hugged me and said, "Ezell Ware, you are one handsome soldier." Doris had been in my class at school. She was a popular girl, tall and pretty and nearly as fair-complected as Annette.

"You did it," she said. "I knew you could."

I asked about her plans, and she said she'd soon be leaving for Chicago.

Before I could respond I saw a white man, wearing a butcher's bloody apron, running toward me, apparently from the butcher shop across the street. In his hand, raised menacingly, was a meat cleaver. He was shouting, "Get away, nigger."

My first instinct was to turn and protect Doris. I pushed her behind me, then readied for the fight. In the last five months I'd learned a lot about hand-to-hand combat, but in none of the training had we practiced against attackers with meat cleavers.

Half of the white men on the Stephens perch ran to stop him. They explained that Doris wasn't white, that before I got there she'd been sitting with the other niggers on the nigger perch, that she was just a light-skinned nigger but a nigger just the same, that the nigger in uniform wasn't hugging a white woman—it just looked that way. And so on. By then, though, the butcher hated me for his mistake, and his anger was too far gone. Which meant I had to get out of his sight.

"Go ahead," Doris said. "You better go before something happens."

I rode the bus up to Tougaloo, stopping first to visit James, but he'd transferred to a junior college with an aggressive math program. Then I tracked down Annette at Tougaloo. When the subject of that homecoming game came up, she said I must've been imagining things, that she was just talking to that football player and hadn't seen him since.

"Well," I said, "if I imagined it, I'm glad I did." And you know what? I knew I'd imagined it. I'd imagined it because I hadn't felt worthy of her and needed a good excuse to leave. I'd left, and now I felt worthy, and now I was glad I'd left. I was going to be a Marine pilot.

The first brown-skinned man I ever saw was at Norfolk Naval Air Station, in Virginia, at radio operator school. I spotted him from afar and wondered whether that was dirt on his skin. Three days later I introduced myself. His name was Lopez—Mark Lopez. We shook hands, and no, his brown color didn't rub off; I apparently looked down at my palm to check, which made him laugh. We became the best of friends in the way that best friends form when you know that one or both of you is only going to be in this place for weeks or, at most, months. It's a different kind of best friend than the ones you know all your life, and a different kind of intimacy. You get used to its limits.

The funny thing about Lopez was that he was the only Latino on the base and, from what we could see, the only one in Norfolk. It was a segregated city, so he never knew what end of the bus he was supposed to ride in. He probably could've ridden up front, but why? He chose to ride in back, next to me.

One day for no particular reason I said to him, "Let's make up our own language, pretend we're talking to each other."

"I like it," he said.

We got on a bus and as we were paying I said loudly, "Henkle mashti pinstop."

"Corpkel radmum intemkapklonfil," he said.

I nodded and we walked to take our seats.

As soon as we sat down, I offered him a cigarette from my breast pocket. "Florpag?"

"Tornole," he said, and took a smoke from the pack.

Seeing the people stare at us, we covered our laughter with more gibberish, and it was such fun we kept it up at the club we hit that night downtown. It was a black club. We'd been there before and knew that some of the local guys didn't like us being in uniform, believing that we thought we were superior. Twice before at spots around town I'd had to fend off jerks who wanted to challenge me to let me know that my being a Marine didn't make me special. On this night, though, there'd be no avoiding a fight—not when they heard Lopez and me speaking a language they couldn't understand and saw us laughing. In their minds, we were laughing at them.

It was two against three, but it could've been two against nineteen and the outcome would've been the same. You don't bring a knife to a gunfight, and you don't swing at a Marine and walk away unless you're Joe Louis. We fought the way we'd been taught, with the instincts that had made us join the Marines in the first place. None of them landed any good blows, but we sure did.

When it was all over, and we were on the bus headed home to the base, Lopez leaned back in his seat and smiled—a satisfied smile.

"What?" I said.

"Plindlsie," he said. And we both laughed.

A week later I shipped out to the Cherry Point Marine Corps Air Station in North Carolina, never to see my friend Lopez again.

My Marine barracks commander was a tall, white-haired man with an angular face and a slight limp from, I was told, World War II. He seemed to like me all right, and admired my work ethic and ambition. He agreed that my test scores and aptitude, by themselves, qualified me for elite status—nearly any assignment I wanted to pursue.

Now, here came the but—which I tried to head off.

"Sir," I pointed out, "I'm already ordered to Cherry Point anyway. I just thought—" I never got to the part about guys with lower test scores than mine.

"Well," he said, holding my application in his hand and not quite looking in my eye anymore, "you can put in for flight school, Ware, but you need to know that you'll be at the end of a long line of, uh, more qualified applicants. It could take a long, long time, and by then . . ."

★ ★ ★ **23** ★ ★ ★

We did not go home today. Today we saw the helicopter in the morning and listened as it came west and then turned north. Today I used up the last of the gauze on Burdett's leg. Today we ate the last morsel of food we'd brought—actually, that I'd brought. And today Burdett's crutches fell apart, as predicted. I tucked the two pieces of torn shirt and the four pieces of shoelace in my vest and trimmed both pieces of wood into canes. For the whole day, we didn't go more than fifteen hundred yards—or say more to each other than fifteen words. Now that we can, it seems, we don't have to. Besides, what does either of us have to say at this point but *I'm hungry* and *I'm tired* and *I'm scared* and, in Burdett's case, *I'm in agony*? He bears the pain well, though, and I admire him for it.

Even at midnight, or whatever time it is now, the air is steamy. It's the kind of wilting heat that feels like it's melting your bones. That can't be good for Burdett's leg. At some point gangrene's going to set in, and in fact I'm surprised it's not there now. We'll know by its smell.

I'm too tired to sleep, and I'm not comfortable enough in this tree to overcome my overtiredness. And that's not good, either.

You need sleep to calm your nerves. Being jittery makes you irrational and magnifies every sound.

What's that?

I pull my revolver.

It's probably nothing, but this afternoon we had to drop to the ground and hold our breath at the sound of voices. Turned out to be three people, including two women, apparently civilians, walking down the trail. They stopped at one point, thinking they heard something in the bushes. I was seconds from shooting all three. If they hadn't started walking when they did, I would've had to.

The map says we're near a village, and I'm tempted to make my way there tomorrow and ask for some food—but I'm only tempted in the way that the devil tempted Jesus on the cross. He didn't take the bait and neither will I. It would be suicide—or worse. But that's the state of mind that's right around the corner. I pray that when I'm standing in that state with both feet, I have the strength to do what's right—and what's right then is what's right today. So I guess what I'm praying for is to stay in my right mind.

Burdett was probably asleep but wakes when he hears me pull my gun.

"What?" he whispers.

I put a finger to my lips.

A long silence. Neither of us can hear anything but normal jungle noises—no approaching footsteps, no voices, no animal growls. I replace the gun in its holster.

"EZ," he says after a while, "what company were you with on your tour?"

"The Sixty-first," I say. "Sixty-first Assault Helicopter Company." Pause. "Why?"

"I was thinking about my own company."

"I know what you're thinking."

"What?"

"You're thinking we'd have been out of here by the second day.

It was like a real team. The war was about doing and killing for each other, and you didn't leave anyone behind."

"Yeah." He says the word in a way that sounds like the sad tremolo of a violin, then leans to the side, farther into the tree's crook, cutting off the little bit of light that might show me his face.

Soon comes the soft crying he doesn't want me to hear. If I say, *You all right, Ron?* he'll know I can hear him. So I say nothing and stop myself from remembering all the reasons we both have to cry.

✶✶✶ 24 ✶✶✶

The touch-typing class I'd taken in high school came in handy in communications, since a lot of the job was typing up Morse code messages. Most guys hunted and pecked at about ten words a minute. I'd sail along at nearly fifty—the best typist there. Of course, that was the boring part of the skills training. The better part was learning how to set up the equipment and wires necessary to transmit the code. My four months there, I saw very few minority faces. No wonder. It was an air station and, as I'd slowly—too slowly—come to realize, Marines didn't let blacks fly. No matter how qualified, we were still niggers. Hell, I was lucky even to be in communications. I kept telling myself that, and I kept believing it. Not to believe it would've meant dying a little inside. I couldn't let that happen, because sooner or later, a little death leads to a whole death—and I'd have ended up like those hollow men in Magee who accepted their own deaths before leaving this planet. It's a choice. Better may not be as good as best, but it sure beats what's below it.

At Cherry Point, I met and made friends with young men I had nothing in common with except the fact that we were Marines (privates, all of us), and that gave us an excuse to soak up from

✦ ✦ ✦

Ma in front of Aunt Lee's home, in Magee, Mississippi, about 1952.

Ma and Pa, proudly showing off their telephone and TV set, 1957.

Aunt Lee and her firstborn, Letha Jean, 1950.

✦ ✦ ✦

Mathematics teacher Jake
Magee, 1957.

The multitalented Roscoe
Pickett, who taught biology
and chemistry and coached
both the football and basketball teams, 1957.

Magee Colored
High School sign.

MAGEE COLORED
HIGH SCHOOL
ERECTED 1956

THIS BUILDING CONSTRUCTED
UNDER THE DIRECTION OF
STATE EDUCATIONAL FINANCE COMMISSION

BOARD OF EDUCATION
SIMPSON COUNTY

D. L. GARRETT - PRESIDENT
JOHN MYERS   J. E. SMITH
A. A. RUNNELS   VILAS AINSWORTH

COUNTY SUPERINTENDENT OF EDUCATION
MRS. GUS P. BROWN

E.L.MALVANEY ▪ ASSOC.- ARCHITECTS ▪ ENGINEERS
CAMPBELL CONSTRUCTION COMPANY - BUILDERS
BETHEA PLUMBING COMPANY -   MECHANICAL
HAROLD EVERETT -   ELECTRICAL

Lollie   Ezell   Sleepy

Annetta

The ninth-grade group photo from the 1956 Magee yearbook with me,
Lollie, Sleepy and Annette.

I was number 24, the smallest player on the Magee football team, 1956.

Coach Pickett (standing far left) was an inspiration to me (front row, sixth from right), 1957.

Ready for action during Marine
Corps Advanced Individual Training,
Camp Geiger, North Carolina, 1960.

Courtesy of the author

Courtesy of the author

I'm in the upper left corner of Marine Platoon 278, boot camp graduation
photo, Parris Island, South Carolina, 1960.

Courtesy of the author

The girl of my dreams—
Jennifer from Port Elizabeth,
South Africa, whom I met on
the South Atlantic Friendship
Cruise III, 1961-62.

Courtesy of the author

Emmalene, my first wife,
1967.

CLASS 67-7 B-4 3RD WOC COMPANY
U. S. ARMY PRIMARY HELICOPTER CENTER--FT. WOLTERS, TEXAS

FIRST ROW:
ISTER, PAUL E.
TREVETT, ARNOLD L.
VIEAU, WILLIAM L.
WATTS, ROBERT W.

WAUGH, DELBERT L.
LOCKE, B. J., CWO
WHITE, WILLIAM D.
WOOLSEY, GEORGE L.

SWIZER, JOHN W.
ZUCCO, ANTHONY J.
WRIGHT, TRAVIS H.
SYELA, JOHN R.
TUREK, JAMES W.

SECOND ROW:
WIERZBA, VICTOR A., III
WORTH, ROY E.
WELLS, WILLIAM R.
TEAFORD, JOHN H.

WRIGHT, JAMES M.
TURNBULL, JAMES C.
WARE, EZELL, JR.
TURNER, WILLIAM D.
SWINT, GREGORY L.

ZUPAN, TERRY M.
TOBEY, ROBERT S.
THOMPSON, EDWARD L.
SULLIVAN, SPENCER F.
TRYON, PAUL E.
THOMPSON, JAMES M.

Class 67-7, B-4, 3rd WOC Company; Ft. Wolters, Texas

Ft. Wolters, Texas, main gate.

Boll Weevil monument,
Enterprise, Alabama.

Adrian Brooks, courtesy of John Conway

Shelley Brigman

Courtesy of the author

Checking out the 40mm cannon turret on my Huey in Vietnam, 1968.

Dee Smith, www.61ahc.org

You didn't want to be on the receiving end of the Minigun when it was firing.

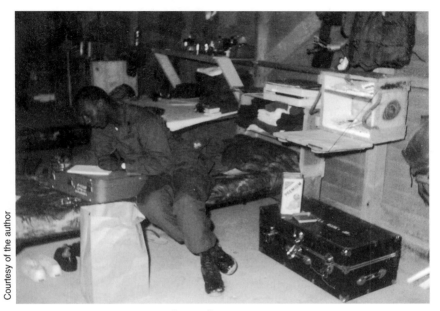

Writing home from Vietnam, 1967

Starblazers patch

This shot of a couple of Hueys from the 61st AHC gives a good look at the type of helicopters I was flying.

Having a little R&R with friends in Penang, Malaysia, 1968.

Dee Smith, www.61ahc.org

LZ English Officer's Club.

Dee Smith, www.61ahc.org

UH-1B 007 lifting off.

Mail call,
South Korea,
1971.

Courtesy of the author

U.S. Marine Corps photo, courtesy of Bob Milby,
www.popasmoke.com

A Marine Corps version of the lethal Cobra gunship I was flying when I got shot down with Ron Burdett.

★ ★ ★

Courtesy of the author

Now in the
uniform of the
California
National Guard,
1974.

Courtesy of the author

Escorting General Westmoreland in 1989.

★ ★ ★

Addressing National Guard troops during the L.A. riots, 1992.

Courtesy of the author

Wearing a fancy dress uniform for a 1997 California National Guard formal event.

Raintree Studios (510) 521-4900

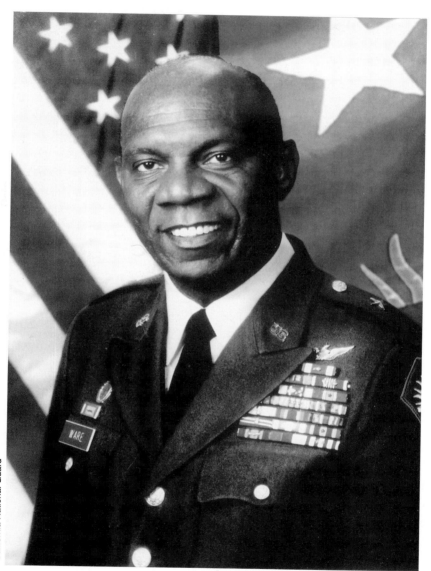

My official portrait as Brigadier General.

Courtesy of Jim Beach

I reunited with some old Army buddies at the 2004 Vietnam Helicopter Pilots Association Reunion in Dallas.

Courtesy of Jim Beach

each other whatever knowledge or experience or memories we were willing to share. Jack Talbot was from somewhere out West—New Mexico, I think—and was a honeybee expert; he knew everything about a hive's intricate structure and society, and how the honey gets made and how much money you could make renting out your hive for cross-pollination. To Steve Clarkson, horse racing was man's most beautiful contribution to civilization. He could look at a horse from fifty yards away and tell you whether it was worth betting on—which is what he planned to do as soon as he got out of the Corps. Harold Thurston was going to be a stockbroker. He had the stock market wired and could explain how to make big money by investing just five or ten bucks a month in certain stocks. Stuart Simon had a phonograph with a collection of classical music recordings dating from Bach to Copland. Anything you wanted to know about classical music, including how to get started liking it, you could learn from him. All of what I heard and saw and read from these guys was new to me, and I tried to soak it up as best I could. From me, too, they heard new stories—stories about growing up in an America they'd never imagined existed. So we all learned from each other—even if what I had to tell them wasn't going to earn anyone a penny or inspire art.

What I remember most about Cherry Point was football. I saw a notice in the base newspaper about tryouts for the base team. Most Marine bases fielded teams that played full schedules of twelve games against other bases, just as if we belonged to the NCAA. There were bragging rights in winning for both the bases and base commanders, so they treated football players better than the average Marine. Road games to bases in other states got you off duty for three or four days, and practice took the place of most other duties. Five of us went out for quarterback. I won the job, we won most of our games, and I was named first team all-Marine.

Those were the days when I fell in love with and considered marrying every woman who talked to me. Like Barbara Andrews. She was one of only a few black WAVES on the base in Norfolk—a gorgeous, sophisticated suburbanite from Detroit who was an aficionado of jazz and classical music, and had an ear and memory for poetry. (Technically, WAVES stands for "Women Accepted for Volunteer Emergency Service," but you can tell by the tortured language that the brain trust began with the acronym and worked backward.) The WAVES barracks were close to ours, so I'd spend evenings in their lounge just talking to her—actually, just listening to her. She thought of me as a sweet country bumpkin, especially after I brought up the *M* word.

"Marriage?" she laughed. "I hardly know you."

I couldn't explain that only married couples could be transferred together, and if we didn't marry, one of us would soon be transferred and we'd never see each other again. She was, and we didn't.

☆ ☆ ☆

In January 1961, PFC Larry O'Doul and I hitchhiked from Cherry Point up to Washington for JFK's inauguration. Larry was an Irish-Catholic from Boston and had spent the night of the Kennedy-Nixon election listening to the returns on the radio, pacing nervously. To him, the future of the free world depended on the Irish-Catholic senator from Massachusetts being elected president, and when the results came in he whooped and hollered and woke up the whole unit—an infraction for which he suffered several days of horrible duty. He didn't care.

Larry took it personally that he and I couldn't go out together on the town—that they wouldn't serve me. If we went to a Dairy Queen and they said they'd sell to him but not me, he'd threaten to beat the place down with his fists. It was especially bad after he'd had a few drinks. Finally he said, "I'm going with you. They'll serve me at black places, won't they?" I took him to all the little juke joints I'd discovered. The people who ran them were fascinated by this redheaded Northerner who would rather be with his friend in a dive than without him in luxury. In those days, a lot of people didn't see anything wrong with calling Larry a "nigger lover."

It's about 350 miles from Cherry Point to D.C. Larry begged for and got three-day passes for us, because neither of us was sure about how difficult it was going to be for a black Marine and a white Marine traveling together to hitch rides in the South. Three cars and a truck later, we got to D.C. the night of January 19 and stayed with a friend of his, sleeping on the floor. The next morning we woke early and found choice spots on the motorcade route. I remember it as one of the coldest days I'd ever experienced—teeth-chattering, knee-knocking kind of cold—and I couldn't understand how President Kennedy could endure the ride without a topcoat. But when he drew near, Larry and I took off our own coats so that our uniforms showed, and when he passed we stood at attention and saluted our commander in chief. Both of us held the salute a long time, and afterward Larry O'Doul didn't hide the tears running down his cheeks.

✭✭✭ **25** ✭✭✭

Burdett's crying has stopped. I light a cigarette and lean over to hand it to him. "Here," I say, reaching.

"No, thanks."

"Come on, take it. It's good for you."

I didn't mean it to be funny, but it is. I laugh, and that makes him laugh. He takes the cigarette and drags deeply. I light one for me. "The smoking lamp is lit, Captain," I say.

"You know when smoking's best?" he says.

"After sex?"

"You would say that. For me it's after eating."

"You would say that."

"Hey, betcha I've lost ten pounds already out here," he says. "My jeans are loose."

"Guess you'll have to get a new wardrobe when you get back."

"Sure thing." Pause. "You really think we're getting back?"

"Absolutely."

"What're you gonna go home and do?" he asks. "Get a job flying?"

"You mean after the war?"

"Whatever."

"I'm a lifer," I say. "In for the long haul. I'm aiming to be a general officer."

As soon as the words are out, I regret not holding on to them better. Some secrets are best kept, even when you haven't promised anyone you'll keep them, because they're not safe anywhere but inside you.

"Jesus Christ, Ezell. A general? That's—I mean, you know, why not president?"

"Because I don't want to be president. Okay? I want to be a general. You got a problem with that?"

"No." Pause—a pause laced with the history of slavery and Civil War and Reconstruction and Jim Crow and all-white juries and lynchings and poll taxes and a military culture run by men who earned their bars when the armed services were still segregated. "It's just that . . ."

"I know what it's just. It's a long shot. But my whole life's a long shot. Me being here now's a long shot."

"Should've bet the favorite," he says.

I say, "I disagree. I think as long as you try, there's more glory in not getting what you really want than in not trying and settling for what you don't want."

"So this is what you want? This? Being here?"

"Well, I believe that what doesn't kill you makes you stronger, and this jungle isn't gonna kill me, so that means it's gonna make me stronger. Right now I don't have any idea what I'll need that strength for, but I'm sure it'll be for something."

"Becoming a general."

"I can't help what I want, and I don't see why I should."

"Damn," he says quietly. It's a strange sentiment now, and I don't understand what he means. Maybe he's drawing back into himself again. Maybe the tears are on him again. Maybe anything.

What seems like a long time passes till he finally says, "Ezell, I have a confession." There's a grave tone in his voice, the kind I imagine Catholics get when they unburden themselves of something terrible to a priest.

But oh, no, I'm not falling for this again. "What? You're sorry about the mongoose?"

"Really, Ezell, this is important." He's as serious as he seemed to be last time.

"Something about snakes?"

"Hear me out. You remember I told you I'm from a small town?"

"In West Virginia."

"Yeah. Well, listen, I—" His voice falters. I can almost see him trying to find his center, and I wonder if he's really that good an actor. "I'm not proud of myself, Ezell. I mean, I used to be proud. But now—"

Just like that, I know where he's going with this. I can almost hear the words before he says them—hear them in my mind just before they come out of his mouth. They're in my own voice, these words, shouting something I should've heard before now but didn't, and the realization makes me gag on the secret I'd just confided to him. I trusted the wrong man. This man isn't worthy of knowing that I intend to make the Army my life and someday be a general—which for a poor black enlistee, already thirty years old and just a lieutenant with no higher-ups behind him to shuffle the right cards, is like planning retirement around winning the Irish Sweepstakes.

I feel sick and foolish that I confided my heart and dreams to a Klansman.

"Back home," he says slowly, sadly, "I was once something called the Grand Dragon. Do you know what that is?"

I don't respond; don't look over at him; don't move; barely breathe.

"You understand what I'm driving at, Ezell?" He sounds impatient, wondering why I haven't reacted. Impatient, probably, for absolution.

"Big deal," I say, "so you're just another asshole in a white sheet. I already figured that."

"No, you didn't. If you did, you wouldn't—"

I can't let him finish, because I don't want to hear my words echoed back to me. I say, "So what're you looking for? Forgiveness?" Well, he's not getting it from me. I can't give him what's not mine to give—and what I wouldn't give him anyway even if it were. Now that I think about things, that Vietnamese woman and her ox who someone said Burdett blew away just for fun when she wasn't even in a free-fire zone—that must've been like something he'd done before; here was this yellow-skinned woman, obviously an inferior breed, undeserving of life. "You best make your peace with God, Burdett, because it's not going to be with me. But first you'll have to fall on your knees in front of all the people you hurt and beg them for forgiveness."

"I wish I could, Ezell, but you're the only one here now."

"How convenient for you."

"What's that mean?"

"Lemme tell you how it is, Burdett. All my life, every time I go somewhere, everywhere I go, there's piles of shit in the road. They're just there, like they dropped out of the sky, big and small, some of them huge, far as the eye can see, pile after pile. And it stinks so bad sometimes I can't breathe, and I get goddamned tired of stepping over them or going around—it's just so far out of the way. So I understand why some men give up. And I understand why some men look at a mouse turd and think it's a boulder. They figure nothing you have to try that hard for is worth it, and they stop believing that they're ever gonna get to a place where there's just clean road ahead, smooth and downhill where they can coast. So they just roll over and die because it's easier, and maybe they'll get to heaven, and then it'll be downhill forever. No piles of shit in the road. It's so much easier to die than to put up with all that. It's easy to give up. But that's not me. I'm not made like that. I'll never give up. I can't. I won't. Never. And I won't die, either. I'll just keep going till I get there, because what I want is worth it, and I don't care how many piles of shit like you I have to step over or go around or through or under or just push out of the way. Could be a thousand, a million, ten billion—I don't care. You understand? I'm telling you right now, nobody's gonna stop me from getting what I want, because I want what I want and that's all the reason I need. Nobody. Nobody's gonna stop me. Especially not you."

Suddenly Burdett's face belongs to Everyman—that is, every man who ever got in my way just because of my skin color.

"Whoa, whoa, whoa. I never did anything to you," he says.

"Then what're you confessing to me for, goddammit?"

Burdett shushes me. "God almighty, why don't you just blow a bugle? Shut up already. There's gonna be gooks crawling on every limb."

"You didn't answer the question."

"What question?"

"Forget it."

I feel inside the kit and hand him the remaining malaria tablet and canteen.

"What're you doing?" he says.

I answer by grabbing on to a banyan sinew and dropping down, hanging for a second until my legs are under me. Now there are only about two and a half yards between my feet and the soft jungle floor.

"Leaving, huh? Hope the tiger don't get you," Burdett says.

"Better him than a snake."

He laughs, and not quietly. "Holy crap, Ezell, don't you know you gotta be Bogart to pull off a hard-assed line like that?"

I let go and drop, landing in a squat, then stand. Now what? It's way too dark to start walking—and I'm already blind with rage—but I've committed myself. Even if I have to feel my way to another tree and wait it out until first light, I can't stay with Burdett now.

As soon as he hears me walking, he shouts, "Watch out for those piles of shit." Then he laughs hard, and keeps laughing—and because he knows I won't ask what's so damn funny, he tells me.

He says, "You know you're not going anywhere—not without me. Tell you the truth, I don't think you'd last a day by yourself. Feeling superior to me is what keeps you goin' every day. You turn and look back at me and think what a poor, dumbfuck whitey I am, and that's what gives you what you need to keep on—stayin' ahead of me. You get to build yourself up on me. But let's say you do go out there now and make it alone. All right? Let's say you make it out of here in one piece and show up back at the LZ, and then they evac you out to Thailand and back to Korea and then wherever. Now what happens? Think about it. You know what happens. They give you another fucking medal and two weeks in a whorehouse somewhere, and that's as far as it goes. No more missions, no more promotions—and when this war ends, no need of you. Ain't that right, E-zell?"

He pauses a moment, like he wants me to answer the question. The answer I won't give him the pleasure of hearing is yes.

"But hey, you walk in dragging your lame captain—well, that changes everything, doesn't it? Yeah, now you tell the whole damn story about how you saved that asshole redneck's life every day, and when you wake up the next morning, there's another bar on your uniform. Captain Ezell Ware, Junior—the man who would be general. Isn't that right, Ezell? I'm your ticket out of Palooka-ville, buddy, and it's the only ticket you're ever going to get in this man's army. You know it and I know it. And that's just gotta be one royal bitch for you, because you want what you want, and you really want it, and you'll just have to do whatever it takes to get it. Isn't that what you said? So right now that big pile of shit in the road you have to go around is making sure that I get back in one piece—and if I don't, you don't, either."

Checkmate. The man has it right. I'm a prisoner of my own dream. What I want most is for my dream to come true; I want it more than I want to make him eat his words by beating it out of there first thing in the morning on my own. Between the two, it's no contest. I don't even bother factoring in how much easier it would be to escape alone, running full speed without him holding me back. No, either we both make it or neither of us does. It's a fact which, as he points out, makes him just another pile in the road.

But he's also wrong, because I know myself—and I know I couldn't abandon any fellow soldier, whether he's wearing a uniform or a white sheet, alone in the jungle to die. Even if no one would ever find out. Even if I someday rose to a five-star general of the Army. The rest of my life I'd be haunted by what I did back when, and the rest of my life wouldn't be worth living. I'd rather the rest of my life be short—and spent trying in vain to save both of us—than long and concerned with only me.

That doesn't mean, though, I can't let him suffer a little—and appreciate me that much more.

"Ezell? You there?"

I don't say a word. I don't move my feet. I don't do anything that might make noise and let him know I've been there all that time, listening.

"Ezell?"

Silence.

"Fuck!"

For an hour I stand frozen in the blackness, enjoying the smell of his sweat and fear, and taking cruel pleasure in his believing he wasted that whole damn argument on the jungle—that I'd already left him. This is the only time in the last week that I've felt proactive instead of reactive; that I'm the master of these ceremonies instead of a spectator at my own show. It's a small victory, true, but it's something.

When I'm sure by the rhythm of Burdett's breathing that he's fallen asleep, I tiptoe twenty yards away, feeling my way carefully through the dark so I won't accidentally wake him. I fall asleep leaning against the trunk of a tree while holding the gun in my lap.

✯ ✯ ✯ **26** ✯ ✯ ✯

Roosevelt Roads Missile Training Center is in Puerto Rico. Our job as radio operators was to transmit target coordinates to Marine and Navy pilots who'd then hit the targets with ordnance on the tiny island of Vieques, just off the eastern coast of Puerto Rico, most of which the Navy had bought in the late 1940s for just this purpose. The twenty of us in radio ops got to be as thick as the Caribbean air that they all complained about. (Not me; Puerto Rican humidity had nothing on the Mississippi summer, when you could sweat while swimming in a lake.) No football team I'd played on had the kind of camaraderie we did, all of us happily suffering the culture shock of seeing beautiful young women holding hands with each other while promenading teasingly in circles around the town square under the watchful eyes of lean and hungry young men—and the Catholic priests whose stern gaze seemed to change everyone's mood.

The Roosevelt Roads assignment treated me to a series of firsts. Puerto Rico was the first foreign country I'd visited, and everything about it—the smell, the look, the light, the music and sounds, the feel of the morning and night, the atmosphere—seemed exotic and pleasingly strange.

It was the first place I'd heard people speaking another language to each other. Before I managed to learn a few words and phrases and adjusted my ear, Spanish sounded like chatter to me—not so different from the made-up language I'd spoken with Lopez, who come to think of it was Latino, just like these folks.

And it was the first place I'd been that wasn't segregated. My goodness, what a revelation. In the same way that you only truly appreciate not being in pain by actually hurting, I don't think I'd ever fully grasped the insidiousness of Jim Crow until its ugly hand wasn't around my throat. Even my visits to Oklahoma as a child had been shaped by segregation. My buddies from radio ops and I could go anywhere we wanted together, into any night-club or sporting event or concert, and actually sit side by side without worrying. For the Northerners among them, this was a return to normalcy. For the Southerners, it was a glimpse of things to come.

So far my assignments had taken me from the Carolinas to Virginia to Puerto Rico—and everywhere in between—places I'd never been and was glad to be, no matter how hard the duty or how miserable the weather. The more I saw of the world, the more I wanted to see. And as long as I wouldn't be learning to fly, I figured I may as well let the Marines show me the world—or as much of it as possible. Even if I didn't re-up after my four years—and that was still an open question, because maybe they'd eventually let me into flight school—I'd always have the experience and memories of traveling to strange new worlds.

One day a buddy of mine named Ettinger—Jeremy Ettinger, a big jolly kid from Missouri with a purple birthmark on his forehead—noticed on the bulletin board that there was a single opening left for a twelve-month assignment on Okinawa. Now, Okinawa may have been many things to many people—an exotic locale and climate, a fascinating culture with noteworthy history (especially to Marines)—but to young, virile men who live in barracks housing with other men, it was best known as a place to mingle with the

Northern Hemisphere's preeminent ladies of the night. Ettinger and I were equally anxious to make their acquaintance.

"Which of us is it gonna be?" I asked our sergeant.

"Oh, no," he said. "You guys decide."

We flipped a coin, and while I was getting over losing I noticed a bulletin for something called a South Atlantic Friendship Cruise, to South America and Africa. Out of the entire Marine Corps, it said, only 240 Marines would be selected for the cruise—and, considering the destinations, the commanding officers were looking for something other than the usual mix. That meant the percentage of blacks on the crew would be higher than our overall percentage in the Marines. On the other hand, as the fine print made implicitly clear, the primary qualification was to be an outstanding Marine. We were to represent our country on an extended goodwill tour to several ports of call that the American military hadn't visited since the end of World War II, and each of us had to be considered an ambassador. That meant we had to have spotless records, several commendations, and no known history of alcohol-fueled antics. I qualified under all of those criteria, but I suspect that what got me on board were my football heroics as the Cherry Point base quarterback during my time there the previous fall. Like the outside world, the Marine Corps, too, admires elite athletes.

There were two ships on the excursion, one carrying mostly grunts and one carrying the mission's commanders, the highest-ranking of whom was a colonel.

After stops in several Latin American ports, we set sail for Africa. I applied for and got the duty as our colonel's driver, meaning that whenever we pulled into an African port I'd be at the wheel of his jeep as it came out of the ship's hold, and I'd be in charge of studying maps and debriefing locals to take him wherever he wanted to go.

As we drew closer to the continent, I became aware of some sort of pull I'd never before noticed—something about being black and African and returning to the land of my ancient ancestors. I thought of my grandparents' grandparents' grandparents, and wondered whether I'd see people who looked like me. The couple of other black Marines on my ship (most of the others were on the second ship) admitted to the same sort of formless excitement and anticipation, though in fact none of us knew the exact country or region of our ancestry.

First stop, though, was South Africa, where we'd certainly not come from. What I didn't know was that South Africa had its own kind of legal segregation laws. Frankly, I don't think our commanders knew that much about apartheid either, which was then about a dozen years old, or they probably wouldn't have selected me as driver. For the first official military delegation in over fifteen years, America would not have wanted to intentionally rub the ruling Afrikaners' white noses in the spectacle of a black Marine escorting and protecting his white commanding officer. In fact, a State Department employee boarded the ship in the Capetown harbor before we debarked for a briefing on where we could and couldn't go because of apartheid, and tried to convince Colonel Morgan to choose a white driver. Morgan refused. He said he'd already selected the best man for the job—and our week in Capetown passed without incident, unless you count the thousands of watchful eyes we attracted, and not a few disapproving tsk-tsks. When I wasn't with the colonel, I could only accompany other blacks—and then only into black areas. Almost like Mississippi.

In Port Elizabeth, around the Cape of Good Hope, I fell in love with a beautiful girl in the crowd who'd come to the dock and waved at all of us on deck. The feeling I had just looking at her looking at me when our eyes met would've been enough in itself, but I was able to invite her on board during the open house, and ate dinner at her family's home every night of the two weeks there. And though she was a good Christian girl, I learned the meaning of intimacy. Leaving her was painful, especially in that country of border-to-border Jim Crow laws.

We then sailed back around the Cape, and up the continent's west coast, with planned embarkations in Congo, Dakar, Senegal, and Liberia. First was Congo, which had recently earned its independence from Belgian rule. The land was just as I'd imagined— tall palms and grasses—and the air smelled virginally sweet. Africa! I could hear the blood pulsing in my ears as we drew near and could see tall, lean, black-skinned people in native robes. It wasn't that I wanted to jump ship and return to the motherland any more than a tenth-generation American of Italian descent suddenly moves "home" after eating pizza in Rome. But all my life the darkness of my skin had defined me to most of the outside world, and I was curious to see what life was like in a country where I'd be in the majority instead of standing out; to be where some people wouldn't mistrust me or hate me without knowing me; where no area was off-limits.

Years before, in 1923, the great black writer and poet Langston Hughes rode a merchant marine ship to West Africa feeling the same jumbled mix of anticipation and wonderment. "But there was one thing that hurt me a lot when I talked with the people," Hughes wrote. "The Africans looked at me and would not believe I was a Negro." In his case, the culprit was the relative lightness of his skin; he had some Caucasian genes in there somewhere. Though that still made him black in America, in Africa he heard cries of, "You white man. You white man."

Me, I wasn't hampered by light skin. I wasn't a white man to these Africans. No, I was an American. They sure got that right.

☆   ☆   ☆

My first week in Okinawa I ran into my old buddy Ettinger. He'd just about finished his thirteen-month duty and was headed home—back to civilian life. "You finally got here," he said. "Believe me, you're gonna love it."

I did. Okinawa is a narrow island shaped like ten after seven on a clock. It was a world caught between two extremes—the agricultural way of life that probably hadn't changed much since the early days of the samurai, and the modern tug caused by Japan's loss in the war, leading to occupation; thousands of Marines were stationed in several strategically positioned small Corps camps, and twice that many soldiers lived in a single large Army base. Naha, Okinawa's capital, is close to the island's bottom on the western coast. My Marine camp was located north of there—a kemshee cab ride from Koza.

Duty on Okinawa came with two taboos. One, you didn't marry a local girl. And two, if you got the clap, you took care of it somewhere else on the island, not through the base doctor, because if he knew about it you'd face an Article 15. This was like a misdemeanor, but a few of these could wash you out of the Corps. Worse than that, though, was being confined to base for thirty days. Other than those two things, if you kept your mouth shut and did your job and were back in your bunk by midnight, you were pretty much on your own during free hours. In fact, there were so many free hours that I rented a little hut, splitting the forty-bucks-a-month rent with another wire operator named Spitzer, a high-strung little guy who kept his black hair almost shaved. We furnished it with a couple of futons and heated it in the winter with coals under the floor. At night we'd entertain ladies for a few hours, or however long we had before midnight bunk check.

Sometimes I'd walk out to the fields and stand on the periphery to watch the straw-hatted farmers and their water buffalo tend rice. They'd already had fifteen years of Americans—white, black, brown, and yellow—in their backyards, so they barely noticed us anymore. When I'd observed them enough times and thought I understood the process, I got down and began tending the rice myself, alongside them. In time, trust developed. They saw I wasn't patronizing them, that I wanted to learn what they knew. Some of them even invited me into their homes for meals. Others took me fishing in the South China Sea and showed me how to catch squid with a knife, by spanking it on the head. They taught me Japanese words and terms, and didn't try to hide their young women from me.

In this extraordinary place the most extraordinary thing I saw was a black Marine officer—a captain. Captain Barry. Somewhere in the Marine Corps there had to be others, maybe even majors, possibly colonels. But I hadn't seen one yet in two and a half years—so unless they rotated another one in here over the next thirteen months, I wasn't likely to see one at all. I'd decided that unless they promoted me to staff sergeant—no, I'd do it for buck sergeant—I'd move on, out of the Marines. But this being peacetime, everybody in the Marines got promoted slowly. And everybody in the Marines complained about it. Most of the guys who'd once thought about being lifers and then didn't re-up after the four years opted out for just that reason. Still, I'd seen white men who I knew had lower scores and worse evaluations step up higher on the ladder that I thought I deserved to be climbing, too. It was hard not to believe that it had *something* to do with my skin color. But even if it did, Captain Barry obviously proved it could be done. And if it could be done by him, I could do it, too. In fact, the idea excited me: By watching him, I was going to be able to pick up pointers and learn what I needed to do. (Talking to him directly, and showing him my scores and evals, would've broken the chain of command.) To me, he became Superman. I'd see him walk across the base and stare—as if he were the ultimate celebrity.

Then came the letter. My base commander—Captain Wilkerson—called me in. He showed the Red Cross letterhead. I didn't have to look to know what was on it. There was only one reason guys got letters from the Red Cross.

In those days, duty and honor were forced on you, just in case you slipped through the cracks and didn't have any naturally.

"Corporal Ware," he said, "do you know a Miss Joanna Duvall?"

"Yes, sir, I do," I said, realizing that the last two words I'd just said would soon have to be repeated to someone else.

"Did you have any involvement with her that might have led to her being with child?"

"Yes, sir, I did," I said.

I'd met Joanna Duvall on a two-week leave after the African cruise, on a visit with my mother and sister in McAlester, Oklahoma. Turned out that my sister had just gotten married and was moving to San Diego with her sailor husband—Joanna's brother. Joanna was pretty, and she was fast, and we got intimate quickly. She was the first woman I hadn't fallen in love with, and she evidently was the one I was going to end up marrying. Did I believe the child was mine? I didn't believe or not believe. And what I believed didn't matter. In the Marines, duty and honor trumped the facts.

Captain Wilkerson explained how the Red Cross would help with underwriting the cost of a commercial flight to San Francisco. It was the only way to get there. The next troop transport ship didn't leave for a week, and if it took as long as the one I'd ridden over on, I wouldn't be in Oklahoma for a month and a half.

I flew to San Francisco and rode a bus thirty-six hours to McAlester, and honest to God didn't notice that Joanna's belly wasn't out to here, or wherever it's supposed to be at about five months—which according to my math was our last intimate night. The size of her belly was not what came to mind when I saw her. When I saw her, I saw the mother of my child—and tried to turn on a switch that would let me care for this woman as a husband cares for his wife.

So on a hot day in mid-1962, Joanna and I stood in the sun on the McAlester courthouse steps and said our vows before a judge. I did not want to be married. But now I was, and with one of the two nights I had left before getting back to Okinawa, I needed to make the twelve-hour bus ride to Magee and tell Ma and Pa they were going to be great-grandparents. Before leaving, I filled out an official allotment so that Washington would be sending her half of my pay directly. Until I got back in another six months or so, she'd stay with her folks, there in McAlester. That was the plan.

"I told you, Ezell," Aunt Lee said when I got to Magee. "Damn, I told you to keep that thing zipped up in your pants."

Well, there was no arguing with that now.

But there was with Ma. She said, "I smell no good. I smell a girl wantin' your money. The girl found a way to it."

"You're wrong," I said. "She's not after my money. Besides, I don't make that much." I made less than ninety dollars a month. "Lots of guys out there make more."

"Hell, boy," Pa said, "you got a job. Lotsa guys got no job's what they got."

There was no arguing with that, either.

Sure, Joanna might've engineered this whole scene knowing that I'd be there, in Okinawa, doing whatever I did there, and she'd be here with half my money. People can be very clever about acting in their own self-interest. Not that I was as clever, but it did occur to me that married Marines tended generally to be promoted faster and higher than unmarried Marines. So maybe this would work out after all. Not that that was selfish; it would work out for all of us better if I got promoted—better pay, better duty, better locales.

The rules kept Okinawa servicemen from having any dependents on the island with them. I didn't know whether that was because they hadn't yet built dependent housing, or whether they hadn't built it because Okinawa was the type of place that didn't jibe very well with having a family around, and it was the type of duty you kept extending if you could.

You will, I hope, not be surprised to hear that I no longer entertained ladies at my bachelor shack. In fact, most nights I worked at the base bowling alley as a pin setter, setting all four lanes, at ten cents a game, for four hours. That came to an extra fifty bucks a month. I'd send it all to Joanna.

Then came the letter.

"Looks like I'm not having a baby after all," Joanna wrote. She didn't say whether she'd lost the baby, or whether there'd never been a baby. "I hope this letter finds you well. Love, your wife, Joanna." There were some other things in the middle, but that was the only meat.

I didn't know what to make of it, so I made nothing. I was twenty-one years old, and the dumbest smart guy in the Marine Corps. I figured I'd transfer for a while from radio ops to temporary additional duty (TAD) in Special Services—meaning I went out for the Okinawa Marines football team.

The Okinawa Marine Corps team had a long reputation for being tough and good. A few years before, Big Daddy Lipscomb, the great pro defensive end, had played on the team.

We didn't have Big Daddy, but we weren't bad. I couldn't even make first-string quarterback. I played halfback, because we had a guy from San Diego who could throw the ball forty yards on a string.

The team competed against bases from all over the South Pacific and Far East, from Japan to the Philippines. Half the time, when not playing football, we traveled on Navy ships that floated around the Pacific, even down to Thailand and Hong Kong, and except for finding someplace to practice on deck, the most we'd do is help scrub and repaint the ships.

My season ended in practice right before the fifth game. Doing hundred-yard wind sprints I felt a pop at eighty yards and hopped the last twenty. My leg was okay to walk—well, limp—but not to play.

A week later the Cuban missile crisis interrupted the season. Like every active American military unit around the world, the 9th Marine Regiment was placed on high alert. Our mission, if it were ordered, was to go to the Himalayas and block the Chinese army from making a move. It was the kind of work we'd trained to do earlier in the year during thirty-day cold-weather maneuvers on

Mount Fuji—done without proper cold-weather clothing. The gear had been delayed in transit, so the regiment colonel in charge announced that none of us had to go on the maneuvers unless we chose to, and then, as we stood there in formation thinking about the option, he'd delivered a stirring speech about what the Marines had endured in the snows and ice of Korea. He turned into Colonel Knute Rockne. Of course, not one jarhead opted out. Every one of us had stepped forward when he asked for volunteers. We were Marines. *Semper fi.* Anyway, we knew the colonel himself was going to go, because that's what Marine officers did. They didn't order you on five- or fifteen-mile runs; they ran with you. They didn't send you out into the belly of the beast, they led the way and lit the darkness. Never did I see a Marine company commander eat until his men had already eaten and he'd watched his first sergeant go through the line, too. Marine commanders lead by participation, and they will not ask you to die without risking their lives, too. In fact, we did risk our lives in the cold of Mount Fuji. That none of us froze to death on those maneuvers was a miracle. So nothing could've been worse than what we'd already endured, because now we had the proper gear; we were prepared for our mission to the Himalayas. But before we could save the world from blowing up that October, the fuse went out in Washington and Moscow. I would be lying if I said that the teeth-gnashing anxiety of possibly being in a real war didn't make me feel more alive than I ever had.

★★★ **27** ★★★

At first light I move to the other side of the tree, where I can keep an eye on Burdett when he comes down.

As soon as he wakes he drops the first-aid kit and canteen to the ground. I realize too late that I've taken this charade too far. If he screws up the leg even more—or hurts the other one—I'll have to suffer, too; he's my responsibility. Burdett grabs on to a banyan sinew and drops down the way I did. But six feet is a long way to land on just one leg. He tumbles sideways and grabs his leg, groaning and moaning, though quietly.

After a minute he manages to get up, hopping on the good leg to pick up the canteen and kit. He stuffs them into his vest, stops to take a leak, picks up the two wooden canes, and heads in my direction. The look on his face as he limps tells me it hurts worse than ever—or maybe that's just the fear of having to do this by himself. I start to feel sorry for him, then change my mind. I come at him fast from the side, putting my hand on his weapon before he can draw it but letting him see right away I'm not trying to take it from him.

"Crap," he says, "you scared the shit out of me."

I say, "Now listen up, Burdett," and reach into the bag for the crumbling map. I open it and point to a spot—a plateau that looks like it may be in the open. "That's where we're going to be tonight. You'd best keep up."

I reach into his vest and take out the canteen and kit, and check the T-shirt "handles" on the two canes. I say, "Let's go."

"I knew you didn't leave," he says.

"Shut up."

I lead the way and at first go too quickly. Without comment, he keeps up as well as he can, and I go more slowly. The pace makes it too easy to think—about how unlikely it is that we'll ever get out of here; about how hot and hungry and miserable I am; about that moment of honesty and where it might've led instead of to where it did. That's right, it's safer to stay away from intimacy and honesty and close friendship, just the way I always have.

After a few minutes I stop and turn over a rotted log.

"What're you doing?" he whispers.

Underneath it are several dozen grasshoppers. The morning dew is thick on their legs and wings, so they can't easily scatter. In another hour they'll be able to scatter fast. I stuff several dozen into the kit bag and remove one for Burdett. "Here," I say, "breakfast."

He doesn't know what to do with it till I show him: You eat the legs, not the body; just chew them right off. They don't taste bad or good. They just taste. Right now, food is anything that can nourish us, and right now anything edible that won't kill us is food.

Burdett gets with the program and reaches into the kit to take out four or five at a time. "I guess that animal instinct kicks right in," he says, chewing.

In truth, our animal instinct had kicked in long before we got shot down.

★ ★ ★ **28** ★ ★ ★

If you don't drink, and you know you're not going to drink, and even so you go places with your friends who believe drinking is the only real way to start a night of recreation and blow off steam, you get used to fights breaking out with no provocation; and you're forced to get used to the overly sentimental, overly hostile, overly everything things that drunk people say to people they know aren't drunk. Over the three years I'd gotten good at nodding my head and laughing, but one night I forgot what I'd learned; actually, I chose to forget. A guy from West Virginia who'd rotated into our barracks snuck in after curfew and shook me awake. He wanted to tell me, he said, "I got no problem with niggers. You understand? I don't got no problems with any niggers. I don't mind niggers at all. You get me?" His breath smelled like a beer tap.

Maybe it was the times—reading in *Stars and Stripes* about the Freedom Riders in the South and what they were risking and accomplishing, and comparing myself to them and thinking about why anyone had to ride buses for freedom. Maybe it was hearing that word "nigger," which I'd heard all my life but now understood, maybe for the first time because it had been so long since

I'd heard it uttered, what an ugly word it was—the ugliest of the ugly. It could've been either of those things, but it was probably the letter from home saying that Ma had died and was already buried. Her heart had stopped and there was no way and no money to get her to a hospital—and no way and no money for me to get there before her funeral.

Oh, it was the hardest I'd ever been hit. My goodness, Ma gone. I could barely think of the world without her. It had been a week and I hadn't told anyone. But keeping it to myself only multiplied its horror. So I was in no mood for this redneck asshole telling me that some of his best friends were niggers.

I sprang up from my bunk and grabbed him around the neck, squeezing to kill. I didn't say, *Don't you ever call me that again. Don't you ever use that word again around me,* because I didn't intend for him to have an ever again. I intended to kill him. And if it weren't for Frank from San Francisco and two others prying my fingers loose and pulling me back, he'd have been in hell before I came to my senses. And then I'd have been in hell, too.

Camp Pendleton was the way station back to America. With just four months to go in my hitch, they put me with a group of guys in the same situation—short-timers, you're called. Same as prison. We had to sit through about half a million reenlistment lectures. They sweet-talked you. But to keep me on a six-year re-up, all the Marines would've had to do was make me a full corporal now. I hadn't gotten even that. Three and a half years of good, hard work at the highest level, and I was still only a lance corporal—just two small steps above where I was the day I finished boot camp. I showed the reenlistment officer my record and pointed out how Buck Sergeant Chandler had selected me out of hundreds for a mission to go on maneuvers with the Taiwanese marines, setting up a relay station on a mountain—which meant climbing eight thousand feet with 120 pounds on my back. I said I'd seen a lot of other jarheads get promoted higher and faster with résumés that weren't as solid. I didn't need to draw the conclusion for him. What was he going to do, admit it? There was no point. Besides, the only thing I wanted to hear was an assurance that I deserved at least consideration for promotions that would let me rise to the level of my abilities and ambition. I wouldn't hear it, because he couldn't say it, but it was true.

They let me out a couple of months early, so I could start school the fall semester at the University of Oklahoma. There was nothing I could do about being black—no way to control how much it would get in the way of what I wanted in life. But there was still something I could do to make myself more valuable—get an education. Earn a degree. That's something they can't ignore and can't take away. Four years on, I thought, I might want to do anything with that piece of paper in hand, even go back into the service—probably the Army—as an officer. Education seemed like the ticket to anywhere.

On the day I was discharged, I conspicuously (as well as petulantly and childishly) threw all my Marine gear into a base Dumpster. That's called destroying government property, and it made the wrong people mad. Since I was still on the base when I did it, I was technically still a Marine, and they intended to throw me in the brig. I said, "I get a call before you do." I called Senator Tom Kuchel's office and said to his aide, "Sir, I'm about to start school. I have a government loan to go back and study, and I need to be in Oklahoma by Monday, and I have to take a bus there from San Diego, which means I have to get started now." My reasoning must've been convincing. The senator's office spoke with the base commander, and a little while later I walked out free.

The date was August 28, 1963. On that day, and at that moment, Martin Luther King was giving a speech on the steps of the Lincoln Memorial in Washington, D.C., that ended, "Free at last. Free at last. Thank God almighty, we're free at last." All these years later, knowing how the "I have a dream" speech has become one of history's most famous moments, the symbolism of my leaving the Marines on that very day had the air of a bad TV movie. But that night, watching the speech on the news at my sister's in San Diego, I shivered. Not because he'd singled out Mississippi as a "desert state, sweltering with heat and oppression," but because I believed his dream could come true.

✫   ✫   ✫

I'd been friendly with Billy Joe Duvall, my sister's husband and my wife's brother, for a few years. Until I told them, they didn't know that Joanna and I had gotten married. Or maybe they did know but just wanted to keep from having to say what I found twenty minutes after getting off the bus and knocking on Mr. and Mrs. Duvall's door. Joanna wasn't living with them. She was living with a guy named Robinson who worked in a gas station. Mr. Duvall said, "If you want to go up there and shoot her, I'll give you my pistol."

I said, "No, I need to go to school, not prison."

Apparently a lot of men in that situation do take out the gun. The rage makes them blind and dumb—dumb as in stupid.

But I was too stunned to feel much of anything. Well, bewildered— I felt bewildered. How could she not see any potential in me? How could she let me go for someone making maybe fifty bucks a week pumping gas?

That's what I do when something goes wrong. I personalize it—not what happened to me, but what I did to make it happen. It's what I was raised to do, to look in the mirror. So I spent a long time wondering how I'd made Joanna think she had a better future with someone who might've already been doing the thing he was going to do for the rest of his life.

I knocked on her door, hoping I might get an explanation. She could barely look me in the eye. And that was it. End of subject. I left and went up to Norman, to start school. In short order, the stunned numbness wore off and the hurt moved in right behind it—a hurt like no other hurt. Ma's death I at least knew was coming someday. But this challenged everything I'd assumed or thought I understood. It was my relentless enemy, and all I could do was try to make peace with it. The hurt became such a constant and wore off so slowly that I can't tell you when it went away. Maybe it never did.

There were tens of thousands of students at the University of Oklahoma, but I don't think I saw another one as old as I was—twenty-two. My living situation was hard. I didn't have much money to spend, and the dorms had closed by the time I sent in my application. A married friend let me stay in his married-housing room—it was a hut, actually—while he was bunking with his wife up in Oklahoma City at her parents' house.

When money's tight, I always think to cut back first on food. It's easy. You just buy about four loaves of bread a day and drink a lot of water to fill your belly. It doesn't mean you won't be hungry for real food. It just means you won't starve in the meantime.

Without knowing it I must've walked around with that lean and hungry look, because on the third day, when I happened to pass a guy doing some carpentry on a storefront half a block from campus, he called me over. Gone were the days when a white man of thirty-five calling me over could make me check instinctively for the work gloves in my back pockets. I'd decided that the way he worked meant he wasn't a real carpenter; that he probably owned the place or was leasing it and wanted to do the improvements himself. Either that or he couldn't afford to pay anybody.

"You hungry?" he said.

"Why do you ask?" I said.

"Want to share my lunch?"

"Uh . . ."

"Come on, my wife always makes too much, and I could use some company." He opened the black metal box and pulled out a big sandwich, already cut in two. He handed me half.

I took it. "Thank you."

"Name's Carleton," he said. "Tim Carleton."

"Ezell Ware." We shook.

"So it's *Ee*-zell, with the accent on the first syllable?" he said.

"That's right," I said. "Most people get it wrong. I guess they don't hear me say it very often."

I bit into the bologna sandwich and almost rolled my eyes in ecstasy over the flavor. It was hard not devouring it like a feral dog.

"What's your major?"

"Chemical engineering."

He laughed, then explained: "I don't think I've ever met a chemical engineering major. Hell, I don't think I even know what chemical engineering is."

"I'll let you know when I find out." We both laughed.

"You a senior here?"

"Freshman."

"Must've been in the Army, huh?"

"Marines."

He snapped a big carrot in two and gave me the half in his left hand. I thanked him.

"A Marine? Geez. A real Marine. That's great. I won't mess with you."

We talked about where I'd been stationed, and I described a few of the places I'd been. He was about the right age for Korea, but he didn't say anything about it and I didn't ask whether he'd served. He said he was opening a restaurant—a student hangout with burgers, fries, malts, beer, and coffee—and suggested I work for him when it opened. "I'm gonna call it Across the Street."

I looked across the street, to see what was there. "Across the street from campus," I said. "Like, 'Let's go across the street.' "

The next day about lunchtime I walked across the street, and again Tim shared his lunch. This time I stayed to help him work, and over the next couple of weeks, until Across the Street was completed, I worked for my lunch by doing carpentry. And as soon as it opened, I waited tables and washed dishes. Too bad I liked the restaurant work more than I liked school. School so far wasn't quite what I'd anticipated. I'd pictured something like Socrates in the town square, guiding eager students through the accumulation of knowledge. But this was more like a degree factory. In a few of my classes, held in giant lecture halls, you almost needed field glasses to see the professor. In others, I didn't know what the problem was. I was getting Cs in the humanities classes and Bs in math and chemistry—and was none too happy about either. As for my love life—well, I couldn't seem to muster enough energy or interest.

Tim tried to improve my mood by fixing me up with a black lady who worked with his wife in a hospital. He invited me to his house to meet her, and when I arrived the living room was filled with white people mobilizing to leave Oklahoma on buses and register black voters in Mississippi and Alabama. It wasn't much of a date.

November 22, 1963. By one-thirty that afternoon everyone on campus had heard President Kennedy was dead. Hundreds cried, and thousands more looked like they wanted to—including me. I only saw one guy laughing and hooting—happy that that "niggerloving president" had bought the farm.

There was no connection between that and my quitting school the following June, three years shy of that degree. Or maybe there was. Maybe it was just another brick in the road I'd been building all my life, but I wouldn't know it till it finally led me somewhere.

The Beatles were the story the following summer, at least in San Diego. If you didn't hear them every time you turned on the radio, you heard somebody talking about them.

I stayed at Dorothy and Billy Joe's with them and their three kids. It was Navy housing on Point Loma, and already too cramped for the five of them before I got there. Billy Joe was a seaman third class. He was sure the Navy was racist—in fact, the worst of the branches. "You know," he said, "when you're out there in the middle of nothing and your life is in their hands, you do what the man says." And the man said, "Cook." Rarely did a black man rise higher than cook.

My mother and Mr. Shorty had moved to San Diego, too, and were living up the highway in Linda Vista. Dorothy had written her about the weather—telling her how the sea breeze smells so good and keeps the air from getting too hot in the summer and too cold in the winter, and that there was no humidity. I slept on their couch and looked for a job. I'd start with the help wanteds in the paper, apply in person, and then, while I was in the neighborhood, knock on doors.

One of them was General Dynamics, on the Pacific Coast Highway. Just so happens the company needed four machinist's apprentices, didn't have any minorities, and wanted one. That meant they hoped a minority took the test, which was mostly math, and finished in the first four—out of three thousand. If he did, they'd gladly take him into the program. I did. And they did.

In a way it was like the military, getting paid to learn. But the pay was a lot better, and the promotion was assured after four years of training. All you had to do was not flunk out of the program. I got my own apartment in a small complex downtown, in a mostly white area, because it was close to work and close to the college where apprentices would be taking classes. My neighbors were working-class people, and pleasant to me. Farther south was the black area of town, Logan Heights. They called it a ghetto, and it was, but it had better amenities than Magee.

At work, you had to go from master machinist to master machinist, to learn all the machines making aircraft parts. Precision meant everything. A tolerance of one one-thousandth of an inch was the difference between flight and failure. So these were no-nonsense guys. As an apprentice, if you didn't act like you knew everything, they'd treat you all right. If you went in with an attitude, you were on your own. Just like everything else in life.

Apparently I was the only black at GD not working as a janitor or at something menial. Most of the others were older, and I could see that familiar dullness in their eyes. But at the same time, they considered me a symbol of hope, and they watched out for me any way they could, like I was their kid. I didn't want to let them down.

One day after a few months I came home and stood on the catwalk between apartments and smelled the ocean and wondered whether this was what I wanted my life to be—learn a good trade, make a decent living, and, well, whatever came next. Whatever it was didn't seem like anything I'd dreamed of. What happened to flying? To leading men in battle? To action and adventure? I was only twenty-three. If I stopped dreaming now, I'd never start again. The image that came to mind was of the hollow men. I didn't want that for me, but I'd already walked away from an education. So now what?

★ ★ ★ **29** ★ ★ ★

A chopper passes at the usual time, and I press the transmitter button. I can tell its battery is losing power; the red indicator light doesn't glow as brightly as before. But the chopper turns north again, so obviously it got the message. Good thing we have a second ETR.

Inside, I feel hope rise the way I do every morning when it passes. I'd like to celebrate the moment with Burdett, as we had before. I'm not ready, though, and may never be again. Even so, I catch a glimpse of his face and notice that he doesn't seem all that happy. I wonder why.

We walk for an hour, maybe more—the most we've walked continuously since the first day. I've decided not to care how much his legs hurts. If we don't get out of the jungle soon, the pain of walking now will be like a skinned elbow compared to what the enemy will do to him and it. And me. I know I have a day or so to press the advantage from last night. He's not going to say a thing no matter how hard I push us.

I see some wild berries of some kind not far away—a mulberry bush. I pick the berry bush clean, stuffing them in the kit. They're not cold but they're as delicious as anything I've ever put in my mouth.

I pull a big mulberry off and hand it to him. Apparently he's never seen one before.

"This is something you eat?" he says.

"It's a mulberry."

"Looks like it's got cancer."

I take it from his hand, say, "Then don't eat it," and put it in my mouth. He hobbles over and cuts one for himself. I clean that bush, too, and fill the bag.

We walk on and I step the wrong way on a tree root, twisting my leg. It sends a jolt through my back.

For the rest of the day we walk an hour and rest fifteen minutes, walk an hour and rest fifteen, walk and rest. During one break I refill the canteen. When I come back Burdett's sitting on his rear and fussing with his wound. It's now an atrocious-looking thing—swollen thirty percent bigger than normal and oozing red everywhere except for the two big pockets that must be filled with pus. He waves the bugs away, but this is their home now; they've found the mother lode. We're out of sulfa and gauze.

"Can you smell it?" he says.

"No," I lie.

"Gangrene or just an ordinary infection?"

"Not gangrene."

"I think," he says, "that I need to lance the pockets. It'll relieve some of the pressure."

"You sure?"

"No. But at this point—"

"Want me to do it?" I ask, taking out my knife and cigarette lighter.

"Oh, I bet you'd like that."

"Here," I say, offering him my knife.

"No, you."

The tip of the knife comes to a lethally sharp point. I heat it to glowing red under my lighter—not that the infection he already has isn't worse than what he might get from the blade.

Burdett removes his vest and says, "Just get it over with," then puts the vest between his teeth and leans back on his hands. He nods.

I hesitate and then jab the first pocket—too big to be called an ordinary pustule—a quarter inch down, though on the side away from me in case it explodes. Burdett's scream is smothered by the vest.

No explosion, just green and yellow pus pouring out.

"One more," I say—and get it over with fast. Same result.

Burdett watches the fluids drain with what looks to me like a kind of detachment, as though, in some way, this is no longer his leg.

"Keep that vest in your mouth," I say before emptying the canteen over the wound. It must hurt almost as much as the knife—and lasts longer.

I tell him to give me his T-shirt. He takes it off, knowing that I'm going to wrap the leg. I do it—tearing it in half to make it longer—before the bugs return. At least now he'll have a little protection against things nesting in there. I run off to fill the canteen again and notice a crayfish in the creek bottom. I stab him with my knife, but when I come back Burdett's not hungry, only thirsty.

"You never had a crawdaddy?" I say. "Good eating."

He shakes his head no and climbs to his feet and grabs his canes. The pain is now permanently in his face.

"Let's get going," he says.

I eat the crayfish myself.

★★★ **30** ★★★

The San Diego Police Department used to recruit heavily in the South. That should tell you what the city fathers thought would please their constituents. Out of 750 officers on the force, only three were black—but there were three more of us who passed the entrance test and made it into the 1965 academy class of thirty.

I like to think that I chose to be a policeman because I'd decided that the war between black people and police would someday lead to another civil war, and I didn't want that.

First thing after graduating from the police academy is apprenticing—partnering with a veteran. That's where the education starts.

My partner was Jim King, originally from Paragould, Arkansas. When he saw me he looked like he'd shown up at a gunfight and been handed a knife. And then it got worse. They assigned us a beat in and around Fifth Street, downtown—a black area. High crime. A lot of nightclubs and prostitutes. More than its share of fights and murders.

Getting a nigger for a partner to work in niggertown, Jim must've thought he was being punished. Maybe he was, by a captain who imagined he could improve community relations. Jim didn't give a hoot about community relations, and anyway figured that I'd side with "them"—the enemy—if things got ugly. Hearing I'd also been a Marine—he'd landed at Inchon and then been stationed at the same Okinawa camp as I had—softened him only a little.

Our first night out we saw an old Rambler run a red light. We turned on the cherry and siren and pulled it over. Three young black men were in the car. Jim started to get out. I said, "No, let me."

"Sure thing, rookie," he said.

I approached the car. "May I see your license, please?" I asked.

The driver turned and did a Jackie Gleason double-take. Black Moses had come to San Diego.

"Lookit that," he said. "Lookit that. Damn, a Negro cop."

"Your license, please."

Shaking his head, he handed it to me. His name was Floyd—Travis Floyd.

I told him what he'd done wrong and began writing the ticket. Meanwhile, Jim was just watching from back in the car, interested.

"Here you are, Mr. Floyd," I said, handing him the ticket and his license back. He pulled his hands away.

"Uh-uh, I ain't takin' it," he said. "I didn't run no red light."

"Just take it."

I pushed it toward him.

"Ain't takin' it from you." He snatched the license. "I'll take this, you keep that."

Jim had seen enough. He stepped out of the cruiser and over to the car. He leaned over and put his face right near to Floyd's. Floyd was a changed man, just like that.

"We got a problem here?" Jim asked.

"No, sir, no problem."

"Good," Jim said. He took the ticket from me, read it quickly, handed it to Floyd. "This has your name on it, Travis. Here."

Floyd took it.

A scene like that happened probably twice a week. It said a lot about a lot of things. "You're just supporting the white establishment." I heard that probably three times a week.

What changed things between Jim and me was *Thunderball*, the fourth James Bond movie. Like all Bond movies, it had a lot of testosterone and attracted young men with a lot of testosterone who don't always know how to control the extra blood fuel. Sometimes things turn ugly, the way they did at a downtown movie theater. Six toughs tried to break in and see the movie without paying, so the panicked manager called the cops. Jim and I showed up, confronted them, and said that they'd have to leave unless they intended to pay.

"We ain't paying for shit," one of them said.

We didn't have time to call for backup—or draw our guns—before a fist landed on Jim's chin and knocked him backward. The brawl was on. It was six against two—six young black men against a black officer and a white officer, both of them former Marines. Jim and I threw punches and took punches, swung our nightsticks and had them swung at us. We might've shot the men if we could've, if only because they were trying to get their hands on our guns and shoot us. That meant we had to do everything to keep our guns out of their hands—which limited how well we could fight. I hadn't seen many people hopped up on drugs then, but it didn't take a genius to see that these guys were mostly numb to pain. The theater owner called in the fight.

Usually when officers are involved in an altercation, back-ups respond immediately, but not this time. The action spilled into the theater lobby after the front doors broke. Soon the candy counter had shattered and pieces of glass were being used as weapons, too. Jim and I stood back-to-back, like the settlers circling wagons until the cavalry arrived. And finally it did.

Later, when we were in the infirmary getting patched and stitched and bandaged, Jim said, "You know, I didn't volunteer to be your partner."

"I know," I said.

"I didn't want a, uh, Nigrah as a partner."

"I know."

He paused. "But damn, you're the real thing. *Semper fi,* Ezell."

"*Semper fi,* Jim."

Pause. "Damn, boy, you sure can fight."

"Jim."

"Yeah?"

"Don't call me boy."

I held off the smile for a moment, and then showed it to him.

"Shit," he said. "I'd rather call you partner."

From then on we worked well together, because he trusted me, and if there's one thing cops need from their partners, it's trust. "You're my foxhole man," he used to say.

One detail we pulled was to protect Bull Connor. The notorious public safety commissioner from Birmingham, Alabama, had come to make a speech inside a school auditorium. This was the man who'd ordered police dogs and fire hoses trained on civil rights demonstrators. Jim and I were stationed outside. We could hear the thousand people liking what he was telling them, about the need to keep Negroes and whites apart forever—at any cost. No, they loved what he was telling them. It sounded like a revival meeting in there. Jim looked uncomfortable as hell—and embarrassed. He shook his head. I considered that progress.

I also pulled the Beatles duty, when they came to play the city college football stadium. A hundred of us ringed the track to keep people away. I remember their vehicle speeding out of the tunnel and delivering them to the stage set up in the middle of the field. The screams were so loud I had to cover my ears. But it didn't let up. For forty-five minutes they might just as well have been singing opera or even nothing at all. I don't think anyone could've told the difference.

☆　☆　☆

The weekly poker game was at my brother-in-law Billy Joe's house. Usually I won, but tonight I'd had a streak of bad cards and pushed my luck, trying to bluff my way into the pot, thinking they'd fold based on my past performance. Time and again my jack high or pair of deuces got called. Not this hand, though. I'd pulled a full house, jacks over threes—and was going to get back everything I'd lost so far. The betting pushed out Bernard, Wilson, Henry, and Tyler; they were Billy Joe's neighbors. Only Billy Joe was left, and he wouldn't budge. We kept raising each other until I didn't have another dime left in my pocket or a penny in my loafers.

"Well, look at that," Billy Joe said, leaning back and puffing on his cigar. "The man's out of money. Hmm, hmm, hmm. But I do believe it's my bet."

"Tyler," I said, "cover me, will you?" I showed him my cards.

"Ain't no need for that, Ezell," Billy Joe said. "I'll tell you what. I'm so goddamned tired of hearing how you wish you were a pilot, and you want to take the Army flight test, 'cause you know you'd pass, and then you'd get to fly. You put your money where your mouth is. Fact, right now your mouth *is* your money."

"What the hell are you talking about?"

"I'm talking about you. You lose, and you drive up to L.A. and take that flight test."

"I'm not gonna lose."

"Yeah, well, we'll see about that. But if you do, you take that test. All right?"

It meant that if I took the test and passed, I'd have to decide whether to go in the Army. If I passed and didn't go in, it would mean I'd given up on my dreams. This was 1966—a time when America was discovering a place in Southeast Asia called Vietnam; thousands of its young men were being sent there to stop the Communist dominoes from falling.

"Sure, Billy Joe, sure," I said. "I may even take that test anyway, but I'm not gonna lose this hand. Read 'em and weep"—I laid down the cards—"full boat—jacks over threes."

"Yeah, well," Billy Joe said, "you're about a jack short, brother-in-law." He laid down his cards. "They may be only twos, but there's four of 'em."

I stared at those twos for a long time. "You're not gonna hold me to this, are you? I was just joking."

"Want me to ride you up there?" Billy Joe said. "Or you gonna fly?" He laughed and raked in the pot.

✮   ✮   ✮

The test was given in the reception station near downtown Los Angeles. It started at ten. I arrived at eight to get the feel of the place. If you passed the first day's tests, you needed a second day, too, so I'd put in for three days' vacation from the SDPD.

There were about forty other applicants, one of them as old as I and most just a year or two younger. You didn't need a college degree to go to flight school, just two years' worth of higher education (I got credit for my year and a half at Tougaloo and Oklahoma, and classes taken for the police academy and machinist apprenticeship). You didn't need to be white, either, though I saw only two other blacks.

When the proctor said, "Begin," I turned the test over and quickly scanned it. Most of it was math, some of which I'd never learned or seen but could figure out just on innate aptitude. But how was I supposed to answer questions about the angle of a wing tilted just so? I laughed to myself, because there was obviously no way I could pass this thing. Apparently I wouldn't be needing that second day off.

At noon we broke for an hour-long lunch, which I couldn't eat, and I kept overhearing guys talk about how great they'd done so far and how easy it all was. At five we finished the test, and the military proctors asked us to stay put while they graded the results. The forty of us sat and fidgeted and I heard some of the same guys bragging about how they'd aced the thing.

Half an hour later, Captain Fryman walked back in holding a

sheet of paper. "If I call your name, please remain seated. If I don't, I want to thank you, gentlemen, for your interest in the Army's flight program and hope that you will be able to serve your country in other, equally important ways."

I recognized after the third name that the list was organized alphabetically, and I understood that when he skipped from Baker to Green to Norton it was going to be a short one. I held my breath as he approached *W* territory. Ware was the last name called—the last of only six.

The others filed out moaning and muttering, and I took some satisfaction in noting that none of the braggarts had passed—but then neither did either of the other two blacks; they stared at me on the way out, not with anger but with admiration. The six of us who'd passed—Remeny and Travers were the other two—looked at each other and nodded and smiled and gave the thumbs-up.

The Army put us up, one to a room, in a fleabag hotel a few blocks away and gave us five bucks to get some dinner. All six of us walked down to Clifton's Cafeteria and pigged out. The subject over dinner was Vietnam—the place we were all likely to be sent if we made it through flight school. By 1965, it had become an air cavalry war. And by 1966, a lot of people our age—and some prominent politicians—were starting to make noises against it.

After dinner, Remeny suggested we grab a few beers.

"Alcohol doesn't sound like something you want in your blood tomorrow, do you?" Norton asked him.

"No," he said, "it's something I want in my blood tonight."

As I would come to see, Remeny had the makings of a real Army pilot in Vietnam.

If I could've fallen asleep that night, I would've dreamt about flying; nothing else would fit in my mind.

The next morning a bus took us to a windowless lab complex with bright fluorescent lighting that made it look sickly sterile. For hours, we went from station to station. Nurses took blood and other fluids and doctors poked and prodded. Remeny stripped to nothing every time he knew a nurse was coming in the room—and laughed when she reacted. The last nurse said dryly, "You're such a child."

"Ah, come on," he said, "it's just a little fun."

"No," she said with a practiced sarcasm, "I mean you, uh, look like a boy." And then *she* laughed.

The test they focused hardest on was eyesight. They were disappointed if you couldn't see the dust on a butterfly's wings at a hundred yards. If necessary, though, they'd settle for twenty-twenty. I had better than that.

I passed. We all passed. They signed us up, swore us in, gave us travel vouchers, and ordered us to be at Fort Polk, Louisiana, in a week—all except me, that is. Seems that because I'd been a Marine, which meant I'd survived boot camp, I could skip the six weeks of basic training and go straight to Fort Wolters, Texas, for flight school. They also had to get permission from the Marines, since technically I had two years to go as a Marine reservist.

"Sir," I told the sergeant, "I'd prefer to go through basic training with my new friends here."

All day the sergeant had looked like a guy retiring that day, eager to punch the clock and get out—which was in fact, I learned later, the truth. But hearing that I'd volunteered for basic training, he looked up at me like I was a poor son of a bitch who'd declined to accept a handful of money on general principles. But I wasn't being masochistic. I was being practical. I wanted to bond with these men who I'd be going through something stressful with, and if I'd showed up after they'd shared that experience without me, it would be like arriving five hours late to a party. I also wanted to feel at home with the Army, which was no doubt a different kind of mule than the Marines. Anyway, Army basic training was, I knew, half as long boot camp—and had to be a tenth as hard.

Jim, my partner, thought I was crazy to quit the police force. He said, "I never thought I'd say this, but I wish you weren't going. Good luck out there." We shook hands for a long time. *"Semper fi,"* he said.

My mother and Dorothy were disappointed and scared. They thought I was walking away from a good job with a future. I was—unless Bull Connor became police chief of San Diego.

They also thought I might either get my butt shot off or crash-land somewhere. Dorothy smacked Billy Joe on the back, screaming, "This is all your fault."

Billy Joe could hardly believe it. He'd been in the Army before transferring to the Navy. Guys he'd known had failed the flight test and reported back that it was impossible. "Damn," he said, "I was just wanting to shut you up, the way you was always going on and on about flying. I'm thinking you'd take the test and flunk and that be that. Wouldn't be any more moanin' about what you always wanted to do. Finally get some peace around here."

Dorothy slapped the back of his head.

A few days before leaving I packed up a box of personal belongings to store at my mother's. The last thing to go in was my service revolver, which I'd had to buy. I remembered that you should clean a gun before letting it sit unused. With my mind focused on leaving and flight school, I didn't check the barrel carefully enough, so I hadn't noticed the .38 round in the chamber that went off when I rolled the wheel. It whizzed an inch from my head—and put a two-inch hole in the ceiling. My first thought was, *There goes the security deposit.*

A commercial airliner flew us to Houston, then a dinky two-engine prop rattled us straight to Fort Polk. It was June, and the air felt like a bucket of warm piss. Wading through knee-deep salt water wasn't much harder than walking through such humidity. That made the training seem more difficult than it really was—especially for guys who'd never experienced it. I saw a lot of fainting the first two weeks, and heard a lot of crying into pillows as training went along—more, even, near the end, as the possibility of fighting in a war became real.

The six of us bound for flight school were spread about evenly across the four platoons of sixty soldiers each. It was all by the alphabet, so only Travers was in mine. A sergeant told me we were the only ones in the place going to flight school, and from what I could tell we were close to the oldest ones there. Most of these young guys had enlisted right after high school, though a few had dropped out of college and that's why they found themselves there, courtesy of their local draft boards. Besides the easier basic training, the biggest difference I saw between the Army and Marines was the number of black faces. In the Army, there were dozens.

I didn't make much of an effort to get to know anyone except my five guys. What was the point of making new friends if you weren't going to see each other again?

I wrote increasingly long letters to Joanna. She'd moved back in with her parents and begun writing to me after I became a cop, saying all the right things, and we'd soon kicked around the idea of getting together. I hadn't had time to date in San Diego, so her sweet nothings landed right on target. But oh, well; I was in now for at least four years, which hardly made me an eligible bachelor. And even if I washed out of flight school, they were going to make me a sergeant and find some useful work, on or off the battlefield. I didn't like to contemplate for even a second the possibility of not earning my wings, but in my darkest moments, when I let myself feel doubt and fear, I prayed that if I ended up as just another earthbound sergeant, that I at least got to serve my country in battle. For America to be at war and me not to be in it would've been a stain I couldn't have washed out, even if no one else could ever see it.

One night before lights out a young white guy came over and sat on my bunk. He said, "I hear you're going to flight school."

"Uh-huh."

"Means you're automatically going to Vietnam, right?"

"Yeah. Maybe you, too."

"Is it true you were a Marine?"

"Yeah."

"So you reenlisted 'cause you wanted to do this?"

"That's right." I was getting a little tired of the grilling, and could see where he was going—a place I didn't like.

"Shit," he said, "if I didn't have to be here, I'd be anywhere else. This bullshit—this isn't my country."

"Don't talk like that—especially around me," I said. "You don't want to be here, leave." By then I'd heard or overheard similar complaints like that fifty times, and they made me sicker every time. It was like a virus, and I didn't want it anywhere in the house. From what I knew of American history, I couldn't imagine soldiers in the two world wars or even Korea talking that way. Complaining about the military in general and how scared they were about maybe getting their asses shot off, sure. Complaining about moronic officers, naturally. But not about how this wasn't their country. Of course, this guy had been drafted. What he was doing in a company of mostly enlisted men, I didn't know. Usually they segregated the two, obviously because draftees require a little different handling.

I gave him a short speech about how many men had died for him, and told him he'd better straighten out. What a waste of breath.

"Man," he said, "I can't believe I'm hearing a Negro talk like that."

"Maybe," I said, "you better stop looking at me as a Negro and start looking at me as an American."

He looked at me like he'd been slapped and walked away.

I grabbed my journal and a pen, and wrote down "DREAMER"—the acronym I'd made up when I was sixteen. It had been kind of a touchstone over the years, a mnemonic way to remember the path home, like Hansel and Gretel's bread crumbs.

D stood for "determined"; success meant you had to be determined and focused.

R was for a "return" to basics, meaning that writing and speaking were the basic communication tools everyone needed to get along better with others.

E stood for "education, education, education."

A was for "attitude"; attitude will determine altitude.

M represented making every "moment" count.

E was for "evolve" by being with those of like mind, people who are going somewhere—people whose attitudes you ought to emulate.

R was for "respect"; respect the opposition and never underestimate your enemies or rivals.

It had been a long time since I'd been through the whole recipe, and I smiled, appreciating my passion at sixteen—and wishing I could sit next to the wild-eyed kid who'd laid out his future in an acronym. I daydreamed memories about Ma and Pa and Aunt Lee; about my coaches and teachers and all-black schools; about Lollie and Annette and Joanna; about the Marines and the South Atlantic Cruise and Okinawa; about Martin Luther King and Emmett Till and Jim the cop. I didn't know what, if anything, they all meant, except that these were all parts of me that I would have to accommodate now and forever.

But so was my father's going off to work in that suit and tie. Maybe that was the biggest part of all.

And thus was born my new recipe, not to replace DREAMER but to supplement it:

Hold on to my dreams.

Outwork the competition to make these dreams come true.

Unlock my imagination to dream even bigger dreams.

Nourish my Soul so that I never wither.

Encourage others, the way Ma had encouraged me.

To my surprise, with a little rejiggering of the "soul" ingredient, the recipe formed another acronym: HOUSE.

How fitting.

It was a good house.

For a moment I wished I'd been nicer to that kid who'd come over to talk. Then I realized I had been as nice as it gets: I'd told him the truth.

The company commander called us to attention as we milled about the yard. We snapped to right where we'd been standing. I could see small groups of blacks together amid larger groups of whites. That was typical. Except for me, the guys hung together by race. The other blacks thought I thought too well of myself; they thought that was why I didn't go out of my way to socialize with them. And they may have thought that going to flight school was the equivalent of passing for white. Which would explain why I once or twice heard someone whisper, "Uncle Tom."

Now came the announcement that an outstanding basic training graduate had been selected. Private Ezell Ware.

Most small communities built around a military installation rely on the soldiers' money for their economic health, and they show their appreciation in whatever ways they can. Leesville was no different. Every season Fort Polk's outstanding basic training graduate was invited to pose for a newspaper photo with the mayor of Leesville and Miss Leesville herself, both of whom got great publicity out of it. This time, though, Miss Leesville didn't show up. Apparently I was the first black winner they'd had, and apparently she didn't feel up to summoning any part of her beauty pageant smile for a black man, even one in uniform. The mayor, God bless him, tried his best to put on a good face. He grabbed my hand and turned quickly to the camera, and as soon as the flash went off he let go and nodded to me and stepped away. In the photo he looked like he'd just swallowed his gum. That was Louisiana.

We had two weeks before reporting to flight school at Fort Wolters, in Texas, a little west of Dallas. Travers found a company in Leesville that needed to get cars driven across the country and would pay you to drive them. He suggested we go together and see new places and make enough money to pay for motels and then for a flight to Dallas from L.A.

Since he'd said the magic words—"new places"—I said yes, and he said "Good deal," and we shook on it. A big, husky guy, he had a grip like a vise and a smile that joined his ears together. I was glad I said yes. We would've had enough time to drive the extra fourteen hours (seven east and seven back west) for a quick visit to Magee, but I hadn't felt like seeing the place since Ma's death. We did stop in Phoenix and spent the night with Travers's folks. They lived in a pleasant tract home on the edge of town. It was hot outside but the house was cool, thanks to something called air-conditioning. His mom was a good cook and made sure we overate. His dad had flown B-17s in World War II and kept up on news from Vietnam—especially now, knowing where his son was headed. We talked about flying helicopters, not fixed-wing planes, because the Air Force was flying mostly fixed-wing; the Army and the Air Cav mostly used helicopters.

"The jungle's a dangerous place to fight," Mr. Travers said.

"It's war, Dad," Travers said.

Mr. Travers excused himself to go clean his glasses.

When he left, Mrs. Travers told her son, "He's so proud of you."

The next morning, on our way out, Mrs. Travers hugged me, too.

☆　☆　☆

The first thing I saw at Fort Wolters was an OH-23 helicopter that looked like it was made out of a little bubble (made famous in Korea as medevac choppers); a T-55, another small helicopter, and a larger Huey slick troop transport.

Each of them was gloriously beautiful, the early fall sun glinting off the polished glass and steel. I caught my breath, imagining myself at their controls, lifting high into the air, as high as Icarus, but not falling to earth.

Four senior cadets wearing their flight suits, walking abreast, came toward me out of the shimmering heat off the horizon. *So that's what it looks like to be able to fly.* I felt like a puppy wagging his tail, wanting to be petted, but they passed me without a glance.

I couldn't wait to get started, but the first week was all processing and procedure—getting your bunk assigned, finding out where the mess hall was, learning what was expected of you. In the Marines, that would've taken a day. The Army took six. On the seventh day we rested, and then we got started.

There were 350 students in flight school, nine of them black, none of them Latino or Asian—not that I was paying attention. I didn't have to. They paid attention for us.

Unlike basic training, all the tactical officers at Wolters were white. That made sense. To be a TAC, you'd have had to go through flight school and flown combat duty—possibly in the Dominican Republic but probably in Vietnam. Which meant they'd just come back.

That first morning, three of them called the nine of us black guys into a classroom meeting. This being the era of church burnings and fire bombings, someone joked that maybe we were in for some of that, too—the Army's way of erasing its screw-ups, the screw-up being that we'd all been allowed to get this far only by mistake. It alarmed me that the TAC didn't tell him to shut up. Then I knew why.

"Gentlemen," TAC Officer Cramer said in a grave voice that didn't match his compact build and close-cropped blond hair. "I've called you together because there's something you need to hear before we begin training to fly." Pause. "Flight school is difficult for everyone. Statistics show that sixty-seven percent of flight school students don't make it. Period. Sixty-seven percent. So you look around you, look at each other, at the person sitting next to you and in front of you. Only two of you, or less, are going to make it through this whole course."

I was sitting in the front row, close enough to smell the man's deodorant. The man hadn't said that two-thirds of *blacks* flunk out of flight school; he'd said two-thirds of everyone. So why had he singled us out as a group? Was someone else telling the other 341 prospective pilots that 228.47 of them, or fewer, would soon be handed another military occupation specialty in the infantry? Probably not. I figured there must've been an edict somewhere to increase the number of black pilots, so they'd cast a wider net from inside the Army. These other eight guys had all been in for a while, maybe in artillery, when word went out that blacks should be encouraged to apply for flight school, as a sop to civil rights. If they passed, they passed; if they didn't, well, then that was that. Of course, as Cramer pointed out, not all the criteria are objective. Some are up to the instructor's discretion. It was code talk for: "Don't get your hopes up."

I stood and walked out. Didn't ask permission.

"You, private," Cramer said. I kept walking, right out of the room and into the alcove. He was a warrant officer, not a commissioned officer; it's the rank I would be after getting my wings.

Noncommissioned or not, Cramer followed me, caught my shoulder, spun me around. "Where the fuck do you think you're going? That was a mandatory meeting."

"Look," I said, "what was happening in there, as far as I'm concerned, was that you're talking to people who are going to fail, and you're helping them fail. They already don't think they can succeed, and you're telling them they're right to think that."

"Everybody should be realistic."

"Only two or three are gonna make it, you said?"

"Yeah."

"All right, well, you're looking at one of them, so I don't have to listen to your damn realistic story. I have no intention of failing this course." He smirked. "You don't believe I can? Look at my record. I don't care how hard the academics are, I'll do fine. Same with the physical stuff. Same with the dexterity. Same with hand-eye coordination." I had his attention now—no smirk. "Trust me, I did my homework on what it takes to pass this, and I will." What it took was a narrow combination of skills and smarts. Guys with two hundred IQs who couldn't tie their shoes would fail, as would guys who could overhaul car engines blindfolded but not calculate wind velocity.

I probably pushed my point a little hard. The man was a tactical officer, so his job was to get students through the overall tactics of helicopter flight. It was possible that I'd be assigned to him as an instructor, and if so, he might just happen to consider those subjective criteria he was talking about a little less leniently and generously. After all, guys could be pink-slipped for almost anything they did wrong. Three pink slips total, and that was it for flight school.

"You're a smart-ass, Ware," he said. "Aren't you?"

"Never have been."

"Well, we'll see if you get through this course."

He pivoted and walked back into the room, slammed the door shut. A while later the other eight black guys came out. Peters, the joker, asked what I'd told Cramer. I said it was none of his business.

He said, "You know what, man? We gotta stick together, the nine of us. We gotta make sure we get through this."

I said, "I'll tell you guys clearly: If I get with you to study, there's not gonna be any fooling around."

They took that as me not wanting to study with them. I ended up forming a study group with my own platoon.

The first four weeks were nothing but ground school—that is, classroom education about the physics and mechanics of helicopter flight. These days went on endlessly. It's not that I minded the eight hours of sitting and paying attention, and another three to five of studying what I'd learned. No, I minded the time because with every fact that fell into place, every concept that began making sense, I longed that much more to climb into the cockpit of a helicopter and lift off.

There was more to know than there was time to learn it. Everybody studied hard, but I probably studied just a bit harder and longer. Not that it mattered to anyone I could see or even to me, but I was the only black in the platoon. And if I was the only black out of the nine in the company who made it through these four months of primary flight school, then so be that, too. It would do nobody any favors to fail out of sympathy or empathy or some other misguided notion. I wanted what I wanted and I was going to get what I wanted. Every moment we weren't required to be somewhere else, I studied. I studied on Friday nights and Saturdays and Sundays, and I studied between surprise inspections, of which there were many—and for no particular reason, so far as I could tell. (In some ways, someone said, it was like West Point.)

On Monday of the fifth week, ground school began lasting only half the day, till noon. The other half, at last, was for hands-on instruction out at the flight line.

Each flight instructor worked with a small group of guys. It was the same group every day, which allowed him to chart progress or the lack of it on someone's flight record.

Now was when guys might start washing out.

My tac instructor was not Cramer. It was Burkhardt, a slightly older man with a jagged scar across his right cheek, which may or may not have come from battle. He'd been back from Vietnam for less than two months and refused to tell any stories.

Standing on the flight line that first day, next to an OH-23, he pointed at a piece of hardware atop the main rotor assembly. "Gentlemen," he said, "that there is called the Jesus nut. And the reason it's called the Jesus nut is that if it pops off while you're airborne, you get to meet Jesus. I've seen it happen. Let's hope you never do. Like dropping a sack of potatoes. Poor guys. They were six inches shorter after hitting. That's what the impact will do to you." Pause. "So who wants to get in there first?"

I did.

If they had hooked me up to a heart monitor I might've triple pink-slipped and 4-F'ed right then and there, it was beating so fast. My excitement was kinetic. I climbed up into the right seat and immediately smelled a smell that doesn't smell like anything else. It's just, well, helicopter smell—the smell of the best toy in the universe; this mechanical dragonfly that can transport you out of reality and put you into a living cartoon.

We lifted off and in seconds climbed to five hundred feet. What gravity? Never laid a finger on me. What noise?

It might've been the most ecstatic moment of my life.

I didn't just watch Burkhardt working the collective in one hand and the cyclic in the other, his feet on the pedals. I studied him. It was beautiful the way his hands and feet all did different things, and this was what happened when they did them right. If I hadn't already known what each piece of equipment was for, I couldn't have figured it out from what the helicopter was doing, so synchronously did he move his limbs. The collective, in the left hand, makes the chopper climb or descend; its motorcycle throttle adds or reduces power. The cyclic, between the legs, is what controls whether you go forward, back, or sideways. On the floorboard, the rudder pedals swing the tail around, causing the helicopter to turn.

He talked as we flew, narrating his movements. The aerodynamics, physics, and mechanics of making the machine climb, hover, descend, fly forward, backward, and sideways are complicated—and seemed more complicated in the cockpit than they did in the classroom. Could I manage this? I looked at this man Burkhardt and knew I could do anything he could do. If he could fly this machine, then I could, too.

The area around Fort Wolters is hardly America's most scenic, but to me the view from up there, seen through the cockpit, could've been painted by Maxfield Parrish. In fact, flying over a toxic waste dump would've been spectacular.

After ten minutes Burkhardt brought the chopper to a five-foot hover on a flat open area the size of a football field.

"All right, Ware," he said. "Make it stay at a hover. Five feet and hover."

Let's see, you tell yourself, *first I have to stay at five feet, so I have to move the collective to continuously increase and decrease the main rotor blades' pitch, but slowly, and then when I get to five feet I'll lower the collective just a little and reduce power to decrease the pitch and the amount of lift—but just enough.*

In a way, it's like learning to drive a manual-transmission car (but ten times harder). At first, your mind sorts through the list of things your hand and feet have to do, but they're not of a piece yet, and the ride is herky-jerky. Soon, you get it down so that it's a smooth ride—but you're still thinking about it. Then at last muscle memory is supposed to take over, and you realize it's become second nature. Well, I didn't have to one day prove myself. I had today.

"Here," he said, "I'll take it to five."

He did, and put the helo into a solid hover, pointed into the wind. "I'm going to give this to you now. Take it." He handed me the collective.

I hadn't even gotten my thumb in place before we spun out of control like a balloon that you let go of. The touch is so exquisitely fine, nothing can prepare you for it. Every movement affects something, so you do what you've been taught in class to do, to compensate, but you do too much—and end up overcompensating. Finding that place where it all comes together, that's the job of flying. And you can't do it when you've got a death grip on the joystick.

I don't know whether my adventure lasted three seconds or thirty before Burkhardt took the controls. By then we were at about twenty feet and swinging side to side like a pendulum.

This was one time I should've let someone else go first. That way I might've seen that everybody—literally *everybody*—does this the first time. Or worse.

Me, I felt sick. I'd failed. I wasn't cut out for this. I'd finally found the thing I couldn't do. *How the hell can I work all these controls and watch the panels at the same time? What made me think I could do this? I'm a fool.*

Yes, I'd heard about training accidents; guys getting killed. So obviously anything could go wrong, and sometimes did. But I'd believed that that wouldn't apply to me. I'd believed that I could take the controls and immediately show the skill and finesse of a combat veteran.

My mood must've showed.

"Take it easy, Ware," Burkhardt said. "You did fine."

I couldn't speak.

Burkhardt guided the chopper back to five feet. "Let's do it again. Come on." He handed me the collective—and again we spun out of control.

He said, "When I said 'again,' I didn't mean spin around again."

Now I was thinking too much—and his sarcasm didn't help. I couldn't get my mind off believing I couldn't do this. Never had I thought such a thing before, but then, I'd never been given reason to; that's the price of always being competent at whatever you try. The first time you're not, you think you'll never be good again. Failure stank. It was in my nose. If I'd been alone right then, I'm not sure I would've minded the Jesus nut blowing off.

"Shake it off, Ware. Let's go again. Come on." He was staring at me. "Hey."

That got my attention. I saw the look in his eyes. Obviously, I didn't really know what the man was thinking. But in my mind, he was thinking he had another colored washout on his hands—one more Negro who just didn't have the aptitude.

That was the moment I understood the hollow men, how they'd lost whatever they'd had inside. It starts just like that, and it can all be gone just like that.

"Come on, hotshot," he said. "You can do it. Just relax."

What a wonderful thing to say, and wonderfully timed.

I realized I didn't have to fly perfectly, just well enough to prove I had a future.

"Let's do it," I said.

"All right, then."

He took the helicopter to five feet and offered me the collective. Before taking it, I inhaled deeply and blew it out hard, trying to expel everything I'd read and everything I'd done wrong. This was about instinct, not thought—like juking and jiving through a team full of angry tacklers. You had to let the controls tell your hands and feet what to do rather than the other way around. It was about touch.

I can't say the chopper hovered steady as a gyroscope, but I did keep it pointed into the wind at no higher than seven feet.

"Nice job, Ware."

"How long you want me to keep it up?"

"How long can you?"

"Long as you want."

"Well, it's a good start."

"Want me to fly her back?"

He laughed. "Not just yet."

When we landed at the flight line, I jumped out and couldn't feel my feet on the ground.

☆   ☆   ☆

By the end of that week I could've flown left seat all the way, from takeoff to landing. I wasn't the first to do anything, but I was among them. Except for Travers, who was in my platoon, I lost contact with the others I'd met in L.A. Maybe if I'd made time for anything other than studying, the way they seemed to, we might've reconnected. They called me an ascetic or a Spartan or a monk, and I became kind of a celebrity in camp—the guy with blinders on and saltpeter in his food; the guy who could go four months without good times and music and women; the guy will-

ing to sacrifice desire in the service of need: I *needed* to be a pilot.
No doubt that's why our TAC officer named me to call the cadence for drills.

One day a letter came from Magee. It was too late to do anything
but feel bad. Pa had died and was already buried. I thought of him
watching me now—at last he could.

There was nothing for me in Magee anymore but memories.
Aunt Lee was having her own babies and wouldn't have time.
That was just as well.

★★★ **31** ★★★

By the end of the day we've covered more than a mile—the best we've done in a single day for that whole week. By my reckoning on the map, we're about three and a half miles from the crash site. Tomorrow we should be able to reach what looks like an open field. So if we're lucky—meaning if the field isn't hot with the enemy, and our friend up in the sky shows himself as usual—we'll be out of here in thirty-six hours.

We're not lucky.

It rains that night—a cool rain made cold by three things. One, neither of us has on more than a vest. Two, there's no place to take shelter; the rain gathers in the leaves and accumulates into drops that seem as large as a fist. Three, there's no warmth between us.

"Can it get worse?" Burdett says.

"It can always get worse."

My back is in spasm, but I know Burdett would gladly trade injuries. Besides, worrying about my back now would be like swimming in a swamp full of alligators and thinking about whether the water's clean.

In the morning, I can't find any grasshoppers for breakfast; the rain seems to have chased them. But an old rotted log that fell over, maybe in the night, is crawling with grubs—dozens of fat ones. I find a small branch, carve out two thin sharp spikes, and impale six on each, then hold my lighter under them for several seconds. It doesn't take long for a grub to go from raw to well-done. If I were in a better mood I'd call them shish kebab and we'd laugh.

The best you can say about eating grubs is that they don't taste like shit. The worst you can say is that you're eating grubs because you'd starve if you didn't.

We eat without comment—not even about what animals we've become and how we don't mind eating anything now. And then we trudge on.

The rain has destroyed our remaining cigarettes. Too bad. It would be good to have one, to get the taste of grubs out of my mouth.

Burdett's not moving as fast as yesterday. He doesn't have to. I'll be happy with half a mile or so, which is about how far I reckon the open field is. It's a hot day, and I can't tell when my pants and vest go from being wet with rainwater to being wet with sweat. The transition is seamless.

My built-in alarm clock goes off about eight-thirty that morning. Our chopper is late. Either that or it's not coming.

Burdett notices, too.

We stop and listen. He presses the button on his transmitter. I tell him to save the juice—and then I wonder if both transmitters might have died in the rain. Can it get worse? That would be worse.

"Let's just keep going," I say. "We're heading the right way."

Piloting a helicopter is complicated. There are eighty-eight things to do, and you always have to do four at a time with your eyeballs split forty-five degrees to the right and left. Plus you have to keep assimilating the classroom work, and it comes fast and hard—avionics, weather, navigation, maintenance. To master all that requires a combination of art and science and discipline—and you get the art and science from the discipline.

I'd broken primary flight school down to its basics. It wasn't four months long; it was 120 days. Each day became a test that I had to pass. And I had to pass them all without a single pink slip. No matter that you could get three. I didn't want one—not for the simple things, like hovering; not for the complicated stuff, like landing on top of mountains or on slopes, setting one skid down, then the other; and not for the manufactured emergencies, like losing a right pedal at five hundred feet and having to fly sideways and make adjustments as you go.

Rules stipulated that you'd have to begin soloing within fifteen hours of log flight or you were out automatically. You could do it sooner, but no matter how gung ho you were, they wouldn't let you unless you seemed like you wouldn't kill yourself and trash an expensive piece of equipment. I thought I was ready at twelve hours, and Burkhardt said fine, go try it. That was about the average number of hours it took everybody who eventually passed to log their first solos.

He said, "At least three takeoffs and landings—and we'll see you back here in an hour."

An hour?

At first you think you can't. The helicopter seems like an untamed tiger. And then you breathe deep and say, *It's now or never,* and you pull back on the cyclic and turn the collective and work the throttle and press the pedals all just right—and you lift off, aiming toward the horizon. And when it happens, the world becomes something you can hold in your hand.

By the third takeoff, you buzz the others to let them see you soloing. And when you land the third time, they carry you to the Holiday Inn pool and toss you in, boots and all. It was better than jumping in a lake naked on a Mississippi August afternoon.

None of us read newspapers. What we knew about Vietnam was only what our TACs, who'd been there, told us. And that was this: "You're going to Vietnam. It's a dangerous place. They kill people there. You listen up or you're going to die."

It was hard to say whether they were trying to scare us, but you couldn't argue that their words weren't true. I think that's why so many guys started washing out, sometimes at the rate of one a day. Either it was a third pink slip, conscious or not, or a towel thrown in; flying had sounded good, killing was tolerable, but getting killed—that was entirely different.

At the end of primary flight camp, only thirty percent of us were still there—fewer than Cramer had said—and only two of us were black. Exactly the number he'd said. Of the original L.A. group, only Travers and I made it.

☆　☆　☆

Advanced flight school would be at Fort Rucker, in Alabama. They gave us a week to get there. A tall, nice-looking, well-mannered young man from Montgomery named Wells—first name Chuck; another warrant candidate—asked if I wanted to drive to Alabama with him in his '65 Chevy Impala convertible, blue with white interior. I said, "You bet," and invited Travers to come along, too, but Travers insisted he wanted to fly home for a few days to visit his parents before we left the country.

Wells and I took turns driving four-hour shifts. We wore our khaki uniforms with gray flight jackets. It was January and a touch cold—actually, it was freezing—but we kept the top down as much as possible, because I didn't know how many more times, if any, I'd get to ride in a car this sweet. The weather got warmer the farther south we went.

Somewhere near Oakdale, which is south and east of Leesville in Louisiana, we stopped at a service station for gas. It was the 1950s rural service station of your imagination, with the old guy in a cowboy hat sitting in a rocking chair against the cinder-block back wall, waiting for someone to drive up so he could crank the arm on that ancient pump, then wash your windows and check the dipstick and tires.

Wells pulled up alongside the pump. We got out of the car to stretch.

The old guy didn't move.

"I'd like to fill her up, please," Wells said.

The man could see we were Army.

"Best move on down the road," he said.

"Oh, you're out of gas?" I said.

"Got plenty," he said. "Ain't gonna serve you."

"Whaddya mean?" Wells said. It took him a second to get it. When he did, his body went rigid, like he'd been ordered to attention. He refused to believe this was happening. "You sell us gas," he demanded.

"Ain't gonna."

"Come on, let's go," I said. "We don't want to give this guy our money anyway."

Wells, it's safe to say, was shocked that this could be happening to him. He'd heard of episodes like this—no, he'd grown up with them all around him, even if he and his family hadn't played a role. But now that he'd been bopped in the nose, the abstraction of its being over there had become reality right here. The way he reacted reminded me of people who lose their faith in God after some painful personal loss or tragedy. No matter that the history of the world is the history of undeserved suffering; until they'd experienced it themselves, they'd assumed that God was alive and well and protecting them. No protection, no faith.

I couldn't blame Wells, though, for reacting as he did. I didn't even blame the old coot who'd been carefully taught to hate.

"How far's the next nearest station?" I said.

"You best find out yourself."

I had to drive; Wells would've driven us off the road, he was so discombobulated. The unfairness of bigotry and racism was all I heard about for the next ten hours, till we got to Fort Rucker.

$\star\;\star\;\star$ **33** $\star\;\star\;\star$

It's a village, a small village not on the map. We spot the thatched roofs of its huts through the foliage. I crawl on my belly for a closer look. No one or nothing seems to be moving in or out. Abandoned villages—those, at least, that hadn't been burnt to the ground for some reason—could mean almost anything. But from my experience, they mean that the people have been warned of an impending assault—by which side, you couldn't know—and have fled to avoid the fighting. It's also possible that Charlie or the NVA had discovered too many villagers sympathetic to the South and flushed them out, though they'd probably have torched the place, too, same as Americans did with Charlie rat nests. Or maybe the village isn't really abandoned; maybe everyone is off somewhere. On this side of the mountains, people lived much as they had for a thousand years.

I report my findings to Burdett.

"Let's go," he says.

"Where? Into the village?"

"Yeah."

"No, that'd be suicide."

"I know."

I'm not sure what he wants me to think about that. Actually, I'm not sure he cares what I think. But I am thinking about it—about what he might mean. I'm thinking that the man would take back the past if he could.

I'll have to remind myself that he can't.

"I'm going in," Burdett says. "By myself."

"You can't do that."

"Why not?"

"Captain, look. I know you're not thinking clearly. Believe me, I'm not, either. But you don't have to think clearly for this one. I'm not letting you go."

"What're you gonna do, Lieutenant, kill me? Be my guest."

His eyes are daring me. Short of shooting him, I could kick his leg—but then he'd scream, which would bring the village to us, and even if I clap my hand over his mouth, what little mobility he has would be gone.

He must be a poker player, because he can see I've got nothing.

"Come on," he says, "it's better for you and better for me."

There, he's just dealt me an ace.

"How is it better for me?" I ask.

"You can make good time on your own."

"Yeah? Not if I'm dead."

"Dead?"

"The minute they see you, they're gonna know I'm out here, too."

I don't let him think about that too long. I say, "I promise you, we'll get out of here alive."

"Shit," he says, lying back.

✶✶✶ 34 ✶✶✶

Fort Rucker is in the southern part of Alabama, about eighty miles south of Montgomery, at the confluence of three small towns—Ozark, Daleville, and Enterprise.

A cop pulled us over in downtown Enterprise—nearly in the shadow of a giant statue of a Greek goddess holding a platter on which sat a boll weevil. This was cotton country. Why would they have erected a statue of cotton's one natural pest, a pest that had sometimes devastated whole areas and driven cotton farmers into bankruptcy? Didn't make sense. It was like honoring mosquitoes outside a malaria ward.

"What're you fellas doin'?" the cop asked, leaning over us—and intentionally ignoring the military sticker on the left side of the windshield that allowed Wells to drive on base.

I answered for Wells, knowing he might say something impolitic that was not in either of our best interests—especially mine: "We're to be stationed at Rucker, for flight school."

"Well, then," he said, "you boys gonna be toolin' around town in the future, y'all keep the top up on this thing."

"Why?" Wells asked.

"I'll explain it to him, Officer," I said, which of course he didn't like because it meant I understood that he didn't want any of the area's wives and daughters and girlfriends to see a black man, especially one wearing a uniform, driving in a pretty convertible. That was too potent a combination for their fear to accommodate. I couldn't help smiling, even though I'd probably made an enemy.

"You put the top up," he said, and walked away—so I didn't get to ask him about the boll weevil statue.

"So what's it about, Ezell?" Wells asked as we put the top up.

I waited to answer until we got back in the car, so no one could overhear.

"Hell," he said, "can't argue with that."

I laughed, knowing he was kidding. At least I think he was. Wasn't he?

✯✯✯ 35 ✯✯✯

Late in the afternoon we hear something, both of us at the same time; and we freeze. Footsteps. Hundreds of feet, stepping in a cadence that could only be soldiers. This must be part of an advance party.

Burdett and I hurriedly take cover deep inside a thick leafy bush above an ant colony. Their crawling all over us is bad enough, but they soon develop an interest in Burdett's leg. Any sort of sound, like slapping at them, would be our death.

I can't help counting the feet of two hundred soldiers, in single file.

The NVA company explains why we didn't see our helicopter that morning. The area is now hot. And if there's one company, there might be another. Might be a full battalion or regiment on the move.

Now what?

We gut it out in the bush two minutes past the last footstep and then Burdett explodes crazily, slapping the ants off and picking them out of his leg. He must be in misery.

I crawl to the trail and peek my head out, looking in both directions for signs of more men. I see no one, but it's clear we better make our way farther from the trail.

"Let's be at that field before dark," I say. "No more stopping."

Burdett nods, and we plod on in silence, our ears tuned to the

186 / BY DUTY BOUND

prospect of more soldiers. I turn back two or three times a minute, to check on Burdett. Hating him—or do I?—doesn't keep me from admiring his stoicism.

Just before the sun sets we reach the field and hide back in the shadows to view it in all its glory.

"Look at that," Burdett says.

We stare at the expanse of green, both of us, I'm sure, thinking how much like paradise it seems, this ordinary sixty-by-one-hundred-foot patch of elephant grass—big enough for a helicopter to land.

For eight or nine days, I've lost track now, we've walked hunched over, slowly slogging our way through jungle thickets that would tire an able-bodied man with plenty of food and drink after just a few hours. And now we've hit the elysian fields.

We have to resist the urge to step into its pure daylight and feel the fading sun on our faces. Instead we stick our noses out and breathe deep. It's not really different air than where we'd come from, but it sure feels that way.

Of course, in some ways we're now in greater peril than before. And not just because of the NVA presence. If that helicopter doesn't show up tomorrow, I won't know how to keep Burdett alive. He's made it these last two days on regret and fear and the fumes from hoping that we'll make it. But now to get here and not— Well, there's no point in finishing the thought.

We camp for the night in a banyan tree twenty yards from the edge of the clearing, and I remind myself that this man's life is in my hands and that, in some ways, mine is in his. No matter what I think about him, I have to keep him alive. That's my purpose. Without it, staying alive myself doesn't seem as important.

I'm so hungry I begin wondering how to catch a monkey. If I could get my hands on one, he'd be dead fast—and I'd find some creative way to get him cooked. Hell, the way I'm feeling, I'd eat him raw. I think I've seen that in Thailand.

"You hungry?" I whisper. Burdett must be. We haven't eaten

since morning, and before we got shot down he couldn't last more than two hours without feeding his belly—which is a lot smaller now than it used to be.

"Not really."

"No?"

"No."

This must be some kind of penitence. But it worries me.

That night I pray. I don't pray for us to be rescued; that seems too far-fetched. I pray that I—we—have the strength to make it through one more day; and if it comes to that, tomorrow night I'll pray to make it through yet another day; same with the one after that and the one after that.

Just in the act of praying I feel stronger. It seems obvious to me that God hasn't kept me alive for thirty years to die here, like this. For that matter, we haven't survived all these days for no reason. I believe there's something larger than what I can see or touch or comprehend, and I believe what Ma told me long ago—that God never gives you more to bear than you can stand; never puts you in a position that you can't handle. For a moment I'm tempted to say, *Well, all right, God, this is how much I can handle. I'm at my limit.* I don't, but it gets me thinking about the other thing I believe about God and the universe—that when your time comes, nothing can save you. Either that bullet has your name on it, or it doesn't. Either that helicopter arrives when you most need it to, or it doesn't. Now, of course you're obliged to do everything you can to stay out of the way of that bullet, and everything possible to put yourself in a position where the helicopter can find you. Everything. Everything and more. Because as long as you're alive, there's something else you can do. Not until you're dead, or you give up, is it out of your hands.

Being dead—that's how you know it's out of your hands. That's how you know your time has come.

But not before then.

Not one moment before.

★ ★ ★ 36 ★ ★ ★

We knew one thing: If, in four months, you got wings pinned to your chest at Rucker, you had a 100 percent chance of going to Vietnam. They weren't training you to patrol the DMZ in Korea or West Germany. On the other hand, if you washed out and got sent to the infantry, you actually had a great chance of not seeing any direct combat. So becoming a helicopter pilot meant that you wanted to go and fight. I know I did. The thought of America being at war and me not being part of it was, well, unthinkable. More than anything, I wanted to serve my country, and I honestly, sincerely believed I could make a difference in the war effort—no, not end it by myself, but be a proud, brave warrior.

This was 1967. The politics of fighting in Southeast Asia never entered my mind other than thinking the protestors had it wrong. We needed to stop the Communists; if we didn't they wouldn't stop themselves. But even if that hadn't been my position, I like to think I would've done my duty anyway and followed orders, knowing that I didn't know what my commanders knew—that they were privy to intelligence I'd never see. You can't have a military without that obedience. Now, some people think it'd be a good thing for soldiers to choke on their orders and for armies to plunge into anarchy. And in fact it would be a good thing—but only if every army in the world collapsed simultaneously. Otherwise, you can bet the bad guys will be left standing and hungry, and they won't have a discipline problem.

I don't think I could've explained it this way in 1967, but the words describe my instincts for what I felt, even then, holds civilizations together. It's a thin, thin thread.

Advanced flight school used mostly civilian flight instructors— good ol' boys who hadn't sworn an oath to honor or duty or anything other than a paycheck. Not that they didn't love their country. They did, but some of them loved it in the way it had been before *Brown v. Board of Education* and desegregation and Martin Luther King and Freedom Riders and the Civil Rights Act of 1964 and the Voting Rights Act of 1965—and they didn't mind being transparent about it.

The protocol at Rucker outside of ground-school classroom was to pair off into permanent two-man teams that flew with the same instructor. Familiarity was supposed to enhance both learning and teaching. My partner's name was Wolf—Gerald Wolf—an otherwise ordinary young man about my age (and already losing his hair) from upstate New York. I remember little about him, because my instructor sucked up all my attention and emotion. The instructor was Morrow, first name Richard, a mean-looking thirty-year-old with a smoker's cough. He'd had two friends killed in Vietnam and talked to others who'd been there and come back in one piece. He understood that, based on the way the generals were running things, this war's progress and the safety of American soldiers depended in large measure on the skill of helicopter pilots—and he believed that putting a nigger out there with so much on the line was tantamount to playing your third string for the national championship. The man was determined to flunk me out, and the excuse he used was the instrument flying test.

They put you in a hooded helmet, like metal blinders on a horse. For an hour, while the instructor sat beside you giving directions and a ground controller yelled orders into your headphones, all you could see were the instruments on the panel, not anything else about the terrain or your location. It's a terrifying feeling—made more so by knowing what the man grading you already thinks.

"We ain't so hard up for pilots that we gonna pin wings on you," he once told me in a rare moment of lucidness between screaming sessions. "You can't fly worth beans."

He pink-slipped me. My first. Said I hadn't turned the heading 135 degrees when he cut the engine. But I'd done it just right—and I wasn't going to wait till my second pink slip to do something about this.

I called the oversight committee and talked to the officer in charge of flight instructors. He was a colonel in his early fifties, which meant he probably wasn't climbing any higher on the promotions ladder. This wasn't the first time he'd heard complaints like this about Morrow, so he suggested we go up together. I was airborne with him for fifteen minutes when he said, "You're good to go, Ware." And that was that.

The Air Force and Army both used Rucker as the place to conduct a week of survival training, because the Alabama swamps are as close to Vietnam as exists in America. After some classroom education about things like how to find water in plants and what goes good with grubs, they dropped you out in the middle of nowhere with a map, a compass, a little beef jerky, one canteen of water, and a live chicken. You then had to find your way back along a certain route, while passing specific checkpoints and specified locations along the way according to preordained coordinates. You used the North Star, the sun, your compass, key terrain features—anything and everything you could in order to make it safely from

A to B to C to D, D being where the friendly forces would take you home. The catch was that there were also unfriendly forces—soldiers pretending to be bad guys—and if you got captured, you might have to start again, from the beginning. The "enemy" tied some guys to trees and left them to holler for help. The humiliation was the symbolic equivalent of torture.

Since both pilots usually survive helicopter downings, they made us pair up for the exercise. My partner was Howard Blatz. He claimed he was related to the beer family—and in fact had something of a beer belly—but I'd never heard of Blatz beer, so it didn't mean anything to me, and he might've been joking anyway. He was suitably impressed with my chicken-carrying technique, which I taught him, and we soon agreed that a live chicken was a nuisance on a long hike like this but that we ought to wait until first light to cook it, so the fire wouldn't be seen. Smoke wouldn't be a problem if we found a place under a thick canopy. It wasn't hard to find.

In the morning I impressed Blatz again, this time with my chicken-killing technique, which I taught him, and my chicken-plucking and -skinning techniques, which he learned reluctantly. Cooked over a small flame, the chicken made an excellent breakfast, lunch, and dinner—and if we'd come upon another chicken during that week, I'd have impressed Blatz with my chicken-catching technique, too. We survived the trip without resorting to grubs or rats or snakes or any other last-resort meals, and made it back without getting strapped to a tree. In some ways, it wasn't much different than how I'd grown up.

Graduation from flight school took place on a huge parade field, to accommodate all the grads and their families (though I was unrepresented in the crowd). There were speeches of congratulations from officers ranked major and up, and short speeches about each of us as the company commander moved down the line to pin the wings and salute you. The whole thing lasted nearly two hours. Too bad it didn't go on for nine. Those wings on my chest felt like they could fly me anywhere I wanted to, but for right then I didn't want to be anywhere other than right there.

Out of a graduating class of a thousand, I finished in the top third. A lot of them would die in Vietnam, including Wolf.

Oh, I found out why there was a statue of a boll weevil in Enterprise. It's because of the year back when the boll weevil ate almost the entire state's crop, and that forced the area to find other crops that couldn't be wiped out so badly. They found a lot of them—peanuts, for example. So the people were grateful for the boll weevil making them stronger by trying to take away everything they had. I felt the same. In my case, there were too many boll weevils to carve statues for all of them, but I was grateful to each just the same.

☆ ☆ ☆

Next stop, Fort Campbell, Kentucky—to meet the unit I'd be going to Vietnam with.

We joined the 61ˢᵗ Assault Helicopter Company, a separate company of the 101ˢᵗ Airborne. Our company had about 250 guys—support units, cooks, administrators, supply people, intelligence guys—of which sixty-four or so were pilots. One other of them was black. His name was Little—Harvey Little—which struck me as funny, considering how big a man he was. He'd been with the 82ⁿᵈ Airborne and flew slicks—troop transports. We didn't go out of our way to get to know or not to know each other. If we became friends, fine; if not, that was fine, too.

People came in and went out of your life so fast, you had to think of them as interchangeable, unless you knew they were going to play a role in your own story. Names, faces, skin colors— they were all the same. Anyone could be transferred somewhere tomorrow, so investing time and emotion in someone who might never be part of your life again was something I'd learned not to do. There were hundreds of guys to choose from if you wanted buddies. I didn't, but if I did I wouldn't have based my choice on just skin color. Anyway, some of us were marked for death. Instinct kept you from opening up. Instinct told you that the more friends you made, the more you'd have to grieve. The irony was that the closer you got to death, the closer you got to the people who were with you. Danger would become an invisible hand that brought you unnaturally close unnaturally fast.

They made me a gunship pilot (flying Bell UH-1Cs), the guy who rains death from the treetops. We spent several weeks doing some more tactical training, like flying in battle formations; more instrument flying, more night flying, more bad-weather flying. We also learned to fire weapons. The cockpit of our Huey gunships, as the UH-1 was known, was fitted with an M5 40mm grenade launcher we called the Thumper. So now flying wasn't just making the chopper do exactly what you wanted it to do, but you also had to fire the grenade launcher while the co-pilot handled the mini-guns. Turns out I had a talent for flying and firing weapons and hitting targets—just like the way I'd imagined wiping out the other side when I played cowboys as a kid.

Getting a warrant officer's pay with battle pay thrown in, I was making almost a thousand bucks a month—and had nothing to spend it on except to send some back to Aunt Lee. I invited myself into a conversation I overheard about stocks between two other warrants. One guy's father was a stockbroker and kept talking about this stock for a company that did something with computers. It was called EDS, and was run by some funny-looking little guy named Ross Perot. IBM was another stock he suggested; same thing with computers. I bought all I could afford of them, and a few others as well. I was buying with the intention of holding on to them long-term. It never occurred to me that I might be one of the ones not coming back from the war. My plan was to fight and win this war, then come back and calculate how much I'd made on my stocks while I was gone.

✻ ✻ ✻

Huey gunship crews consist of a command pilot, copilot, crew chief, and gunner. Pilots didn't see much of the crew chiefs' and gunners' training until we practiced hitting targets together, but we knew we were going to have to trust these two guys with our lives, in that they were the ones primarily responsible for the air-worthiness of the chopper and its preparedness for battle as well as the operation of our weapon systems. Among other things, they learned mechanics, ammo handling and loading, and armament; once we were up there in battle, they'd be firing the big-boy guns—M60s.

From somewhere in the chain of command came the permanent four-man assignments—permanent meaning that we'd fly together until we got to Vietnam and probably, though not definitely, there, too. About four weeks in, the permanent assignments were made. My gunner was Dave Cleveland—"Like the city," he said—a twenty-two-year-old aspiring car mechanic from Buffalo ("Like the animal," he said). Crew chief was Michael Somers ("Not like the seasons," he told Cleveland). Smart and sassy, he'd already graduated college and could've gotten a deferment to go to grad school, but his father and grandfather had both been war heroes and he didn't want to break the chain, so he'd enlisted; it was a common sentiment and reaction among the guys I met.

My pilot-in-command was Lieutenant Joseph McCullough, who was also the platoon leader. I didn't know why he and I had been paired off, and I didn't ask; for one, it wasn't my job to question, and two, I might not have liked the answer. The truth might've been that in assessing the pairings, the officer in charge of making them had noticed that he had a black pilot and couldn't just pair him off the way he would a white pilot. It might've been that they'd given me to McCullough for McCullough to act as a watchdog. It might've been that the officer had asked McCullough, who was from Oregon, whether he minded flying with a black pilot and McCullough had said no, he didn't mind. I'd seen no evidence to support anything having to do with racism, so I chose to believe that I'd been made his copilot because the right-seat pilot was in charge of shooting the mini-guns, each one capable of four thousand rounds a minute—and the left-seat pilot usually fired the 2.75-inch rockets, which had a burst range of ten meters and so were easier to fire. On the test ranges, I'd become one of the company's more accurate triggermen, and I'd also apparently earned myself a reputation for being unusually fierce—not belligerent, just gung ho. By then there'd been enough of the war in the books for officers to know that timid (we used the word "coward") gunship pilots were a danger to themselves and everyone else.

Anyway, no other assignment could've made me happier than to fly with McCullough. Not just because he was platoon leader, which was an honor, but because he was genuinely a pleasure to be around. Nothing he did grated, and everything seemed to come from decency.

I called him "Lieutenant."

He called me "EZ."

☆   ☆   ☆

Waiting for your orders—knowing they're coming but not knowing when—is a good time to smoke. There's nothing else to do. I can't think of another member of the company except the lieutenant who wasn't smoking now, even if he hadn't been before.

Finally, the orders came from company commander Rinehart. He said, "We've been directed to go to Detroit." Detroit?

Actually, we were supposed to fly in formation to Stockton, California, to drop our helicopters for the long ride to Vietnam. But riots had broken out in Detroit's ghettos; people were dead and buildings had been set on fire. Our whole company was to fly there.

"Gentlemen, it's a necessary show of force. We are the most

highly trained unit in the country right now." It felt good to hear that, but the idea of using what we'd learned and rehearsed on fellow Americans, even if they were breaking the law, was disturbing.

Surely the National Guard would be able to quell the violence—and let us just watch. Michigan's governor, George Romney, had called the president, and LBJ had opened the vault. At that point he was still running for reelection in '68, and had to show the country he hadn't lost his grip.

No one knew how big or out of hand Detroit might get. There were a lot of poor blacks in the city, and a lot of angry blacks. I wondered whether there'd ever be riots in the South, and I prayed that I wouldn't have to think about following orders there.

Every moment of those ten hours felt alive with drama and significance. I was twenty-six years old, on my way to war but making a detour to a civil uprising, flying over my country at a perfect altitude to see both the lay of the land and its smaller details, and just off my flanks was the next line of a thirty-helicopter formation. We'd left in the dark of morning and flown with the sun at our backs all day, stopping only to refuel and eat at an IHOP. McCullough let me sit left seat at least half the time.

It was six o'clock in the evening, July 24, 1967, their second night of rioting, when we reached Detroit. Flying over the city, you could see how much of it was on fire. Looked like all of it. You couldn't tell the sunset from the flames' reflection. For the first time I believed that big changes were coming—I mean, for others, too. Even those who weren't going to do what it took to change their destiny were going to have it changed for them anyway.

A show of force, Rinehart had said. Imagine being on the street and about to throw a Molotov cocktail when you hear the hurricane roar of thirty helicopters and look up and see the whites of the pilots' eyes.

We showed our fully armed helicopters to the rioters and then kept going, landing in a stadium and going by bus to a hotel in a rich suburb and eating room service for a week, but never really doing anything again. The whole thing reminded me of getting sent from San Diego to Los Angeles during the Watts riots of 1965, and riding with undercover L.A. cops past National Guardsmen aiming their machine guns at rioters.

Thank God the orders to shoot never came. If we'd fired on those people from our helicopters, there wouldn't have been a major city in America not burned to the ground—or that's how it seemed in those days when violence was in the air like static electricity. I still wonder sometimes how many of us would've refused the orders. It was hard not to wonder then, and hard not to think that maybe I should've been doing something else.

✭   ✭   ✭

We flew on to Stockton in formation by squad, with different helicopters taking turns leading and following. In V formation, the hardest positions were just off the leader's right and left flanks. You get his rotor-blade draft at the same time as the real wind pushing on you—but you'd better not react with someone right behind you. In trail formation, being behind anyone was tough, because you couldn't see. McCullough and I took turns flying left seat. There wasn't much for Cleveland and Somers to do.

The flying took three days. Bakersfield was our last night in transit. My sister drove up from San Diego to see me for a couple of hours. The second she saw me run up the restaurant stairs, she began crying. You could tell she was already planning my funeral and eulogy. I said, "I don't want to hear it. I don't want to see you sad. I don't want any part of that stuff in me." I explained that I thought people get what they visualize, and I didn't want to ever visualize or imagine or dream that I wasn't coming back in one piece.

Destination was Sharp Army Depot in Stockton, where our helicopters were partially disassembled and crated for the thirty-day

trip. Buses took us to San Francisco. They put us up in a downtown hotel and gave us two days to walk around. I stuck with the
gunship pilots. We'd heard a lot about the "Summer of Peace and
Love" and whatever else the newspapers were saying every day, so
we headed to hippie central—Haight-Ashbury.

"I don't believe what I'm seeing," Peters said. "I don't think
Detroit and San Francisco are on the same planet." Girls lay top-
less in the grass and those who kept their shirts on didn't wear
bras anyway. Meanwhile, you could easily trip over couples making love in the bushes. Even the postman wore flowers in his hair.
It was a groovy sea of long hair and pot smoke and good vibes—
and with our buzz cuts and ramrod posture we stood out like men
in a women's locker room. We were from all over—Georgia, Indi-
ana, Southern California, Texas, New York—but we may as well
have been born of the same mother. We had each other's back, and
when we joked about "wasting the gooks," it was out of camaraderie for each other, not hate—gunship pilots were getting hit
hard in the jungle.

Nobody in the Haight called us baby killers, though they did
flash us the peace sign and say, "Make love, not war."

Typical military, we then flew American Airlines from California
all the way back to Nashville and rode buses to Fort Campbell,
Kentucky, to wait for our orders. Any day, any minute, they could
come—and the next time we moved it would be straight to Vietnam. The military's the best rumor incubator ever devised, and
some guys got their jollies making up stories that we were leaving
in ten minutes or ten hours or ten whatever. This was when you
could see a lot of buyer's remorse among the men. I saw one mechanic wet himself with fear.

One night the platoon commander came into the barracks
around midnight and said this is it, "Be on the flight line in ten."
Fort Campbell is headquarters of the 101st, so the runway was big

enough for a 707. We got to Oakland by three in the morning and boarded buses for the short ride to the Oakland Army Depot. There were hundreds of us, units from all across the States. We were all on board ship before first light. Apparently the antiwar protestors didn't get up that early.

Tugs began pulling us from the dock. That was when the smell of war got strong. Most of us stood almost at attention on the top deck as we went under the Golden Gate Bridge. Some ladies in dresses were standing on its pedestrian walkway waving handkerchiefs. I guarantee you that every one of us thought of our wives, girlfriends, mothers, sisters—and wondered if we would see them or this again.

We were a month on board ship, and if you didn't watch it you could end up with something like mess officer duty, bakery duty, or laundry detail. I'd taken care of that. I'd volunteered to be education officer for my company, meaning I went around to enlisted men and officers and noncommissioned officers with information about correspondence courses the Army had in order to help guys if they wanted to bump up their rank and pay. Me, I wanted a commission, and pulling this duty was a way to stand out. Warrant officer wasn't commissioned, and without a commission there was no way to climb to the top of the ladder of the commission ranks. In fact, there was no ladder at all. Closest I could get now was taking the precommission course—just one more piece of the mosaic I was building.

The troop transport moved slowly, stopping for a day in Hawaii and two days in Okinawa—not that it mattered; we couldn't get off the ship or pull near enough to ogle the girls anyway. Apparently we were killing some time. Arrival in Vietnam had to be at a certain hour, certain day, one determined long ago, according to a master Pentagon schedule. I spent the weeks studying and writing letters home and playing pinochle.

The night before we got to Vietnam almost everybody lost his appetite, and not just because—even long after sunset and even at sea—the air had become oppressively hot and heavy. Company commanders called their men together and gave out the orders that only they'd known about since embarkation. My company was headed to Qui Nhon, and from there would be taken to Lane Army Airfield. The grunts of the 101st Airborne were being dropped off at Phamrang. Rinehart pointed to it on a map he'd posted. It was about midway up the country, nearer to the east coast—the South China Sea.

At first light the shoreline became visible and quickly got bigger. We were aiming right for the sunrise, with the rays scalloped into layers of orange and yellow and pink by the prism of thin clouds. It was a thing of beauty utterly incongruous with the hell of that little country's war.

The water was calm, not like the Normandy coast of France on that June morning in 1944, but guys were throwing up just the same. The rumor mill had ground out news that we'd be storming the beach, like D-Day. We got our packs and weapons ready, but as we got close enough to hear, there was nothing to hear—no bursting bombs, no small-arms fire, no artillery—and nothing to see. Maybe the enemy was waiting and hiding, and we'd have to run a gauntlet.

No. When we got close enough, we could see Americans on forklifts, waiting to unload the boat's cargo. They were wearing T-shirts and waving. "Hey, newbies!"

Behind them were buses—for us.

Obviously, this wasn't like any other war.

"Hey, dudes," a forklift driver called. "Y'all still got all your time to go. Three-sixty-five and a wake-up. Not me. I'm outta here this week. Six and a wake-up, dude!"

✦✦✦ 37 ✦✦✦

Morning comes and we work our way to the edge of the clearing again. We stare at it as though watching a movie. We can do nothing now but wait—actually, hide and wait.

First I find us some breakfast—grasshoppers, wild berries that I can't name but know aren't poisonous, and a few grubs, everything chased down by a canteen of fresh water that's probably not so fresh. We've both got a bad case of the trots.

Eight-thirty comes and goes, then nine, nine-thirty, ten. The chopper's not coming today. We're where we're supposed to be. This is the place—and there's no chopper. After all that.

"Maybe tomorrow," I say.

Burdett doesn't say anything. He turns and finds a place to sit on the jungle floor, sticking his leg out ahead. If I had to write a caption for the image, I'd say that the man's heart had just been broken.

I sit down next to him. I say, "We'll wait here for the day. That'll be good for you. You just sit and relax, and I'll go stock up on some food. All right?"

He just nods.

"You be okay for a while alone?"

He just nods.

I'm worried as I go off with the bag. I find a few more berries and take the canteen down to a stream and look for some crayfish. There aren't any, but there is a large fish, something resembling a perch, hiding in a shadow. Too bad I don't have a silencer on my gun. If I had a long spear of some kind . . .

Over there is a long skinny branch. I snap it off its tree, then hurriedly whittle the tip into a lethal needlepoint. I'm already impacting the environment more than I want. Enemy soldiers or VC passing by might notice the change and be alerted that someone new is in the neighborhood.

I hold my breath in a prayer that the fish is still there. It is, just hanging out. I've got one shot at this thing, and my hands aren't too steady now, so my aim better be true.

I jab. Bull's-eye! I pull the fish out. It's still alive, tail flopping wildly. I keep it in the water while I fill the canteen, and then carry both back. This can't help but lift Burdett's mood. I'll fillet the fish and lay both halves on a rock at the clearing's edge in full sun. Shouldn't take more than fifteen minutes in this heat before we have a proper fish supper.

It's strange how excited I am—and not just to find such an incredible treat. No, I'm just as excited to be sharing it with Burdett.

Goddamn me. I don't want to be excited that way. I want to keep hating him the way I have been. I think I need to. Or I'm supposed to. Something like that. But why? What's the point? I'm out there, and he's out here. He's a changed man—isn't he? He'd die without me, and he knows that—and it would be a lot harder for me to stay alive if he weren't with me. I believe that to be a fact. Doesn't matter whether I like it. True is true.

I'm sixty yards from the spot where I left Burdett when I hear Vietnamese voices jabbering. Closer now, I can hear Burdett's voice saying something to them.

I pull my revolver and cock the hammer, then sneak near, careful not to be heard. Two men wearing black pajamas and wielding machetes flank Burdett. He's still sitting just as I left him, except now his head is resting on his chest.

"Go fuck yourselves," he says, igniting a machine-gun conversation between them. They're either farmers or VC—or both.

I haven't picked up enough Vietnamese in my time in the country, but I think I hear some talk of money. I'm guessing it's about a reward for bringing Burdett in. I'm also guessing that these two guys have heard enough English over the years to understand what "Go fuck yourselves" means, and to feel that the insult trumps the reward.

They twist Burdett as if looking for a better angle on his neck. Obviously, they're going to kill him. Burdett, I can see, knows that, too. His face shows no fear.

Thank God I don't see an AK-47 or any other kind of firearm—except Burdett's revolver, which the one on the right has taken from him.

He's the one I shoot first with my .38. He falls in place as the other man whirls in my direction with the machete. I don't have any choice but to kill him. One shot in the chest does it.

Burdett barely reacts. Maybe he's in shock, or had already resigned himself to death—welcoming it, even. Or maybe, like me, he's accepted the law of the jungle, literally—kill or be killed. He stares up at me with blank eyes. I snap my fingers in front of him, make him blink. I pick up his gun and replace it in his holster, gather the spent shell casings, then put rounds in my gun's two empty chambers.

"Come on, Ron, get up, we can't stand around here. We gotta go now."

In the meantime I drag the first body deep into a thicket, and cram his machete in there with him. I do the same with the second body, though I'm tempted to keep the machete to help me hack through the thick brush. If only it didn't make so much noise.

"Captain, please," I say.

He notices the impaled fish. "What's that?" he says.

"Lunch," I say. "Was gonna be."

He still seems not to comprehend what's happened. I hand him the two canes and take his arm.

"Listen to me, Captain, we have to get out of here right now. Anybody who heard the gun is already on their way here, and we can't be here when they get here."

"How can anyone tell where the shots came from?" he asks.

I say, "They know the general direction."

"So how do you know where they're running from? We might run into them running to us."

It's a good point. I don't have an answer.

He says, "I don't want to go anyway. I like it here. I wanna stay. By this field."

"Captain, you're talking crazy."

"This is as good a place as any," he says.

"Unless you want to go home alive."

"You don't know that."

No, I don't. Moving for the sake of moving may not be the best strategy. "All right," I say, "we'll make a deal."

"What?"

I tell him we can spend the day here, but it has to be hidden way up and back in the tree, so anyone walking by looking for where guns were fired or for missing friends can't see us. I say, "Tomorrow is when I figure those bodies'll start stinking bad in this jungle, so anyone walking around here won't need to see them. Their noses'll lead them. We'll stay here all day, and stay in the morning long enough to hear if the chopper shows up. If it doesn't, we have to move on."

There's not much chance of the chopper showing up, not with the NVA on the move. We both know it.

"Deal," he says.

We manage to get him up the tree. He had to put the vest in his mouth again, to keep from crying out. No wonder. The leg is getting harder to recognize as a leg. The infection is climbing.

I eventually get up there with him; I take the fish, too. We both settle in.

Burdett just stares at the bad leg, disgust on his face—like it failed him.

"I have to ask," I say. "What happened, why didn't you shoot them? You had a gun, they didn't."

He thinks for a second. "I didn't have permission," he says.

I hope he's kidding, because this is a very funny line—and I want to think that he had the energy and impetus to try to be funny. That's a good sign. Besides, I don't mind laughing. It's hard not to when you remember how many times you called in a rich, lethal target and couldn't get permission to fire on it—targets like an elephant lumbering up a trail loaded with a ton of explosives, or an entire NVA company racing across an American runway.

He says, "I had to wait till they fired first. You can't fire a machete."

I laugh again, but he won't break his deadpan.

"That's quite a fish," he says.

"Yeah."

For a moment I imagine it hot off the stone, like the way they cook it some places in Japan and Thailand. Oh, to have a hot meal, even in this jungle heat. Real comfort food—refreshment for the spirit.

Do I say anything? No. It would only be cruel to tell him how I'd planned to cook it.

"Here," I say, cutting the fish in two and handing him half.

★ ★ ★ **38** ★ ★ ★

The buses had chicken wire over the windows to keep street kids from running alongside and lobbing in hand grenades. The trip to Lane Army Airfield was twenty miles on dirt roads. None of us talked. We stared out at the people and the ravaged villages and saw how much of their lives was taken up with accommodating war and violence.

Lane was a good camp to be assigned to. The Koreans had sent their storied Tiger and White Horse Divisions to Vietnam in support of their friend America, and kept the White Horse Division at Lane—which in fact had a Korean commandant. Koreans were known for their ferocity in tactics; they had no mercy. That's why they were there—to fight under rules of engagement less stringent than ours and put the fear of heinous retaliation into the Vietcong guerrillas and sympathizers who spent much of their time trying—and often succeeding—to sneak into military installations and create violent havoc. Vietcong caught by the Koreans were in for an unpleasant final few days of life—fewer if they were lucky. Because of that, on the ground Lane was likely to be safer than most big American cities. Only the most devoted guerrillas would risk trying to sneak through the fence for an attack knowing that their home villages might be destroyed both as collective punishment and in pursuit of collaborators.

To pacify ordinary Vietnamese, the Koreans occasionally organized karate matches in the streets between some of their country's biggest and best black belts—not one of them under six feet tall. They would pass them off as ordinary Korean soldiers.

Lane Army Airfield was named after a helicopter pilot, Chief Warrant Officer 2 Robert Carl Lane. He'd been killed on a mission January 5, 1966—the first 1ˢᵗ Air Cavalry Division Sky Crane casualty of Vietnam. The camp was the size of a Midwest city. Trenches and pillboxes marked the perimeter. On one side was a sloping hill. Besides us, there was also another American helicopter unit. We divided up by platoon and moved into Quonset hut hootches that had just been built, each holding about twenty guys.

The outhouses were closer to the hootches than our privy in Mississippi was to Ma and Pa's house. Guys complained immediately. I laughed, thinking how posh this was compared to back home. I visited the toilet and was glad I'd carved out my niche as education officer; latrine officer would not be good duty to pull. Underneath the toilet seat was a fifty-gallon drum that had been cut in half. Every time one got half full, the guys in charge would have to yank it out of there, burn it with jet fuel, and put it back in place.

You can imagine the smell in that heat. It was so hot you couldn't take a shower except late at night or early in the morning, before or after the sun boiled the water in the big steel drums on the roof.

We began our long in-country training: This is east, this is west, these are the mountains guys have flown into, these are where pockets of enemy are known to be located, these are emergency landing sites, these are where friendlies are located, these are your radio frequencies.

Topic one was the weather—that is, the humidity. Major Ellroy was our gunship company commander. He said we'd almost have to relearn flying because of the wet air, which drains power from the rotors; the hotter and denser the air, the less lift you get. "All that high-altitude training you had—forget it," he said to the gunship pilots. "You're not gonna be up seven, eight, ten thousand feet. You're gonna be fifty feet, just above the treetops. You come in low, and you come in fast, and you come in hard." Our missions, he said, were to engage the enemy and fire at them. We were to shoot and keep shooting until no one shot back. There would be times, he explained, when we'd have to fire on a Vietcong or North Vietnamese Army platoon of maybe fifty men—and there'd be times we'd have to kill that many. Or more. If we didn't, they'd kill us. So there could be no hesitation in our actions.

The officers' club at Lane had of course been the first building erected on the camp when it was built two years before, and it was impressive both for the structure and its location on the side of a hill, elevated above everything else. On one side were the bar and tables and gambling tables—craps. When I walked in the first time, loud music was playing through tinny speakers—the Rolling Stones' "Paint it Black." As soon as it ended, on came "We Gotta Get Out of This Place," and everybody stopped what they were doing and sang drunkenly along with the chorus—"We gotta get out of this place, if it's the last thing we ever do." It was obviously their anthem. None of us FNGs, fucking new guys, as we were called, joined in. We didn't want to get out of this place. We'd just gotten there.

Against the wall on the other side was a large glass window that acted like a giant TV screen on the war. You could see explosives going off and orange streaks of mortars, and could hear the booms and blasts. All of the newbies noticed it, but the drunk or on-their-way-there-fast officers crowded at the bar and tables—most of them in their early and mid-twenties—took no notice. That told me something important. Apparently this had become like a show they'd seen on reruns too many times. That first night, I doubted I would ever find it less than fascinating. I couldn't move my eyes off the action, thinking about how I'd soon be out there in it; same with the other newbies I'd gone there with.

By the third night, though, maybe because I didn't drink, I was the only one of us still fascinated. And maybe because I was the only guy not wanting to be a doctor, lawyer, teacher, Indian chief, or airline pilot (which was the most common aspiration), nothing I saw through that glass window made me hope that we wouldn't be out there in it sooner rather than later.

But for a while on that first night, lying in my hooch, on top of the cot in just skivvies, trying to breathe air as thick as paint and as hot as steam, what I heard gave me second thoughts. It was like the sound track to a horror movie that was scarier in my mind than on the screen. I doubt any of us slept that night. Not that we could have anyway, with helicopters taking off and landing all night almost right outside the windows and the whine of shells exploding somewhere that always seemed too close. In time we would learn to ignore the sounds of war, the way people in big cities hardly register honking and screeching brakes and noisy mufflers and sirens. But not tonight, and not soon.

They gave us thirty days to learn whatever we needed to kill the bad guys fast and get back to camp in one piece. Nobody had to be reminded to pay attention. Besides the weather and topography, and figuring out the boundaries of the AO (area of operation), nothing mattered more than map-reading. Bases didn't have their own beacons to guide us in, so if you lost your way visually, the map was the only way home.

You'd see guys gathering around pilots from other companies who'd been there awhile. Three months was enough to have advice, and stories to go with it. These were young men, with young men's braggadocio—and they seemed like grizzled old veterans. To them we were the FNGs—and would stay that way till we'd been shot at and lived to fly another day.

Sometimes you'd just eavesdrop, listening to pilots talk about the action at landing zones like LZ English, and you'd get out your map and try to put what they were saying to a coordinate and remember what you could about it.

From everything I heard and overheard, there was no safe mission. Maintenance problems—malfunctions—could just as easily kill you as Charlie could (Charlie or the NVA, or any bad guy). The mountains, too; we were near the Central Highlands, which were often hidden behind curtains of fog. There were enough stories about pilots who never saw what killed them. Of course, that was better than what Charlie had in mind for you. Charlie didn't have the temperament or resources for prisoners, unless he was getting something of great value back in exchange—and since he didn't often have anything of great value to lose, he didn't need you. He might, though, express his loathing for America by having this young man who'd just been captured stand in for his country. The Geneva conventions never came up in conversation.

A week in, we walked to the officers' club and saw half the pilots from another company holding a wake for two of theirs who'd touched down in a landing zone surrounded by Vietcong armed with AK-47s they'd received from the Chinese—and two others who'd died in the firefight that followed when an assault team led a mission to recover the bodies.

The only time I ever felt chilled in Vietnam was hearing news like that—but only for the first few months.

On the Korean side of the compound I passed a caged area where Vietcong fighters had just been captured. They were chained together by a necklace of barbed wire. I didn't think much about it except to wonder in general what happened to prisoners of war.

Early the next morning I happened to see a Korean slick hovering at about five hundred feet. By the open door were two Korean soldiers and two of the VC. The VC were shouting and screaming, and the Koreans were shouting, and then one of the Vietcong came sailing out of the side—his screaming becoming a terrified shriek. And then the terrible jerking, and then swinging. I was far enough away so that he sounded to my ear to be still screaming when my eyes could see he was already dead, his neck snapped by the rope whose other end was twenty feet up.

From what I could see of his reaction, the other Vietcong fighter was likely to be cooperative now.

The Vietnamese were gooks, just like Italians had been wops and dagos, and Germans krauts, and Japanese nips or Jappers. Epithets help you put a mental mask over your enemy's face, which you have to do when your job is to kill him. Gook was a good word for this particular enemy in Southeast Asia. It didn't sound human at all. Everybody was going to be wasting gooks or had just come from wasting them or couldn't wait to get back out there so they could waste them some more. That was what you did with gooks—you wasted them. The only good gook was a wasted gook. It's what gooks deserved.

Gook, gook, gook. Hearing it and saying it made me part of the majority. I was the only black pilot around, but because of the gooks, I was not in the minority. When it was the Americans against the gooks, the yellow gook made all Americans the same color. Having a common enemy turns you into brothers.

But the Koreans were gooks, too (actually, gook is derived from a Korean slang term), because they always seemed to know before we did when the PX was going to open and they'd buy out everything before we could get there—radios, stereos, tape recorders, records, whatever and whenever. They'd send stuff home for a quarter of what it would've cost them in Seoul. I don't doubt that their families sold a lot of it on the black market. That was the smart thing to do, and they were smart. They were still gooks, though—but only behind their backs, of course. I wouldn't let myself wonder whether, behind my back, I was a nigger to any of my guys. It wouldn't have surprised me, because a lot of them were from the South, but my attitude was that if I didn't hear anything and didn't notice anything, it did me no good at all to suspect the monster that may not have been there. There was no point. As long as someone wasn't in my way, he wasn't an obstacle.

★ ★ ★ 39 ★ ★ ★

I don't know exactly how many days we've been out. I'm not even sure how many days it's been since the chopper last flew over. Four? Five? Six?

Our progress is sometimes measured in yards per hour. But that's all right. At this rate, we'll still be within the chopper's range if it comes in at the same angle; the pilot will be able to hear our signal—assuming we still have a signal. Assuming he comes back.

Burdett throws his weight forward onto the canes and drags the leg along, the scraping of it on the jungle floor as painful as the dentist's drill on a nerve; I smooth the trail from behind. A lesser man than he is would've given up by now—especially knowing that if we'd been the Special Forces guys instead of just the bus drivers getting them there, they'd have dropped a Long Range Reconaissance Patrol (LRRP) team long ago to rescue us.

You can't figure out or second-guess the politicians and generals and colonels and majors in charge of making these decisions. They're the same people who chose not to bomb Haiphong Harbor at the beginning of the war when it might've ended things quickly; and the same people who from time to time stop bombing the Ho Chi Minh Trail, even though letups lead to more enemy supplies and munitions coming into the country—that is, more dead Americans.

For me, it's harder every day—not just every day, but every minute—to stay positive and focused on the job instead of on what-ifs and why-nots. Mostly what keeps me going now is Burdett. For him, well, I'm not sure what keeps him going. Just when I think he's reached hopeless—and I want to take his revolver from him so that he can't use it for what the Green Berets claim is its only real purpose—he gets a spark in his eye. Even if it's only anger, that's good enough for me.

⋆⋆⋆ 40 ⋆⋆⋆

The thirty-day in-country orientation seemed to take twice that long—and no wonder: It had been almost a year and a half since flight school began. We sat in on daily briefings where officers went over new call signs and frequencies, enemy sightings in the area, weather forecasts, and whatever else the fresh intel happened to be—and watched other fire teams go off to fight. We all felt impotent—anxious to get on with it already. Knowing that we wouldn't even be on a twenty-four-hour standby alert until after the thirty days were up—meaning we might not be going on an actual mission for who knows how long after that—made all of us almost obsessive about losing our rookie status. By the time we'd taken some practice flights and felt comfortable with how the helicopter behaved in that humidity, the only thing that pacified me, ironically, was calibrating the guns—"zeroing them"—by test-firing at a range. The other guys at least had drinking as a salve. Me, I'd have to be content with sipping Cokes in the officers' club and watching the war through that window.

Part of me hoped that I'd be named command pilot of our gunship, but the assignments stayed the same. McCullough could've changed them, making me CP of the second helicopter in the fire team instead of, say, Gerardin. Of course, he didn't choose Santusi, either, Gerardin's copilot, to be CP. The way I looked at it, two of the three of us aside from McCullough had to be copilots, so until I saw or heard reason to believe otherwise, I'd believe McCullough wanted me on his team because he wanted the best. Besides, if anything happened to him, I'd become the fire team leader.

On the thirty-fifth day I'd begun thinking we'd come to Vietnam for nothing when at last our team was put on standby. It happened at about five one night. For the next twenty-four hours we'd be on alert—which obviously meant no drinking for the others.

Standby teams report to the operations center just off the flight line for a briefing of what's known about the whole area of operations. We heard that there were several areas in which ground troops already had or might face opposition from either the North Vietnamese Army or the Vietcong—not that it mattered which was which, since the NVA frequently fought as VC, using guerrilla tactics and Chinese weapons. There were sometimes Chinese soldiers fighting, too.

Both teams went through the tedious preflight procedure to make sure the choppers were airworthy. The checklist ran several pages and could take half an hour, which was why you wanted to do it as soon as you were placed on standby, so that you wouldn't have to do it again when the call came to fight. That way, you could just untie the rotors, push the start button, and wait for clearance.

"Helmets?" I said.

"On," McCullough said.

"Battery?"

"On."

"Warning lights."

Push to test: "Working."

"Master caution panel."

"On."

Engine out audio, governor rpm switch, fireguard, radios, gen switch, door, hydraulic boost, pedals, throttle, shoulder harness, altimeter, magnetic compass, engine and tranny oil pressure— nothing was too big or small for the checklist.

After we'd finished, Somers and Cleveland loaded the ammo and rockets, tied up the rotor blades, and camped out in the helicopter. Most crew chiefs and gunners did this. Two reasons why: To protect against sabotage from infiltrators and fraggers (choppers on the flight line sat side by side in twenty-foot-wide revetments of sandbags stacked four feet high), and because you couldn't drink alcohol for the twenty-four hours of standby—so the chopper was as good a place as any to hang out.

McCullough and I and the other two pilots were at the officers' club sipping Cokes, probably to calm our stomachs. I couldn't stop pacing along the width of the picture window, my head turning to look outside each time I changed direction. "EZ, give it a rest," McCullough said. "You're not on sentry duty."

"Sure thing, Lieutenant," I said. But ten seconds later, I was back up and pacing.

The call came at about nine. Someone at the bar answered the field phone, and he yelled for our fire team.

We ran down to the flight line, about two hundred yards away. McCullough stopped for a last-minute briefing at the ops center. Somers and Cleveland untied the rotors and when they were clear I pressed the button on the cyclic. We were ready to ride.

McCullough came over to our chopper with what he'd been told. The other two pilots in our team joined us. McCullough unfolded the map and pointed.

"Friendlies here," he said, "encountering resistance. Once airborne, we'll make contact with the FAC and get further instructions before attacking. There appears to be no weather of note, except for low clouds. Remember, if you get in trouble, head east to the South China Sea. And here"—pointing at the map—

"remember not to let this mountain kiss you in the face. Any questions?"

None.

I was in the right seat. McCullough climbed in.

We made voice contact through our headsets with the other chopper. They were ready. We checked our radio frequencies—one for talking to each other, one for talking to the forward air controller, and one assigned to the friendly forces on the ground, which on this mission were Koreans from our camp; they all checked out. On the intercom, McCullough asked Cleveland and Somers if they were ready. He turned back and saw they'd taken their seats on some metal armor called a chicken plate, which had actually been designed to be worn as protection around the chest. But all gunners and crew chiefs sat on them instead, the idea being that they could kill us a hundred ways—with mortars and bombs, and bullets in the head, chest, and neck—but they're damned sure not going to shoot off our balls.

"Ready," Cleveland said, his mouth dry.

Then McCullough asked me.

"EZ?"

It would have been literally impossible for me to be more excited. This moment was the pinnacle of my life—everything I'd hoped for and dreamed about. I didn't show it, but I'm sure he could see it anyway.

"Ready, Lieutenant," I said.

"Starblazer one-six, ready to go," McCullough said into the mic on his helmet.

"Starblazer two-three, ready to go," Gerardin said from the other gunship.

The air tower hadn't yet been completed, so it was up to the operations officer to give us the go-ahead to leave.

"Roger, Starblazer one-six," came the voice. "You're good to go."

McCullough brought us up to four feet. "Clear right, clear

left," he said, and we eased back out of the revetment. "Tail coming right. Clear right."

Cleveland, Somers, and I had the job of looking every which way to make sure we didn't hit anything—not that there was anything to hit.

"Clear right."

"Clear left."

We turned straight to the runway and McCullough moved us about fifty feet along. Helicopters don't usually take off straight up, the way you see in movies—especially not in that kind of humidity. They require a certain amount of airspeed going forward before you get transitional lift, and once you do, you can feel it happening. That's why pilots try always to keep their crafts' noses into the wind, whether it's during takeoff or landing or, with gunships, on a run—because wind creates lift that you might need at any moment.

McCullough hovered for a moment, letting the other chopper back out of the revetment. I pointed when I could see them.

"You ready, Starblazer two-three?"

"Ready, one-six, ready to go."

McCullough eased the nose forward and added some collective. We hit thirty knots fast and could feel the transitional lift. Now, more power, more speed. We climbed gently at five hundred feet a minute—which isn't that fast; it's slower than a high-rise elevator—and at two minutes leveled off.

Our objective was to ease the assault on the squad of Koreans from the White Horse. We'd been instructed to fly to a particular coordinate and circle while making contact with the forward air controller (FAC)—a one-man recon unit in a one-man plane whose job is to scout the action and direct the air attack. At that point, we didn't know how big the enemy contingent was or what they had to fire.

I'd flown practice missions in this part of the jungle, and had been seduced by the alluring beauty and mystery—a canopy of trees that hid the ground. Now clouds hid the moon, too, so there was nothing to see below. We may as well have been in a closet with the door closed.

"Starblazer en route," I radioed the FAC.

"Roger."

It was another five minutes till we hit the coordinate. McCullough tuned in the FAC's frequency. "This is Starblazer one-six," he said.

The FAC answered. I pointed him out at ten o'clock, catching a glimpse of his controls in the cockpit.

He said, "I'm gonna fire a willie peter"—white phosphorous grenade—"at the bad guys' position and then direct fire. Friendlies will be one-eighty off where it hits."

"Roger that."

A burst of light cut through the air and hit the ground. He said, "Thirty yards from my fire is where Charlie is located." About three hundred yards away from us.

"Roger your fire," I said, my hand on the trigger.

"Fly west to east," the FAC said.

"Roger," McCullough said. "We're headed to target." And to the other helicopter: "Roger, we're coming in, descending to five hundred feet for the gun run, going west to east."

"Roger that."

We descended to five hundred feet and made a pass at eighty knots. I fired the mini-guns thirty yards to the right of where the willie peter had hit. Meanwhile, McCullough pulled the rockets and Cleveland and Somers were firing 60mm machine guns. Such remarkable violence; in the dark it took on a kind of surreal beauty, with the colors of the explosives bright enough to illuminate our faces. If there were human beings anywhere in that radius, they were no longer alive. I could not think anything about that now.

Gunship attacks are run in a daisy chain. Just as the first helicopter completes its pass and breaks off, the second one comes in on the target, keeping the heat on so the enemy can't take out the first chopper from behind. The gunner pivots his machine guns and pummels the target even as his chopper comes about in order to protect the second chopper and keep the punishment unrelenting.

Our first pass took approximately forty-five seconds. It appeared that everybody hit bull's-eyes with their weapons, but I had so much adrenaline coursing through me I could barely feel my body in the seat—as though I didn't need a machine to fly. We came about and I had a fifty-yard-line seat for the second helicopter's pass. All that rehearsal, all that training, had paid off. We felt exhilarated—we'd lost our cherry and lived to tell the tale—but there were no cowboy yee-haws or rebel yells or attaboys. This was deadly business, not pleasure.

Now we waited to hear from the FAC. Seconds passed. He said we needed to make a second pass, a little west of the first one.

We descended and began our pass—and saw the stroboscopic lights from tracer rounds headed straight toward us.

"Holy shit!" McCullough said as we headed for the run.

To me, the tracers seemed to come in slow motion, but that's because the illuminating charge is on every fifth bullet in the clip—and I was looking at them through the scope on my miniguns.

We could hear the ping of the bullets tearing through the helicopter skin and the plastic nose. Their deadliness is disguised by the surprisingly soft sound they make—like rain on a roof.

I forgot to breathe and then, when I tried, air wouldn't go in. My first thought was, *Welcome to Vietnam; this is war.* Well, actually my first thought was what McCullough had said. My third thought was, *You're going to die on your first mission.* But I kept firing just the same—as the others did, too—and I realized that tracers not only light up the target, they light the source. That's where we trained our weapons.

We completed the pass and banked hard left for the third one, not letting the other Starblazer gunship get too far ahead of us. I couldn't see the tracers anymore—and then I couldn't see anything at all.

The clouds had been moving all night and by flying into the wind we'd been swallowed by one that blotted out everything. Uh-oh.

The FAC had seen us disappear into the cloud and called. "Starblazer one-six, come in."

"Starblazer one-six," McCullough said. "We're in the shit now."

"Well, get yourselves out of it."

That meant instrument flying.

"Jesus Christ," Somers said, "I can't see a thing."

"Lieutenant," I said, "that mountain's west of us. We've gotta turn back, toward the sea."

"Yep," he said.

I said, "Now I'm glad we had that blind training—with the hoods on."

"What training? What hoods?"

I must've blanched, because he snorted a laugh as he turned back east.

I said, "Just let me know if you want me to take over, Lieutenant." He couldn't see the smile.

"Starblazer one-six, this is Starblazer two-three. We're circling here, waiting for you. You all right?"

"Fine," I said.

"Roger, good luck."

We'd need it. At eighty knots with no visibility, we could hit a mountain and be dead before we knew to be afraid.

Somers and Cleveland sat tight in the back, straining to catch a glimpse of light—a break somewhere in the cloud.

We kept the radio on the FAC's frequency. "Starblazer two-three, you guys head home. Mission accomplished. Friendlies in control of battle zone. Good job, guys. Starblazer one-six, good job, guys. Just get yourselves back."

"Roger that."

I opened the map and studied it, looking for another mountain that we might kiss or something else to worry about not mentioned in the briefing.

There wasn't much talk for a while. McCullough and I were thinking the same things: Heading out toward sea, which we may very well have been over now, could increase the cloud size—or take us into a cloud bank. By the time we broke through, assuming we did, we might be so far out that we wouldn't have enough fuel to make it back to Lane. I calculated the time and distance.

At its widest, from Pleiku, which is near the Cambodian-Laotian border, to Qui Nhon on the coast, Vietnam isn't even a hundred miles across. The math wasn't difficult. We descended slowly, believing that we'd reached the South China Sea and weren't still in the jungle, home to some tall trees. Where was the water, though? We couldn't see it.

This went on for fifteen minutes. Every minute of flying out meant a minute back. The fuel gauge was now our enemy, too. It was time to start thinking about making a water landing—assuming and hoping that I hadn't miscalculated and that we were really over water—and trying to hang on till first light.

But just like that, we burst through the cloud. It was clear, and the sliver moon glistened on the water.

"Thank God," Somers said. "It's like he scared the shit out of us, and now we get to go home."

"Roger that," McCullough said.

He turned to me and smiled, and I realized I hadn't been even a little scared. God help me, I was going to love this.

We took a roundabout route back, to avoid the cloud, and there was a reception waiting for us at Lane. The Koreans had overrun the enemy position, thanks to us and the other unit. We all inspected the floor and nose of the chopper for bullet holes, and saw about a half dozen. One of them had apparently missed me by the amount I'd been leaning into the mini-guns' sight.

The maintenance crew took the chopper to the repair shop to patch the holes and gave us another Huey. We spent a half hour getting it ready to go, should the call come again in the next twelve hours. We were still on standby, so the only reason to go up to the officers' club was to sip more Cokes and get patted on the back. This was a fine first mission—a mission accomplished. We'd cheated death, and we weren't newbies anymore. I don't know about my crew, but I was hoping we'd be called back out there before our alert status ended in a few hours. I didn't want to wait another few days to do this again.

★★★ **41** ★★★

Burdett's no longer able to climb trees, so we find the safest place possible on the jungle floor to catch a few hours of sleep. It's a full moon and a cloudless night, so some of that brightness finds its way down to us the way light from the hallway sneaks under bedroom doors. We can see each other's faces with slashes of moonlight across them. His skin looks as dark as mine. We're eating grubs. In silence. I'm thinking about how much my back hurts and about my crotch rot and blisters and how angry I am—angry enough to burn down this whole goddamned jungle. But what's the point? I don't have the energy to waste on being angry. Besides, half an hour from now and in the morning and tomorrow night and the day after that, I'm going to be in the same predicament— and all the righteous anger in the world isn't going to change a thing. No, anger only gets in the way of survival.

Burdett heats a grub over his lighter and says, "I wish I had me a big steak, 'bout yea thick, smothered in onions and mashed potatoes and a giant slice of sweet potato pie."

"Mmm, that sounds good. I guess I could do with about a pound of pork chops, some black-eyed peas and okra, and a whole pan of corn bread."

"That sounds good, too. Hell," he says, "cooked dog sounds good right now."

"Man, I don't even need to cook it," I say.

More silence. Again, Burdett breaks it. He says, "You know what kills me? Just fucking kills me, goddammit."

"What?"

"We volunteered for these fuckin' missions."

"Hey, you volunteered to go in the Army, period."

"I didn't want to, really."

"No?"

"What I wanted to do was go to LSU—get my history degree, then go to law school. Couldn't get in."

"Grades?"

"You gotta know somebody to get in, and I didn't know anybody."

That doesn't sound right to me; I suspect white men with good enough grades get in wherever they want. But now's not the time to argue protocol and custom. "Come on, your dad was an Army officer. That had to help."

"You kidding? To them, we were just poor white West Virginny trash that they didn't want at their pretty school."

That, I think, has the ring of truth. I tell him about when I tried to get into West Point.

He laughs. "Poor black man from Mississippi at West Point— 'specially back then. You really are a dreamer, EZ." Then he stops laughing. "But you'd have made it through."

I'm not much for taking compliments and can't say thank you to this man, so I have to change the subject. I look up at the little bit of sky I can see.

I say, "I used to stare up at the full moon when I was a kid and make wishes on it."

"Bet you didn't wish for this."

"So far, most of my wishes have come true."

"Yeah, well, none of mine have." He pauses, shakes his head. "I stopped making them."

"You sure feel sorry for yourself a lot."

He has nothing to say about that—at least, not directly.

After a long minute he says, "You know what my old man's gonna be doing tonight—probably doing right now, in fact? He's got his mouth around a bottle of whiskey and whinin' about how life's not fair. And you know what? He's goddamned right about that."

I don't respond.

But something else soon does—the concussion and burst of a bomb strike, far in the distance. North.

"B-52," he says.

"What're they doing flying on a full moon?"

"Probably wanna make sure some more pilots get shot down."

"Maybe the action's moving south. That might be good news for us."

"Come on, you know what the fuck it means. Means we're closer to more of the enemy. They'll be coming this way, maybe back into Laos."

He's right. But that doesn't change our situation or what we have to do about it.

★★★ **42** ★★★

New Year's Day, 1968. Ho Chi Minh had written a new poem and Hanoi Radio broadcast it:

> This spring far outshines previous springs
> Of triumphs throughout the land come happy tidings
> Forward!
> Total victory shall be ours!

We hadn't flown more than half a dozen missions, I think because there were more experienced gunship platoons in the A-O. Anyway, it had been like an intense game of musical chairs to get a mission. Everyone wanted one, and there weren't enough to go around.

But now someone somewhere in Central Command decided that an artillery unit living in a permanent encampment of tents and bunkers about thirty miles out there in the back country needed to be paid that day. Why, I don't know. It wasn't as though the soldiers had anything to spend it on, except maybe gambling with each other. When these guys went on R&R, their commanders called in helicopter units to shuttle them out of there; that's how isolated they were. Anyway, the mission was to bring them their Military Pay Certificates (MPC). Psychologically, I suppose, it was a morale boost for guys who spent their lives wet, muddy, and miserable.

Normally gunships accompany the slicks on a mission like this, to provide offensive cover and protection. But there'd been a declared lull in the action—a semi-official cease-fire because of the yuletide, not unlike the Christmas 1914 cease-fire in World War I that saw soldiers from both sides getting out of their trenches to show off photos of their girlfriends and exchange cigarettes and treats from home, and to play soccer. Gunships stayed home as two slicks from the 61st were sent out there, both with full four-man crews. I knew the four pilots, though not well because they weren't gunship pilots, and the crew chiefs and gunners by name and face.

On the way back, their mission accomplished, they took heavy fire and one of them went down. Four men dead, all from the same company; men we'd known for almost a year since Fort Campbell; four out of 250 in a single incident.

Our unit's first KIAs.

A chaplain led services at Lane's chapel. Everyone attended. Not a man didn't feel the loss and sadness, but no one cried. Two reasons: One, we were young men who'd grown up at a time when men didn't cry, especially men like us, and most especially not in front of each other; we weren't teenagers bawling for our mamas in basic training. And two, the emotion had turned into macho anger. Yes, we should've known already that this was war and things like that happened in war. We should've known a lot of things. But what we'd known until then was that killing was easy. What we learned was that losing someone was hard. And we took the lesson personally.

"Total victory," the chaplain promised, "shall be ours."

☆　☆　☆

A platoon of bad guys had been spotted closing in on an ammo dump northwest of Qui Nhon and an infantry unit had them trapped in a V-shaped valley with mountains to the north and south. My fire team got the call to flush them out of there—or kill them.

We started the gun runs from west to east, broke hard left, pulled pitch, and went back and around. Each run lasted one minute, with the whole cycle almost three minutes. We'd just completed the third run when the panel lights started blinking and the alarm sounded; it's an awful sound, even apart from what it means. In this case it meant we were losing power just when we needed it most—to get over the mountains.

"We're hit," I said. "Engine failure. Going down."

"Roger, we're covering you and calling in a mayday," Gerardin said on the radio in the other chopper.

McCullough and I were in perfect sync. What followed took at most a minute, but in our perceptions it seemed to take an hour. We bled the motor speed, cut the throttle, and put the collective all the way down to gain rotor speed.

We barely made it over the mountain and then started into a free fall.

"Clear right," Somers said.

Cleveland said, "Clear left." They'd already begun looking for a place we could come down.

I called out the rpms to McCullough, so he'd know whether to push or pull back on the cyclic, and at fifty feet of altitude he pulled back on the cyclic. It's called flaring the aircraft, and to pull it off we had to jerk up a little on the collective, because we didn't want the rotor blades to overspeed the redline. Now the helicopter nose was pointing up about fifty degrees, and now we weren't looking at the instruments anymore, we were looking outside for a place to land. All I could see was treetops, which is the same as seeing your own grave.

We talked to each other and to the guys in the other helicopter the whole way as we kept falling—forty feet, thirty, twenty—the skids dragging branches but not catching anything. At ten feet we pulled the nose up and put the tail down, and then at five feet landed the aircraft and slowly pulled the collective all the way up, sucking in the speed and maximizing the angle on the rotor blades to set down as softly as possible. Just as if the hand of God had guided the helicopter, we didn't land as much as slosh down without a jolt—right in the middle of a rice paddy.

Somers and Cleveland jumped out to secure the site.

McCullough turned to me and smiled. "Damn, EZ," he said. "I guess we know what we're doing."

"Just like they taught us, Lieutenant."

The rescue chopper was already in sight.

It's said that danger's the greatest aphrodisiac in the world, not that you need something to get you going when you're in your twenties. Where we needed to get going on this particular night was to the whorehouse on the other side of the perimeter fence. Risking being shot at by the Koreans, we sneaked out. In all that testosterone, deprivation seemed like a kind of death anyway, so we figured the risk was a push.

By some miracle, we made it safely to the house—or what passed for one. The whole thing was the size of an ordinary master bedroom. It had bamboo walls and hanging bamboo curtains as separators between the, uh, service areas. Standing on the little walkway outside the door, you could hear the sounds of young men and younger "women." Five, ten, fifteen minutes at the most—they'd be done. I didn't care if it took me one minute, I was going in when my turn came. Then my turn did come and from the doorjamb I could see a young girl come out and squat over a little washbasin that looked like a bedpan filled with dirty water. She picked up a dirty washrag, squeezed out the excess water, wiped herself, and said, "Next," while looking at me. And suddenly, all that saltpeter the Army had been putting in my food began working. I thought, *Never mind.*

The Koreans had bought out everything at the PX again, so on a day we weren't on standby Somers and I rode a jeep to Qui Nhon, to shop at the much bigger PX. I hadn't spent any money on anything except Cokes, so I had plenty of dough to spend on gadgets and cigarettes and whatnot.

I drove. We parked along the side of the road near the PX and did our shopping inside. When we came out I absentmindedly laid a carton of cigarettes I'd bought on the jeep's hood and reached into my pocket for the keys. Just that fast, a Vietnamese kid—not more than twelve—grabbed the cigarettes and ran off. In Vietnam, American cigarettes were more valuable than gold.

Without thinking, I unholstered my .38, raised my arm, and aimed at him. Somers said nothing, I think because he couldn't believe I'd actually pull the trigger. But I almost did. I was that close. And then I came to my senses.

This was what battle did to you. Or to me. Life wasn't even worth a carton of cigarettes anymore.

Maybe two other pilots didn't drink at Lane. All the rest of the pilots and officers thought we teetotalers were strange, and some of them, when they were drunk, didn't like being around us—as though we couldn't be trusted. They thought we thought we were better than they were. To them, it wasn't just a bond that we couldn't share; to them, it was a bridge that we wouldn't cross. There was no point in explaining I'd grown up seeing my grandfather lying in pools of puke, and that I couldn't tell what it was about alcohol that was supposed to be fun. To me, being in control of yourself and your faculties was a lot more fun than losing them.

Never having been drunk, I can't say whether the way people act when they're plastered is the real them or just some alchemy catalyzed by the alcohol. I suspect the answer is a little of both. But I saw and heard some ugly things that made me glad I'd chosen differently, even though in commanders' reports I'd sometimes be referred to as "odd." Guys who were so drunk they could barely form words would spot me across the room—the only black there—and stagger over to tell me, "You know, Ware, you're not like them. You're different. Other people, they might hate you 'cause of the color of your skin, but not me." Uh-uh. I'd stop them before they got to the part about me thinking I was better than they were, which I of course must think, because I was Mr. High and Mighty, always in control, never getting even a teensy-weensy bit loaded. From there, it would be just a short step to, "You know, Ware, we used to call people like you niggers."

What was I supposed to do, throw a punch at a drunk man? Take him aside the next day? Or ask him, *Now* what do you call niggers?

In time I stopped going to the club at Lane, unless there was a mandatory officers' meeting. That was when my commander's reports starting noting how "antisocial" I was. I didn't care. This was a small price to pay for the privilege of being a pilot.

It came to be called the Tet Offensive because it began at the end of January 1968, during Tet, the Vietnamese new year. The North Vietnamese Army and the Vietcong joined forces to launch surprise attacks on every major city and provincial capital in South Vietnam. At first the toll on South Vietnamese troops and American troops was heavy, and American news agencies reported the losses with alarm. That the offensive followed President Johnson's call for higher taxes to pay for the broadening war may or may not have been coincidental, but between that and the dispatches from Vietnam of the carnage—including nightly newscasts of ferocious fighting and pictures of young men being carried out feet first—more Americans began turning against the war every day.

The truth was that we successfully repelled the attack with our own counterattacks, and in military terms the offensive was an absolute failure for the enemy. In fact, we all but wiped out the Vietcong as an effective fighting force, an effect that some people believe Ho Chi Minh and his generals had intended all along, in order to consolidate his power. Whatever the truth of Ho's intentions and whatever the truth of battlefield wins and losses, the perception of victory belonged to the North, and from then on the landscape became progressively surreal and disconnected from the ordinary rules and aims of war. Maybe it was the press. Maybe it was the era in general, with the world exploding in psychedelic colors and music. Maybe it was the Pentagon, insisting on calling the shots for a war nine thousand miles away. Or maybe it was just the jungle. As John Ford said, when the legend becomes myth, you print the myth. In Vietnam, it was perception that got printed. And no gunship or Marine battalion or B-52 was powerful enough to fight it.

✴ ✴ ✴ **43** ✴ ✴ ✴

A thick tree branch snaps back after I move through, hitting Burdett's leg. He howls in agony, drops to the ground, and rolls around until the sharpest pain subsides. Then he begins crying. Not mere soft whimpering, this is the sobbing of a terrified child who's just lost his mother.

"Burdett, sssh," I whisper. "Stifle it." He doesn't. The tears and blubbering rise up from someplace deep inside, gaining momentum and power on the way so that they explode as they reach his mouth. It's loud—too loud for our circumstances.

"Burdett," I say, "shut up."

Nothing changes.

I slap him.

"Shut up!"

No change.

I kneel down and cover his mouth with my hand. He doesn't seem to care, and it has no effect on how hard he's crying.

I look away from his face, not wanting to see something private I believe I'm not meant to see. It embarrasses me, makes me wonder whether that kind of pain is inside me, too. Have I paved over the place where my memories of being a terrified child used to be?

He continues crying for long minutes, until he's exhausted himself and reaches a clearing in his emotions.

"We're not gonna get out of here," he says when I slowly take my hand off his mouth. "They're not gonna pick us up."

"Yes, they are," I say.

"No, they're not."

"Well, then, we'll make it home ourselves, without them."

"I can't."

"Yes, you can."

"I can't. I'm done."

"You can and you're not."

"Why haven't they come back for us?"

"I don't know. I'm sure there's a good reason."

"What good reason? Even if they can't land, they coulda sent a jolly green giant and have some guys rappel down to get us."

I don't have an answer for that, because it's true. Reminding him that the mission is more important than the people wouldn't be helpful right now.

"I want to give up," he says. "There's nothing left. What's the point? You don't have to, EZ. You go on. I'm slowing you down. Just get me to a village, and I'll take my chances."

I've heard enough of this. No rational argument I can make is going to get us past this place—and anyway there are no rational arguments anymore. My only weapon is whatever vanity and pride he has left.

I say, "Get up, you goddamned pussy. You get up right now. I mean it, when I get back to the States—and I *am* getting back—I'm gonna go tell that Imperial Wizard of yours, and every other cracker in your little town, how you let a nigger beat you. I'm gonna tell everyone everything. You understand? And don't think I won't love doing it. I won't leave out a thing. When I get done, your own mother's gonna be ashamed you were her son. For the rest of time, they're gonna think about you out here crying and giving up and rolling over and dying. Now get your fat white ass up."

In a way, I'm just repeating a version of the same pep talk I keep hearing in my head, to keep me going when I feel I can't take another step. I kick my own ass every half hour, imagining how General Patton would do it if he were here, and pretending I have to keep up with him so that he doesn't disgrace me in front of everybody. Sometimes the voice in my head belongs to Job, reminding me that what he went through makes this seem like Eden. Of course, I also have to remember that whatever I'm feeling just can't compare to the misery of Burdett's leg. Doesn't matter, though. Giving up isn't an option.

Burdett stops crying. The tears have left streaks on his grimy face. He looks straight up at me. "My whole family's Klan," he says sadly.

Apparently in his town the Klan was like the Rotary Club. It's what you did to get ahead and to be accepted. I don't know whether it's an excuse or an explanation for this: "Daddy," he admits, "used to be Imperial Wizard."

"Look, Burdett," I say, "right now I don't care if your father's Adolf Hitler. But if he is, you've got one more reason to get going. You don't want another Jesse Owens thing happening here." I try smiling at the joke—a little sugar with the medicine.

"EZ, I can't," he says, tearing up. "It hurts too much. Every time something touches it—"

"We'll fix that," I say.

From now on we'll have to take our chances on the trail.

★ ★ ★ 44 ★ ★ ★

Qui Nhon was popular with American troops stationed in bases within a few A-Os of there. Three of our squad members had driven down for the day—January 30, 1968—to listen to music and enjoy female companionship in someplace a little swankier than that rat's nest outside the gates of Lane Airfield. The best place in town had a big bar downstairs and private, reasonably spacious rooms upstairs with young women who didn't look like someone's baby sister with dead eyes. These ladies could actually smile—and had white teeth in their mouths.

It was early evening. We were upstairs, each in separate rooms, when the shooting started in the streets and got audibly closer—mortar blasts, artillery fire, and gunshots. Squads of VC, some with AK-47s, were running in and out of bars and restaurants and anywhere else they thought they might find Americans—which was everywhere. I don't know how many, if any, Americans were killed that evening in those streets.

I threw on my pants and ran out to the landing above the bar area, getting there the same time as my squad mates, who were also in various states of undress. We could make out VC knocking over tables and chairs and hassling the people who ran the place, for catering to American soldiers. Each of us up there only had a .38 sidearm—standard issue for pilots—so we were pitifully outmatched. We had to get to the street and out of there, because they'd soon work their way upstairs, but there was no way we'd be able to fight it out cowboy-saloon-style—shooting, hiding behind tables and chairs, saying, *Cover me!* and making a break for it.

From outside, we could hear the street violence getting louder.

That left the roof as our only escape choice if we were going to get out of there alive.

We motioned to each other to climb. Surely by now word would've reached one of the base camps in the area that this was no disorganized street demonstration; this was a full assault, and at least one of the bases would've sent out slick ships to pick up the stranded.

When we got to the roof there were already four other American soldiers from another unit at another camp huddling together. They weren't pilots, but they weren't any better armed than we were.

Looking down, we could see the fighting. I counted at least two Vietnamese shot dead, probably for being "collaborators," in a scene not much different from that famous photo of Saigon's police chief executing a Vietcong.

Soon the skies offered a welcome sight—three American slicks. They'd no doubt brought troops to beef up the security at the MASH and ammo dump. We all waved our arms, trying to get their attention, and at last we did. One of the slicks, nearly full already with evacuees, came our way. The pilot didn't have enough room to land on that little roof, so he hovered as close as he could, turning the helicopter into the wind, nose up, meaning that the tail rotor was barely four feet off the tarpaper. We huddled on the north side of the main rotor, to keep from getting eviscerated, and jumped up onto the skids to pull ourselves inside. We beat it out of there just before Charlie made it to the roof, firing.

I can sometimes amuse myself by considering how, if we'd been downstairs at the bar when Charlie burst in instead of upstairs, we would've been killed. It was our sex drive that saved our lives.

☆　☆　☆

We wanted missions, we got missions. Lots of them.

But first we got briefings—all sorts of briefings on Tet and how these were the battles that would come to define the war, or maybe end it. Early losses had been heavy on the American side, with some bases completely overrun. Like the one at Kontum.

Kontum was a small town with a strong French influence located near where Vietnam, Laos, and Cambodia come together. It was mostly under the control of the American 4th Infantry Division, but when the American base was overrun by waves of fierce and heavily armed Vietcong fighters, only the South Vietnamese army prevented the attackers from taking the entire city before reinforcements arrived. The Americans lost about a dozen helicopters in dynamite attacks, and there weren't enough remaining to make a serious dent in the assignment load. My fire team went to pick up some of the slack, expecting to be back at Lane in two or three days, when a replacement company arrived at Kontum.

It was a few hours' flight to get there. We reported in, got our hootch assignments—an eight-man tent for us plebes, and a one-man tent for the officer, Lieutenant McCullough—and went to get some chow. The place still looked like, well, a war zone. On the perimeter of the camp, the offensive was still raging. We huddled in our tents and talked about how great we had it at Lane compared to the poor guys stationed here. Even the privies were rat holes—literally.

Not five minutes later we heard screaming and hollering, then shooting, then more screaming and hollering, then more shooting. The camp was being overrun again—and everybody was beating it into the bunkers. All we had for weapons were our revolvers, which weren't much better than arrows. So the four of us joined the stampede. We sprinted like Bob Hayes—and I didn't make it.

I stepped on a rotted board covering a dried-up well and fell in, not knowing I'd fallen until I hit the bottom. In the daylight I would've seen it. Not at night.

It was a ten-foot drop, and the only reason I didn't break something or kill myself was my adrenaline parachute. For half an hour I huddled in there, my .38 drawn and ready to blow the face off some Vietcong who leaned over—or worse, fell in. I could hear fighting and shooting and shouting, and then it was over and the all-clear signal was sounded. When I heard American voices I yelled for help. That nobody razzed me when they lowered the rope meant the damage had been bad again. It was—though fortunately no one had been killed. But two more helicopters had been destroyed; not ours.

We started flying missions the next day in support of the Special Forces bases and fire bases in the area, flying every day. Sometimes we'd accompany slick ships dropping off or picking up Green Berets on what are known as long-range reconnaissance patrols (LRRP, pronounced "lurps"), where they're left all on their own in the jungle to accomplish whatever their mission happened to be.

Most of our missions were in or around Dakto, a dense jungle area in the Central Highlands near Pleiku that had been heavily damaged by B-52 strikes and napalm and herbicides. Three months earlier, throughout most of November—*before* Tet was considered to have technically begun—one of the war's ugliest and bloodiest battles had taken place there. About forty-five hundred members of the 4th Infantry Division and 173rd Airborne held off six thousand heavily armed NVA troops over three weeks, and when the NVA finally retreated, they left nearly fifteen hundred dead—at a cost of 285 Americans killed and nearly a thousand wounded.

Ten years later, no American who'd survived action in or around that A-O didn't recognize the essence of what they'd experienced when *Apocalypse Now* was released—meaning that the uniquely psychedelic insanity of this war was in its full glory there.

The NVA would steal our tactical radio frequencies, probably off a dead soldier, and hack in like Tokyo Rose, so just as we'd be communicating our position to ground forces or base camp we'd hear an Asian-accented voice butting in: "You dead person. You going to die, Amelican." Meanwhile, detachments of the South Vietnamese army would stop fighting and insist they be airlifted out of hot zones. They'd hold guns to the heads of Green Berets, whom they were supposed to be accompanying, and warn, "If we don't get out of here now we're going to shoot you," as the Green Berets would try to convince them to keep fighting. If they wouldn't, we'd have to come in to pick them up. By contrast, you could shoot a VC between the eyebrows, and even stone-cold dead he'd get up to fight you.

Some nights we couldn't make it back to Kontum and had to stay at the Dakto base, which made the discomforts of Kontum seem like a Hilton Hotel. It was a fortress, and it had to be. At various times after dark every night our guys would fire artillery at nothing in particular outside the perimeter, and in the morning you could count a dozen or two would-be infiltrators, dead where they'd fallen in the surprise volleys. Sometimes the mortar blasts were like flashbulbs that caught the frightening frozen image of NVA running straight for us, and then shots would ring out. Every time someone shouted, "Incoming," we ran for the trenches and were handed M-16s. Our own .38 sidearms, a Green Beret once pointed out to me, "are only good if you wanna commit suicide."

I felt safe with the Green Berets around. Inside Dakto, they had their own compound within a compound—a kind of fiefdom. These guys were kings of the jungle. They ate meals that the rest of us who'd been stuck with cold C-rations considered as good as home cooking (freeze-dried meats and stews in foil packages to which you added hot water), and slept on cots with sleeping bags in roomy tents. After dark they'd manage to bring in beautiful young women, whom they'd sneak out before first light—though I'm not sure they even had to sneak anything; they did pretty much what they wanted. And best of all, they liked pilots; no, they loved pilots, because pilots bailed their asses out of trouble. That's why they made sure to take good care of us if they knew we were in for the night. They shared everything they had, including stories of courage and skill that made us proud to be on the same side. I would look at these gigantic, smiling, focused young men, most of them younger than I, and feel a deep appreciation for their confidence and foolhardiness. They had no fear and a deep dedication. We formed a mutual admiration society, each of us knowing that this night and the laughter could be the last any of us experienced.

☆　☆　☆

Coming back from a LRRP mission one afternoon near Bong Son near the coast, we looked down and saw an American engineering company in jeeps and trucks being ambushed by a large NVA contingent. Usually a company of that size would've been accompanied by some kind of air support, because they're rich, easy targets. This one wasn't protected. It was only by accident and luck that we happened to be there.

Well, it was a little too early to say they were lucky. You see, outside of free-fire zones in which pilots were allowed to—and in fact ordered to—shoot at anything human according to the understanding that they were probably bad guys who had AK-47s under their black pajamas, the rules of engagement prohibited us from doing the right thing without permission. The rules stated that, unless specifically authorized by the A-O commander to fire on the enemy, we could only fire when fired upon. So we had to hold fire until we received that authorization. I called it in to the ops officer at LZ English, who called the A-O commander for final authorization. While waiting, I recalled the time when we'd seen an NVA squad at the end of a base's runway in Pleiku and couldn't get permission to take them out. But with our guys getting slaughtered, this would be only a formality—right? Wrong.

The answer came back: No, we couldn't fire. Because this was a week or a month or whatever the changing season happened to be when the A-O was being controlled by ARVN, the South Vietnamese army.

On the radio, I pleaded to let us fire away. Here we had two loaded gunships circling over the enemy, who were already killing Americans—and we couldn't get permission. It was insane. I shouted, "Don't they understand? American soldiers taking heavy fire and heavy losses."

The ops officer was sympathetic, but the issue was out of his hands. We were ordered to return to base.

McCullough suggested that we buzz the enemy, to draw fire. Once they fired, we'd be within our rights to fire back and kill them all.

We made several low provocative passes. And you know what? The enemy didn't fire back. Not one bullet. Which told us something we'd rather not have known. It told us that the NVA understood our rules of engagement as well as we did; they understood that we couldn't do the jobs we'd been trained for unless they made the first move. It was even possible that the ARVN commander who wouldn't give us permission to fire was playing for the other side, or that spies had tipped the NVA off. To this day I can only wonder and imagine what our guys getting killed and maimed down there were thinking when they saw us. *Why don't they fire? Go ahead, you sons of bitches. Fire! That's what you're supposed to do!* And to this day, I'm sorry that we didn't lie and claim that we had been fired upon by the enemy. Who was going to say we hadn't been?

Our anger was like fuel. We were borne home on it and raced into the ops officer's quarters to tell him.

"Their blood's on your hands," I said.

I couldn't sleep; none of us could. How many Americans would be sent home in body bags because of the rules of engagement—or because of treachery?

At four a.m. came the order to go back out toward Bong Son and chase the NVA unit that was now on the run, thanks to land units of the 173rd that had been sent out there in their own slicks to help repel the attacking NVA. Now the NVA were trying to escape. By the time we got out there at first light, we saw somewhere between two hundred and three hundred NVA soldiers either wading into the South China Sea to climb into sampans, or already in sampans hoping to paddle away. Many had AK-47s. All had weapons. We fired into the water just east of the farthest sampan, letting them know that they needed to go back to shore and give themselves up to the 173rd. They didn't. We fired again and waved our arms and pointed toward shore, letting them know that that was the only way to live. They refused. We tried again. And the answer came in a volley from their weapons.

After that came an orgy of shooting from our gunships. One soldier at a time, all turned down a personalized offer to surrender—and for that they died. The whole thing took an hour or so. Their bodies floated in the tide, oozing blood. They'd all chosen this end, so I couldn't feel bad except to think that no American should have had to die before this.

$\star$ $\star$ $\star$ **45** $\star$ $\star$ $\star$

The line of infection looks like a snake crawling under Burdett's leg. It's now halfway to the top of his thigh. Actually, I'm surprised we've gotten this much time before having to decide.

"It's definitely moving," Burdett says in a kind of fascinated voice. "Look at it."

But I only look at him looking at it. I've sneaked plenty of glances when he's asleep. That thing on what used to be his leg is the ugliest, angriest wound I've ever seen on a human being who's still alive. I don't know if it's staph or E. coli or some other kind of bacteria, but whatever it is, if it climbs three inches higher we won't be able to stop it before it reaches his heart—and kills him.

For a week we've talked now and then, nothing serious, about where the cutoff line is. And every day we agree to put it off another day; we don't want to strangle the leg if there's a chance we'll be rescued. But today's the day without a tomorrow. Common sense and what we remember from first-aid class say that once it gets higher than his pelvis, there's no other place to make a last stand. You can't, after all, tourniquet an abdomen.

But will he let me do it? I'd rather not make the decision for him. After four or five hours with the tourniquet on, that leg's going to be lost forever—even if we're picked up right after that and flown to a MASH unit.

Burdett keeps staring at the leg. Maybe he's imagining looking down and not seeing it anymore—trying to get used to the idea.

I say, "Look, Captain—"

"Uh-oh," he says, "now I'm a captain again."

"If you don't do it, it's suicide."

"It may as well be if I do."

"That's stupid."

"Yeah? Well, you're not the one who has to live without a leg."

"You just said it. You said 'live.' I can't believe you'd rather die with both legs than live with one."

"Well, you're not the one who has to."

"But I would. I'd be grateful for having one leg, two arms, and a head."

Burdett stares at me. He says, "I bet you would." Pause. "But I don't know about me."

"There's only one way to find out."

He thinks about that and says, "I envy you, EZ. Right now, I wish I'd grown up a dirt-poor nigger in Mississippi."

Strangely, I know what he means.

"What's it going to be, Ron? Life or death?" This time, I can't make the decision for him; I can't force him to do anything.

He pauses a long time, thinking, his eyes darting back and forth. I hope for a certain answer that has nothing to do with the Army and promotions. I know I can make it alone here; I've been flying solo since I was six weeks old. But I don't want to anymore—not even if it means being rescued faster. Or at all.

He looks at me and reaches for my hand. I take it, first in one and then in both of mine. I've never held hands with a man before, but it feels perfectly natural. For this moment, I'm not hungry anymore. I'm not tired or in pain or frightened. What I am is completely in this moment. With him. And him with me. In fact, it seems like the whole universe is here with us—everything that's ever happened and is yet to happen. It's all right here, right now.

"Do it," he says as the tears start to roll down his cheeks.

And mine.

I don't let them go too far, though. I look away from him, losing the moment. But I need to. I can't afford to feel anything. I have a job to do that doesn't care how I feel.

I remove the T-shirt from one of his canes and rip off a shred. He watches me.

"You look like you've done this before," he says.

"Sure, to all my partners."

"Hell, I was in damn good shape before I met you."

"Except for that big, fat belly."

The trick now is to tie the tourniquet above the top of the infection tight enough to stop that particular vein from carrying it to the heart but not so tight that there's no arterial blood at all flowing to the leg. That takes some experimenting, tightening and loosening it until the pulse I feel in his ankle is the weakest possible. I don't even know if that's proper protocol, but all I have to go on is what seems right. After more than two weeks out here, I'm glad something still does.

When it's all done, Burdett manages a grim smile and says, "I guess the good news is, we probably won't make it out of here alive anyway."

I don't have the energy or heart to scold him.

$\star\star\star$ **46** $\star\star\star$

The Kontum commander wouldn't release us yet to go back to the rest of our company at Lane, and he wouldn't let us check in via radio. So every time a mission was accomplished, we'd take the choppers up to ten thousand feet and try to make contact with Lane ourselves. This went on for another three weeks. We missed the comforts of home. Funny, Lane had at first seemed to most of the guys like a hellhole, and now we all woke every morning hoping this was the day we got to go back.

That day refused to come.

After a month at Kontum we received new orders. We were to go to LZ English—a relatively new base not far from Kontum. The whole 61st was transferred, and from what we figured out, the move had been planned all along. Flying out of Lane was for new companies in-country, because it was safer than most bases and allowed FNGs to work into the rotation at a good speed. Now that we were old hands, we could take the more rugged assignments. English certainly offered that. The place itself was huge and growing. I rarely ventured away from our little area—hootch and flight line and ops center—so I don't know for sure, but I'd bet there were four or five officers' clubs. All someone had to do was put a wooden plank across two fifty-gallon drums, call it a bar, get some booze and soft drinks, and that was that.

✷ ✷ ✷

Most of my mail came from the precommission correspondence courses I was taking. Once a month, maybe once every six weeks, a letter arrived from my wife. Yes, my wife. Joanna and I had reconciled before I'd shipped out—but reconciliation to what? The prefix implies a return to where we'd once been, or the establishment of a kind of cease-fire. But in truth I'd met her halfway because I'd romanticized having some sort of anchor back home, a connection to the States, and I'd hoped that the time and distance might bring us close for my return. For her, though, I'd come to believe, reconciliation meant bank deposits, meaning that she got half of my $1,400-a-month pay sent automatically to her, plus a lot more when I didn't have anyplace to spend the remainder left to me. She also got the new car I'd bought before leaving, a green '67 Ford Fairlane with a 428 engine that accelerated like a dragster.

My letters to her were long and detailed about what I'd been seeing and doing, where I'd been, the young men I'd met, the nature of war and man, the fear and loneliness and boredom that magnify the time between missions. Some of these communications were recorded on those small reel-to-reel tape recorders that were popular in Vietnam then because they were cheap to buy at the PX—and because everyone knew how to talk, even if they couldn't write well. Joanna's letters to me were like form letters sent to God's complaint department: the car needs new tires, the sink is backed up, she wants a new winter coat. I never stopped writing to her—or speaking to her on tape—because it was good therapy for me, like keeping a diary. But with every one of her letters that arrived, I knew more clearly that this was not someone with whom I wanted to spend my life. Her world was small, and that was fine for her; its boundaries were whatever brought her comfort. My dreams were of glory and honor, not clean laundry.

We'd accompanied a LRRP dropoff of Green Berets and were heading back to LZ English. We radioed the ops center and the order came to check out some particular coordinates. That was code, since the map coordinates corresponded to a free-fire zone that lay just on the other side of the mountains between us and the LZ if we took a south heading. According to free-fire zone rules, anyone we saw should be considered armed and deadly. The question pilots had to answer when they saw people in these otherwise unpopulated areas which they'd been warned to avoid was whether to pull the trigger. Everyone had heard stories of gunship pilots who'd seen old men and women—it's sometimes hard to tell who's under the straw coolie hats and in the black pajamas—walking down by creeks with their water buffalo and dismissed them as harmless, and then when they passed overhead were shot down with some concealed weapon.

To keep the element of surprise we stayed below the mountain peak until the last moment and then rose just high enough to clear the treetops at the ridge. Yes, anyone in the valley below could've heard the chopper coming, but it would've been impossible to know exactly where it was coming from.

Two people and a water buffalo were walking slowly. Both wore coolie hats and black pajamas. One of them glanced up quickly, then went back to walking, as though we were a common sight.

What to do?

I did not want to kill them, and yet I was supposed to.

If McCullough had been command pilot, I don't know what he would've ordered, but he was letting me fly today—and letting me make all decisions. I decided to fire rockets as a warning—to scare these two out of the free-fire zone, where they knew they weren't supposed to be; or if they didn't know it, to send them a message to get out.

There is no turret on the rocket sight. It's a fixed sight, like looking through a peephole, that can only be aimed by pointing the nose of the helicopter at the target so that where you're heading lines up with what's inside the sight's concentric circles. We were a thousand meters away. I didn't aim right at them; I aimed just over their heads—and pressed the fire button.

Two rockets shot out and then did something I'd never seen before and would never see again: they crossed in midair—and continued on their way to the targets. All four of us watched in astonishment as these two people exploded and evaporated into ash. The water buffalo kept walking.

There was nothing to say—not *Good shot* or *Nice job*. And there was no sense of exultation. Were they VC? I didn't see an AK-47, but it might have been hidden in the animal's pack. I felt sick to my stomach, nauseated by my second thoughts. Maybe they were just working the fields, and maybe they had kids who needed and loved them and parents who depended on them. Maybe the VC or NVA forced them to work there. After all, there weren't any villages in the area.

Back at camp, guys cheered me and toasted to me. The best I could do was force a smile, and the next many nights were long and dark and sleepless, the noises of war outside not as loud as the voices in my brain. When I thought my head would burst, I visited the chaplain.

"This is war," he said, "and you were in a combat zone. You followed orders, you did your job, you protected your own men. That's something to be proud of. Think how the infantry feels—looking men in the eye before shooting."

It was nice to hear but I couldn't stop wondering whether I should've fired those rockets. At the same time, I knew it was suicide to start guessing. I had to find the strength to know I could fire those rockets again in the same situation—because many of those who hadn't in the same situation hadn't come back, and neither had their crews. The chaplain was right. This was war.

A week or so later, coming back from another mission, we saw a sampan in the middle of a lake paddled by a woman wearing a coolie hat and black pajamas. Something was in the sampan with her. Probably a sack of rice. We were the lead helicopter.

Okay, let her be, I decided. We pulled off her and moved on— and then I heard the mini-guns from the other chopper. We looked back and saw that she was dead, blood oozing into the sampan and water—the hidden AK-47 still in her hands.

"She had you in her sights," Gerardin said. "Damn VC."

The difference between pilots and almost everyone else you met in Vietnam was that everyone else had dreams of being butchers and bakers and candlestick makers and anything else you could think of. But we pilots were already doing what we wanted to be doing the rest of our lives. We were flying, and that's how we wanted to earn our livings, whether it was in the military or for the airlines.

We'd chosen a high altitude, about ten thousand feet, for the flight from Dakto to the Air Force base at Pleiku, near where the first truly bloody battle of the war had been fought in 1965, in the Ia Drang Valley. It was that battle that convinced the generals to make the helicopter the war's primary tactical weapon. We were taking our time, McCullough reading aloud to us a *Stars and Stripes* that was no doubt going to piss off the brass, about how this wasn't going to be a fast war after all. Again, McCullough had let me fly left seat, preparing me for the flight test given to certify me as a command pilot.

Somers had remarkable vision. The man could see the veins in a leaf at thirty yards—and from two miles up he spotted a jeep traveling unescorted through this dangerous country hit a mine and overturn.

"Holy shit," he said, reporting what he'd just seen.

I took us down to about twenty-five hundred feet so we could confirm the sighting. The two soldiers, sprawled across the road, were conscious but obviously unable to move, their legs mangled.

We also saw two or three VC running toward them out of the jungle. They may have been by themselves, or they may have been part of a so-far-unseen platoon.

"We have to pick these guys up," I said

"We can't," McCullough said. "We're gunships."

"Lieutenant, please," I said. "We can't just leave them there."

We debated the rules against doing what's right for a few seconds. He pointed out, correctly, that landed gunships are almost as vulnerable as jeeps, and that we still had a full load of ammo, so the extra 370 pounds or so might make it hard for us to take off—and if that happened we'd be in deep kimchi. But I think the memory of leaving that engineering company to the slaughter was still fresh, because I just nodded yes to everything he said—all of it being true—and soon he said go ahead.

I told the other gunship to hold its altitude at about a thousand feet and cover us while I spiraled us down, focusing on a spot about thirty yards ahead on the road to land. At the last second I turned the chopper in the direction of the VC so that if they rushed us we could fire both the rockets and the mini-guns.

The dust kicked up from the road by the rotors was so thick I had to guess where the ground was by staring through the bottom of the bubble.

As soon as we hit, Somers and Cleveland jumped out and ran to the soldiers—who were MPs heading toward Kontum. One at a time, they carried them to our aircraft and put them in the back; the poor guys were in bad shape and moaning. We took off before the VC shot at us, and flew to the hospital at Pleiku.

McCullough gave the corpsmen our names, unit, and base, in case they needed to know anything else. We never heard from the MPs. Judging from the way they looked, I suspect that their war was over.

The Army awarded our whole crew medals—an Army commendation with "V" device for valor.

$\star\star\star$ **47** $\star\star\star$

We should've been on the trail all along. We're making much faster progress now, almost a mile and a half a day, even though we have to duck off and hide in the bushes whenever we hear people coming. It's easy to hear the small squads of NVA troops marching in single file but not so easy to hear a farmer stepping lightly. That's why we walk in complete silence—no whispering, no groaning, no leg-dragging—so that we can listen for any sound that's not our own. Actually, that's my job; Burdett's is just to keep going. His face is permanently contorted into a mask of pain and tears, but his weeping is soundless. We stop once an hour for ten minutes, not counting the three or four times a day I give the signal for us to duck into the bushes at the sound of something or someone. When that happens, he grits his teeth and I cover his mouth.

We eat what I can find and sleep what little we can twenty yards off the trail. Burdett complains constantly about his leg hurting and being numb at the same time. He says the tourniquet makes him claustrophobic. So I spend most of the night whispering pep talks to him that I can hardly believe myself, crap along the lines of, "You can't lose faith, Captain. There's no way we're not getting out of here alive. You just have to take every moment by itself and know that we're going home soon." It's as hard summoning the energy to speak as it is conjuring the imagination, which is where these words live now. I'm torn between my belief that the universe isn't so much our enemy as it is indifferent to suffering—not just ours but everyone's—and believing that God has something in mind for us; we are, after all, still alive. I pray for the strength to stay alive and free for another twenty-four hours, and I pray for guidance and inspiration.

Guidance comes when I notice Burdett staring blankly ahead in a way I interpret to mean he'd rather be dead than suffer anymore. I reach over and take possession of his gun and knife—something I should've done when we first saw that village.

Inspiration comes when I decide we'll rest during the day and walk at night, when there aren't so many civilians on the trail.

Moving in the dark isn't a problem, not at that speed. I walk half a step ahead, clutching his right hand with my left, which I hold behind me as I poke at what's in front of me with my free hand. We only have to get off the trail about once a night, which is a lot easier on Burdett. The air is cooler, too. Which is easier on both of us. At first light we find a safe spot in the overgrowth and settle in for the day, dozing in and out, hardly noticing the bugs that feast on us. We're feasting on them, too, and drink sparingly from the canteen that we know has given us dysentery. Our situation is still a misery, but at least it's manageable misery.

"When can I get my gun back?" Burdett asks one morning.

"When I'm sure."

He shakes his head and falls back asleep.

I should've been inspired before. Maybe we'd be home by now.

$\star\star\star$ **48** $\star\star\star$

We were escorting slicks carrying guys for a LRRP. We were at about five hundred feet, a hundred yards behind the slick, when the pilot radioed that they were taking fire from the ground. Below them was a village.

"House at two o'clock in that clump of grass," he said.

"Roger," I said. This was my fire team now. I was the command pilot.

We lit up the area with rockets and mini-guns, and then there was no more ground fire aimed at the slick, so we continued on with the mission.

The next day I was called in to see the commander of American forces—a general. Apparently some villagers had complained that we'd been too brutal and killed innocents.

I was in no mood to be contrite. The rules of engagement changed from A-O to A-O, and I'd just had a *Twilight Zone* experience chasing half a platoon of NVA soldiers into a village that was being temporarily evacuated. As the villagers were leaving, the NVA was streaming in—and my fire team was helpless to fire on them unless they fired on us first. To provoke them, we tried flying low and hitting them with our skids. But they'd just kept walking, not even in a hurry, knowing we were powerless.

"Sir," I said, "I don't know what else I could have done. I believed the mission was in jeopardy. I'm truly sorry and regretful someone innocent on the ground might get killed because he's near where the enemy is firing on Americans, but between that outcome and the chance that my guys will be killed because I'm too cautious or timid, I'm not going to apologize for choosing my guys. I'll do it every time."

I stood straight at attention and looked the general in the eye.

"All right, Ware," he said. "You're dismissed."

That was the last I heard of the complaints.

War brings out the best and the worst in a man. It's full of defining moments. It tests your loyalty, your commitment, your beliefs. It asks you to consider whether you're strong enough to die for what you believe—and to kill for what you believe. They're intertwined and inseparable.

War also unleashes the beast inside you—the viciousness that you've spent a lifetime trying to civilize.

In war, death is arbitrary. You could be killed by an enemy or friendly fire or something falling on you. If you survive, you take every day for the rest of your life as a gift and wonder why you were left alive when the man next to you—a good man from a good family with hopes and dreams—died. This was the man you were fighting for, the man you depended on, and when you pull everything else out of the bag, your devotion to him was what kept you going. Patriotism, country, even your family—those all become abstractions once the bullets start flying and the mortars explode. The only thing that was real and counted was this man— and you didn't even have to know his name.

☆ ☆ ☆

It's the waiting that gets you. It gets you thinking, and it gets you scared. The busier you are, the better off you are.

Whenever there was fragging—soldier slang for killing officers—or race fights, boredom was probably the instigator. To a young man whose sex hormones were already raging and whose kill-or-be-killed instinct was on hair trigger, idle hours weren't just the devil's playground, they were hell itself. It was in the quiet and stillness that dark thoughts would snatch his mind.

Me, I tried never to be idle. In that, I had company. Most of us volunteered for every mission we could, but the rules kept you out of the cockpit if you'd flown 140 hours in a given thirty-day period. Then you had to stand down for at least five days. Most guys went on R&R to the Philippines or Thailand or whatever exotic place the postings board listed quick flights for. I did that, too; after all, our MPC bought an awful lot of fun. But I also liked to go along on other missions if they had room, to see how other pilots did what they did. Obviously, there wasn't any room on other gunships, but there was on slicks, in a third-row seat that instructors and evaluators sat in between the back and cockpit.

I'd gotten to know one of the slick pilots from 2nd Platoon, a guy named DeMann, first name Allan; poor fellow, every time he met someone new he'd have to endure the same joke about how he was "da man"—the jokester thinking it was an original line. Anyway, DeMann was about to leave on a mission as one of a huge formation of slicks delivering South Vietnamese army troops to a combat zone. I asked if I could ride along and watch; I said I'd just bought a new Nikon at the PX in Qui Nhon and wanted to practice. I figured that the formation in the air, something like a flock of birds, and the images of dozens of men in uniform jumping out of helicopters hovering four feet off the ground and then into the wilds, would make for some great first photos.

It was odd to be inside the slick instead of one of the escort gunships—and especially as a passenger, not a pilot. I liked the view but didn't like not having my hands on the controls. Good thing I had the camera to occupy me. I composed a few shots I thought might be good enough to get into *Stars and Stripes*.

We came to the LZ of the combat zone, a wide flat field overrun with elephant grass. Nobody I met liked elephant grass. It was sharp and could grow higher than six feet—perfect for the enemy to pull an ambush, or for snakes. I'd known soldiers who said they'd happened on angry, hissing cobras, their hoods out wide, in the elephant grass of the Central Highlands. Even tigers had been spotted.

The most deadly menace, though, was booby traps the NVA and VC liked to hide in the grass. They were ingenious little devices—not mines, exactly, but small mortars, buried an inch or so in the ground, with attached plastic propellers that stuck up just above ground level. The helicopter rotors' downdraft made the propellers spin, activating the time-delay trigger mechanism. You didn't even have to step on these things to make them blow. Just being in the right place at the wrong time would do it. No wonder the infantry hated these missions.

Our turn had come to descend to about four feet. On both sides of us and in front and back, other slicks had done the same. "Come on, go, go, go, go, go," the crew chief shouted, pushing the ARVN soldiers out the doors so we could beat it out of there and let the next choppers in. Simultaneously, one through the right door and one through the left, pairs of soldiers hit the ground running and ran through the grass. Most of them would've disappeared from view if the rotor blades hadn't pushed down the grass. I was sure I was taking prizewinning shots. One of them was of an ARVN who tripped as he hit the ground and rolled over, my lens accidentally lighting on his frightened face as he tried to get up and get out. I clicked—and as I did I felt the camera snatched from my hand. The man who stole it was the last South Vietnamese soldier leaving the slick. He'd obviously been planning and plotting his move since first seeing the camera. No doubt a new Nikon like this would fetch a good price on the black market—probably more than he made in three months. Still, it was my camera, not his.

"Hey!" I shouted. Getting off the slick and racing him down—which I could've easily done—would've endangered the mission. I was a guest here.

I watched him run. And then I watched him die. It must've been one of those mortared booby traps, because one moment he was running, and the next he was just pieces of body flying through the air like debris in a storm. I did not see my camera land.

We've been two hours under a tree when we hear that familiar thwacking sound.

"Listen," I say.

A helicopter, coming from the east.

I snatch both transmitters from my vest and push the buttons, not knowing if either is still working. A thumb on each, I tap out the code over and over.

Even on the trail, the jungle canopy is still too thick to see much of the sky. I don't know if it's wishful thinking, but it does sound like the chopper has changed vectors enough to pass directly overhead. Then comes the flash through a narrow opening.

Now, will it turn and go north? I close my eyes and listen.

Yes.

This is excellent news.

I grab Burdett's shoulders to celebrate the happiest moment—actually, the *only* happy moment—we've had in many days.

Burdett doesn't see it that way.

"How the fuck much farther north can we go?" he says. "What do they want us to do, walk to Hanoi? Fuck them. We were already at that field—and then three others just as good."

I say, "Shut up, Burdett," because what he said echoes exactly what's in my mind, and I don't need any more reinforcement. Every minute of every day, my rage at our situation roils in my stomach like a cauldron of acid. If I give in to it and take the lid off for even a second, I may never get myself under control again—and then we're dead for sure. I sure wish Burdett would be strong for me now.

"You know what I think?" he says. "I think they want to know where we are so they can fire on us—so we can't get captured."

"Well, if that's true, then you oughta be happy. You've been ready to check out since the day after we went down."

"Fuck you," he says.

"I told you to shut up," I say, and that does it for conversation the rest of the day.

I open the map to see where the next rendezvous point with a rescue team might be—and wonder if maybe Burdett's right.

✯✯✯ **50** ✯✯✯

There was an orphanage in Qui Nhon that I used to visit every time I had to be down there. I don't mean visit as in pay a visit. I mean visit as in pass by and look and wonder. It was surrounded by cyclone fencing that offered a view of the ragged yard inside where the kids seemed to do nothing but stand around and watch the people pass by who were watching them. Some of the orphanages were full of Vietnamese whose parents had been killed in the war, the father probably fighting and the mother in some other way. Most of the orphans were the product of an encounter or an affair, occasionally even a marriage, between a GI father who was now either dead or back in the States, and a Vietnamese mother who was now—well, anywhere or dead. The kids were three, four, seven, ten, and their faces already looked old and hopeless. One thing always stuck out, and this was why I think I kept feeling this compulsion to stop by there: The full-blooded Vietnamese kids and the Eurasians would mix with each other. But the children of black fathers always kept to their own group. I never found out if it was by choice or necessity.

✯ ✯ ✯

LZ Uplift was south of LZ English. It was mostly an artillery base and didn't have its own aviation company. Every night another team from English was assigned to protect Uplift. A team consisting of two gunships and one flareship arrived in the evening and stayed till first light. A flareship was a regular slick with its four-man crew, but instead of ferrying men, it carried flares that would light up the combat area. The flares were enormous, at least three feet long and four inches wide. They worked by twisting their tops and dropping them out of the chopper from a height of about a thousand feet or less. After a few seconds, the timer would ignite the powder and these giant things would fall to earth like meteors. You almost needed sunglasses to fire at the target once someone had turned on the lights in the outfield.

Ten percent, maybe twenty percent of the time we saw action when we pulled the Uplift duty. We'd arrive around six, check in, get whatever kind of briefing they had, preflight the helicopters so that we'd only have to quick-start them in case, then hang out in the hootch—same as at English or any other base. The six pilots stayed together, the six crewmen on the choppers.

All three crews had been together since Fort Campbell and had gotten to the point where no one could surprise anybody else with a new side of his personality. We knew everything and nothing about each other, and that's the way we liked it. It's also the way we loved each other.

One night at Uplift we were playing pinochle—our usual game—and Davids, first name Mark, the slick pilot, pulled out a can of Schlitz. Being on standby, he wasn't supposed to drink. But it was only one beer and from the briefing it didn't sound like anything was to happen that night. Lieutenant McCullough didn't say anything. He might've probably liked one himself.

We went to sleep as usual in our flight suits with our boots on the floor. The helmets were left in the aircraft.

The call came on the field phone at about ten. We jumped up, zipped on the boots, grabbed our sidearms, and ran the fifty yards to the flight line. McCullough was fire team leader and got a quick briefing while we untied the rotor blades and fired up the engines. As soon as he jumped in we were ready to take off.

It had been less than five minutes since the call came in to the hootch.

"Starblazer one-six," he said into the radio, "on the go."

He pulled up on the collective.

"Negative," Davids said from the slick, "let us go first."

McCullough shrugged. "All right, Lucky Star three-three, go ahead."

Davids wanted to get up to altitude first, being the heavier flareship.

"Roger that," he said, and we watched his slick from the next revetment back up and move forward, then rise at five hundred feet a minute. So he was only in the air about six seconds—at an altitude of fifty feet—when the rocket-propelled grenade hit the slick and ignited the flares. Just like that, the thing burst into a ball of hot white light that illuminated half the camp.

"Holy shit!" or worse, we all shouted in unison.

For a second you could see Davids, his body aflame, trying to land the chopper, but it crashed to the ground about seventy-five yards away.

We jumped out and ran to the site. We could see the four guys inside, looking like Roman candles, moving slowly—surreally slow.

We were screaming their names, except for McCullough, who was trying to hold us back.

"Stop," he said. "There's still ammo inside." Not the flares, but .60-caliber. "You can't save 'em anyway. They're gone now, they're gone."

One of the guys, I don't know which because it was going to take dental records to identify each of them, managed to make it out of the chopper before falling to the ground. The best I could say was that they were lucky not to survive.

The next day or the day after, I totaled up their ages and divided by four. Average age wasn't quite twenty-two.

"You know," Somers said to me, "if we'd gone first, that would've been us."

"I know," I said. That's what kept me awake.

I volunteered for every mission and apparently said almost the same thing every time: "I wanna go eat 'em up." So that became my nickname. They called me "Old Eat 'Em Up."

The body count. Every mission in which we saw combat we had to bring back a count of bodies. Let's say there was a squad of VC in the bushes. We'd fire, they'd die, and we'd estimate—not based on tallying up the corpses but by imagining that we'd killed, hmmm, half. All right, if the squad was thirteen, that meant seven. Yeah, seven, that's right. We killed seven. That was the number we'd bring back.

It was the noise that didn't sound like any other vehicle I heard in Vietnam—the growl of an eighteen-wheeler fighting the ruts with its full load. You only had to hear it once and see what it was carrying to not want to see or hear it again. And so you'd turn away, but once you knew it was there you made yourself look, like an obligation, and you stood at attention while you did it. The load was dead bodies—Americans—in body bags, stacked like a cord of wood, every cargo inch taken.

The 61ˢᵗ had lost so many aircraft in battle or to maintenance that twelve of us—six pilots and six crew—were sent down to Vung Tau in a slick to pick up two new slicks, fresh from the States. It was a long flight from LZ English, nearly three hundred miles, but it was worth it. As soon as we saw the place, we were sorry we'd only be there until the next morning. Vung Tau is a tropical paradise on the coast near Saigon marred only by the fact that it served as a major South China Sea port for American matériel—and that the war had driven thousands of destitute people, many with multiple missing limbs, to beg on the streets. We checked in at the base, changed into jeans and T-shirts, and started to head into town for the copious fun we were told was possible there. Then a staff sergeant ordered us to check our sidearms; soldiers weren't allowed into town with weapons. And then with a smile he gave us directions for the best places in town to get a drink and some soft companionship.

The enlisted men went one way, we officers another—toward the establishment underlined on the sergeant's list.

The town was still pretty, its French colonial past and Asian heritage giving it a kind of giddy feel that contrasted with the vistas of white unspoiled beaches.

Beggars would tug at us, and every time I saw cripples—obviously from the war—I tried not to think how or when they'd gotten that way, or by whose hand. That was the kind of thing that could drive you crazy, and no good could come of it.

There were some older American men who looked at you without wanting you to see they were looking at you, which meant they were either CIA or private contractors. Judging by the number of MPs, the town saw its share of trouble.

Our destination was a small house surrounded by a grimy cinder-block wall eight feet high. The mama-san was glad to see us. So were the girls. They were prettier than usual—a little bit older but not harder; less weathered.

We sat on soft upholstered sofas, and they brought us drinks and sat on our laps. "You no want whiskey?" my girl asked. "Black soldier no like drink?"

"Coca-Cola," I said. "Cold, please."

Behind us in the hall were small rooms with rice-paper walls that did nothing but give you some visual privacy. Saunders and Chandler had guzzled three or four drinks and were about to take their dates in for a little R&R when the mama-san came rushing in. "You go, you go," she shrieked.

It looked like she was reacting to the guys tugging on the girls, but she wasn't. She was frantic with fear. "VC coming. VC coming now. Wrong night. Must go. Must leave now. You, all go."

Apparently she'd had an arrangement with the Vietcong that they would take their pleasure on certain days of the week, and this wasn't one of them. If it had been, she wouldn't have showed us in. But now, she'd been told, a group was on its way—unscheduled. Between telling us to leave and telling them not to come in, she chose to eighty-six us. It was the smart choice. We wouldn't kill them—and unlike the Vietcong, we didn't have weapons, so we couldn't fight back.

But that didn't stop Gerardin and Santusi from wanting to. They were blasted enough on mama-san's cheap whiskey to make a stand. It would've been a short, ugly stand, so we dragged them with us over the back fence before we had to—and laughed all the way to English in our new choppers.

McCullough rode me to Cam Ranh Bay for a C-130 flight to the Philippines. I was way overdue for R&R and figured I needed somewhere to spend all the MPC that was bulging out of my jungle fatigue pockets. I'd never been there but heard it was big enough for five days of exploring, which meant more to me than the excellence of the women, though one would certainly enhance the other. As it turned out, I was senior officer aboard the plane, so technically I was in charge. According to custom and practice, they treated me like a pasha flying first-class on a Pan Am Clipper.

When the plane landed, a car pulled up on the tarmac and whisked me to one of the city's better hotels—not one I would've chosen myself—where an intelligence officer briefed me on the area. It was hard not to laugh. What came to mind was the scene in *The Dirty Dozen,* which we'd just watched at the base, when Donald Sutherland impersonates a general inspecting the troops.

The hotel's clientele was, shall we say, controlled, so my romantic options were limited—at least for the first night. I went down to the hotel bar, hoping they'd let me eat there. If I'd sat at a restaurant table, I'd have spent the night alone; at least at a bar you might meet someone.

I did. He was two stools over, nursing a drink of some kind and enjoying the people coming and going. I was suspicious of him, though. He was a little overdressed—like James Bond in a tuxedo at a sumo match.

"Let me guess," he said. "R&R from Vietnam."

"That's right."

"Well, then, let me buy you a drink."

"Coca-Cola."

"You don't want any rum in that?"

"No, thanks."

"Sure?"

I had to explain that I never touched the stuff, which impressed him enough—and then when I answered his question that I was a Huey helicopter pilot, his face lit up and he moved a barstool closer. He coughed a one-syllable laugh and said, "And you don't drink? Now I've heard everything. Name's Sterling—like the silver."

"You have a first name?"

"Well, if you must know, it's Arnold."

I introduced myself and we made small talk. He said he was an expatriate American, the son of a career officer and World War II vet, who'd actually spent most of his life in the Pacific region. He spoke flat California English.

"You live here, in Manila?" I asked.

"Yeah. Been here six, seven years."

"Doing what?"

"Little bit of everything. I own several businesses."

It was the kind of generic answer I figured CIA agents might give. I pulled back a little, and he sensed that.

"Actually," he said, "I own a lot of real estate, and I'm about to develop a shopping center just outside of town. You want to see it?"

I hesitated. He didn't wait for me to answer. He said, "Come on, I'll pick you up at oh-eight-hundred. Believe me, you'll like what you see, and you'll like how you see it."

"What's that mean?"

"Come on, take a flyer," he said, laughing at the joke I didn't get till the next morning when he picked me up and we drove out to an airfield where he kept his French Alouette helicopter. He laughed again when he saw my wide eyes and dropped jaw. The Alouette was a beautiful and elegant machine, and I couldn't help thinking that if the U.S. Army had equipped a thousand or so of them as gunships, we could've ended the war in a week.

As we flew, Sterling explained what was different about the Alouette, and listed its advantages in tough situations.

He let me fly it, and I didn't want to land.

We stopped at hotels he said he owned, and the way they treated him, I had no reason to believe he didn't. He took me to sites he was planning to develop, and explained his vision for them. He knew the whole history of the Philippines—and narrated it as landmarks appeared, both from the air and ground. And on the third night, at the bar, he popped the question. "So, what're you gonna do when your tour's up?"

"Not sure yet," I said.

"You wanna come work for me—flying my chopper? You'd be like my personal pilot, flying me, flying my associates, flying people who come in to do business with me. You'll love it, and I'll pay you two grand a month. To start. And if you keep your eyes open, which I can see you do, you'll have plenty of business opportunities."

Two thousand dollars a month was a lot of money then—the

equivalent of at least ten grand now—especially for a young man of twenty-eight or so. But it didn't tempt me; not really.

"I'm not leaving the Army after my tour's up," I said. "I'm going for a commission."

"Really?" There was an undertone of *You poor dumb jerk* in his voice, though he tried to make it come out smooth. "Gonna be a lifer, huh?"

"I want to be a general," I said.

"A general?" That took him by surprise. "Well, Ezell, you got your work cut out for you, then."

"I'll make it," I said.

He was silent a moment before smiling and sticking out his hand. "I'll bet you do," he said. He walked away and then turned: "Hey, Ezell. Your parents should be really proud of you—your accomplishments and everything."

Ever since, every time my memory replays those words, I wonder how much he was telling me about himself—about what his own father did or didn't think of him.

✯ ✯ ✯ 51 ✯ ✯ ✯

I've identified a place where a chopper might be able to pick us up. Looks like it's only two miles away—two nights' walk, maybe less.

But it's raining now. Not just rain. Monsoon rain—biblical rain. Liquid fucking misery. It started suddenly and hasn't let up all day and probably won't for a while.

We're squeezed under the branches of a spreading tree, but there's no place to hide from it and no point resisting. I don't even want to look directly at Burdett to see if he's still alive. Surviving this is a moment-by-moment proposition. You have to use your mind to leave your body behind.

For the first time, though, my mind offers no help, no refuge. None of the homilies I've been telling myself for nearly three weeks has the power to inspire or transport me somewhere far away, to a place of hope. Instead, the more I think about this, the more I start to take it all very personally. I'm sure that God and nature have conspired together to torture me. Burdett doesn't even factor in. This is about me now.

The more I think about things, the more enraged I get. All the emotions I've had to push down are now pushing back. I can feel them physically building and rising out of me—lava spurting from the earth's bowels to the volcano's mouth.

But what comes out isn't shouting; it's laughter—wild, uncontrollable laughter that describes better than any screaming or cursing how absurd this all is. I don't have any say in what's happening now, and I've never laughed so hard. Never. It's actually funny to me—hilarious, really—how miserable I am and how much I want this to be over. And how unlikely we are to get out of here alive. The thought makes me gasp for breath. My sides hurt.

Burdett doesn't know what to make of me. He glances over and I meet his eyes, and now everything is even funnier. His not laughing, not seeing this for what it is, strikes me as hysterical. He gets mad at me, which only makes me laugh harder. There's no bottom to the laughter.

"Shut the fuck up," he says.

Stop it, I want to say, *you're killing me.* I fall over into the mud and leaves and manage the words, "Can't get worse than this."

Burdett still doesn't get it.

"Asshole," he says, which is pretty funny when you think about it.

I don't know how long I laugh. But I stop before the rain does. Long before.

★★★ **52** ★★★

On R&R I always noticed two things about Americans, and both made me feel strange. The first was that the races tended to segregate. Rare was the black soldier who'd hang with white buddies, or vice versa, in the streets of Manila or Bangkok or Honolulu, or even Saigon. It was as though race was the most important factor in who guys made friends with, and I could tell sometimes when I was with the other pilots—all of them white, of course—that the groups of young black men who saw us considered me some kind of an Uncle Tom. The laughs and smiles would drop away, and their bodies would go rigid. They were thinking, *What's that brother doing with those honkies? He's not a real brother.*

The second thing I noticed was the Ugly American acting in ways that, to me, weren't so easily excused by the tension of war and killing, and the easy access to alcohol and girls, in places whose sole purpose, yes, was to separate drunken young soldiers from their money that they couldn't wait to be separated from. The drunker they got, the stupider they got, and the stupider they got, the uglier they got, so that even the places that were raking in their money couldn't stand them being there. And I couldn't stand seeing them. Black or white, they all made me uncomfortable. I'd

sometimes pull a black soldier aside—blacks more than whites—
and point out quietly that he was disrespecting himself and his
country with his behavior. "You're not my fuckin' father," was a
common reply.

That's why I sometimes took the less-traveled path, like my
second visit to Bangkok, a city where that kind of ugliness stuck
out in Technicolor. I'm not sure the Thai language has a word for
anger. It's considered the height of disrespect to show such emotion or to make a fool of yourself in public. The people are so exquisitely polite and pleasant, they must all be related to Buddha
himself. Walking to my hotel, I winced as I passed a bar where a
group of soldiers was singing drunkenly "I can't get no sa-tis-fac-
tion . . ." Maybe that made me a party pooper, as it said on some
of my commander's reports. If so, I could live with it.

When I got to my hotel I struck up a conversation with one of
the housekeepers, a beautiful woman in a country of beautiful
women. I said I was interested in getting out of the city and seeing
parts of Thailand that most people miss. She volunteered to be my
guide, and I volunteered to pay her—a hundred bucks a day,
which was probably more than she made in a month of cleaning
rooms.

We hired taxis and rode mopeds and took sampans to primitive
parts of the country. I said I wanted to see the bridge on the Kwai
River, and that required an elephant. I made the mistake of wearing shorts that day—it was a mistake because you sit on the neck
of an elephant, where his hair is short and bristly, like copper wire.

One day we were in the country north of the city, in an area so
primitive it seemed we'd gone centuries back in time, to see arti-
sans make clay pots on potter's wheels that a coolie turned by
hand. As we walked back along a winding jungle lane, I saw a
black-skinned man wearing a straw hat and Western clothes coming toward us. Since there are dark-skinned Thais I didn't think
much of it. I said hello in Thai, and he said hello in English—In-
diana English, to be precise. Turned out he was an ex-

anthropologist who'd come years ago to Thailand to study the culture but had fallen in love with the people and become a potter. Now, he said, he made the trek to this place because in its soil was the perfect clay for his pots. We talked for two hours in the jungle, then for another hour at a bar in the nearest small town. The talk was only of the moment, and of his work, and of the Thai culture—and it was only after I left to go back to my hotel in Bangkok that I realized we hadn't once spoken of race or the war or America. He really had found the perfect soil.

We'd just escorted a LRRP and were on our way back to English. Passing over a five-mile-wide valley surrounded on three sides by mountains and the fourth side by Highway 1 stretching down the coast, we spotted a vicious battle going on between much of a full NVA regiment and elements of an American mechanized infantry regiment. Even from a few thousand feet, we could see blasts and smoke and bodies falling. For some reason, the friendlies hadn't been assigned any air support. We called it in and asked permission. The answer came back yes—and we began making daisy-chain runs. There were so many NVA soldiers—many more than a hundred—that we could've fired almost anywhere in their direction and hit some of them.

On the fifth or sixth run at them we were hit. The red lights went on and the alarm sounded. We had diminished power and oil pressure but didn't know how long either would last. It was time to land—but where? The closest safe place was a mile away, at a tiny fire base that was firing artillery at the NVA in hopes of repelling the invaders but also in preparation for evacuating.

Gerardin's chopper covered us from behind. We found a safe spot on the fire base amid the rolling trucks and went into a controlled autorotation, with just enough power to set her down and not break our legs from ten feet up. We hitched a ride on an evac truck filled with soldiers that was headed for LZ English, and as soon as we got there jumped in another chopper. Gerardin had followed us the whole time, and together we formed another daisy chain and made runs till dark, when the ground forces called us off. The two sides were too close to each other, and in the dark we could've accidentally nailed friendlies instead of the enemy. Reluctantly, we pulled off, and by the time we checked back in the morning, the battle was over. I said to McCullough that I didn't understand why the troops hadn't been assigned air cover—that we'd only come upon them by accident—nor why the artillery unit just a mile away had evacced to English instead of staying to fight.

McCullough laughed and he said, "That's because you're Old Eat 'Em Up."

☆ ☆ ☆

I don't know how many hours earlier the event had happened, but when I heard the news it came from Armed Forces Radio. We were returning to English from a mission at eight thousand feet, where the reception was better. McCullough was in the left seat that day, Somers and Cleveland sacked out in back.

It was April 4, 1968—or at least it was back in the world. "Martin Luther King has been shot dead by an assassin's rifle in Memphis, Tennessee," the announcer said, adding as many details as were known at the time. No others were needed. It was the news people knew was coming someday. King himself had apparently known.

I closed my eyes and pretended not to be there—or anywhere.

"I can't believe that," McCullough said. "I just can't believe it."

"I can," I said.

There were riots in Vietnam over the next two or three weeks. It was mostly the troops in support positions, the ones with a lot of time on their hands; and it was mostly members of what became known as "McNamara's Hundred Thousand," the kids Defense Secretary Robert McNamara had put in uniform—some of them straight from reform schools and all of them with emotional and psychological problems—by lowering the Army's entrance requirements just enough. The war machine had needed feeding, but politics said not to call up the National Guard and reservists.

There were briefings up the wazoo about how to protect ourselves from sabotage—committed by Americans. Apparently guys had figured out that if you put a rubber band over the pin of a grenade and dropped it down a helicopter's gas tank, the heated jet fuel would slowly expand the rubber band and cause the clip to pop, exploding the grenade and igniting all that JP4. That would be it for anyone inside the chopper or near the vicinity. We'd heard of several crews who wouldn't be going home alive because of this.

The riots were over by the end of April, and a few weeks later I made my first pilgrimage to Long Binh Jail—LBJ—which was a vast fenced-in area that looked more like a Japanese internment camp than a stockade. From the perimeter fence you could see dozens, if not hundreds, of soldiers—or ex-soldiers. Most of them—probably ninety-five percent—were black. I have no reason to believe that they were put there unjustly, but the sight of them saddened me, which was why I stopped by whenever I was in the Saigon area.

In the officers' club the night of the day we'd heard about King's murder, I sat sipping a Coke—the only black face there—and feeling sorry for myself that the best of what we were was now gone. There wasn't the usual frivolity, that's for sure, but neither was there talk of the assassination, at least that I could hear. One officer came up to me. "It's a shame," he said, shaking his head. "Just a cryin' fuckin' shame." I recognized his accent. He was from Alabama. And he was serious. As far as I was concerned, that was progress.

I'd filled out my commission application, then held on to it for several weeks before handing it to my company commander for his own comments and forwarding. I could think of no reason to believe his remarks wouldn't recommend me strongly—echoing, I felt certain, McCullough's—but I held on to the app until I could feel the planets in proper alignment, or something like that.

The commission panel met in Nha Trang, a coast town just above Cam Ranh Bay. I went through a series of one-on-one interviews and then faced a three-man panel of two majors and a captain, all of them posing questions about why I wanted to be a commissioned officer and what I thought I could bring to the Army as a leader. The questions were specific, not generic, and the answers had to be specific. I was worried that I wouldn't get a chance to tell them other things they wouldn't have known, like the fact that I'd been a Marine and number one in my boot camp class, as well as number one in my basic training company. For some reason, those were the kinds of things that were sealed.

When they'd finished asking questions, one of the majors offered me the chance to speak. I went on for five minutes, telling them everything I thought was pertinent that they hadn't already heard or known, then walked out feeling like I'd aced the test.

"We'll let you know," they had said.

On the way back to English, McCullough asked me if I'd mentioned race.

"Didn't come up," I said.

"You didn't raise it?" he said.

"No."

"Good."

☆   ☆   ☆

The Green Berets told stories—true stories. And we heard them, too, from infantry units. Nearer to the North, captured soldiers would be taken or marched to camps like the Hanoi Hilton and tortured both psychologically and physically. In the South, getting prisoners to North Vietnam was too difficult, too expensive, too time-consuming, so the NVA would take the pleasure in the moment. They had three favorite methods. First was to push a man facedown on the ground, tie his hands behind his back, and pull his arms over his head. Second was to attach one end of a wire to a crank generator and the other to his testicles. Third was to yank out his fingernails with pliers. Then, if they could, they'd exchange the broken man for their own prisoners, or whatever else they could get.

We also heard that the enemy liked to make a special example of pilots. It happened to Jason Woodruff, a slick pilot I'd gone to flight school with. He'd been assigned to another company, so our paths didn't cross too often, and then they didn't cross at all. He'd been shot dead, I heard, and when the rescue party got there, they found his head on a stick.

★ ★ ★ 53 ★ ★ ★

The helicopter doesn't show up in the morning, but of course it wouldn't because of the rain.

We start making our way at dark and I'm determined to get as far as possible, just in case the rain starts again—or Burdett's tourniqueted leg gives out completely.

We make our way slowly in the dark, with me using a tree branch to stay on the path the way a blind man uses a cane.

We've been out for about four hours when we can hear water—the rushing of a stream. The farther we walk, the louder it gets. And what I fear is what I find: The rain has swollen a gentle creek that cuts across our path into a raging torrent. In the dark, I can't see how far to the other bank it is, but wading is our only way across. I use my stick to gauge the depth—about waist-high.

"Damn," Burdett says.

"We don't have a choice," I say. "Come on, let's not think about it. Let's just get it over with."

I put the two gun holsters on my neck to make sure they don't get wet, then take his left cane and put my right arm around his waist. His left hand grabs on to my right shoulder. "Put as much weight on me as you can," I say. If he can take the water on his leg, I can take his weight on my back.

It's my job to make sure we don't lose our footing; that would be sure death. We progress with small steps, in unison, with me calling out the cadence. I use one of Burdett's canes and my stick to make sure we don't hit any sudden drop-offs. I can hear Burdett's groans over the water. The farther we go, the more I hold him up.

It takes at least five minutes to cross what I'm guessing was twenty meters. We reach the far shore and collapse. After a while I ask Burdett if he can go on some more tonight. He says no. I find a small clearing off the road and coax him into it. In the morning, I'll find us something to eat and then risk leaving him alone, with his gun for protection, to see how far we have to go yet. It'd sure be a boost to hear the helicopter.

Both of us fall into an exhausted, dreamless sleep and wake a couple of hours later, at dawn.

I walk a few paces away to relieve myself, and take down my jeans. In the fuzzy light and behind fuzzy eyes, I'm at first not sure I'm seeing what I think I see. But it's true.

Leeches. All over my legs.

I was wrong the other night. Things can always get worse—and this proves it.

I scream out in horror and start slapping at them, both hands.

Burdett says "What the—" and then checks himself. As many are on him.

I'm jumping around like a man on fire, slapping at myself as hard as I can, not caring that I'm whacking my own flesh. If Burdett is less frantic, it's only because he's more compromised. It's all I can do not to howl like a coyote.

One by one the leeches fall off, though some of the heads stay in. I pick them out with my knife and can hardly feel the cuts. I just want the damn things gone from there. When they are, I turn and vomit—and then help Burdett finish the job on him. We can't slap at his bad leg, so I have to pry them off. It must hurt, but he's as stoic as though he were already dead. In fact, he's laughing—at me.

He says, "You looked like Mr. Bojangles there for a while."

When the last leech is out of his leg, I collapse backward and put my face in my hands.

I don't know what to think. I don't know what to do. I don't know if we can take any more.

And then comes the sound of the helicopter.

★★★ 54 ★★★

I still remember sleeping through the sound of eight-inch howitzers being fired from fifty yards away outside our hootch—but waking up the second someone opened the door.

And I still remember Straczynski, first name Henry, a matinee-idol-handsome pilot from Jersey whose beautiful wife stayed on the bases with him during flight school. When he was off duty, he never let go of her hand. He spent the first half of his tour talking about her and reading her letters aloud, and the second half sneaking out at night to be with the Montagnard prostitute he'd fallen for—a girl with black teeth from chewing betel nut. And I don't remember him going back to the States—"the world," we called it.

I remember a lot of pilots coming back from missions cut up and bleeding badly, and I remember Towne—Dan, I think—a slick pilot assigned to the 61st to replace a pilot who'd been killed. His first flight, the slick took a direct hit and by that night his legs had been amputated.

I remember running into Chuck Wells, the nice young man I'd driven down to Fort Rucker with—the one with the quick smile and easy manner. Not anymore. When I saw him at Bong Son he was the walking dead, his eyes barely registering recognition except when the barkeep poured the vodka in his glass. He would've mainlined it if he could have. I said, "What's wrong, man?" and he said, "It ain't nothing but a thing."

I remember guys all the time saying, "It ain't nothin' but a thing," when they didn't have the words to describe what was in their mind and heart and knowing that they could say everything they needed to say by uttering these six.

I remember rubbing my skin and having it fall off.

I remember money and maps crumbling in my hands, because of the humidity.

I remember loving dozens of guys—and not wanting to get too close to any of them, in case something happened.

It was one of those things that seem like nothing when they happen. We'd gotten back to English after a mission and in sliding out of the helicopter I'd scratched my behind on a protruding screw that wasn't there when I'd slid in. If I hadn't been flying left seat— if McCullough had been there instead—well, there's no point in pointing out the if. As scratches go, this was a pretty good one, good enough to tear my flight suit and a couple of layers of skin. But it was a scratch—not shrapnel, not a bullet. A scratch. I didn't even say anything about it for a while. I also didn't clean it properly. Not that I could've anyway; that would've taken a medical professional, since the thing probably needed stitches. Had I done that, I'd have been grounded for a while, which was something I couldn't tolerate. I just wanted to turn the other cheek, as it were, and get on with the business of war.

The infection had other ideas. Over the next weeks, and then months, the moist Vietnam air, lack of soap, and less-than-pristine conditions conspired to form a fistula that looked like my intestines had dropped down a foot and were emerging through the skin. I'd kept rationalizing that it would get worse and then better, but by the time I realized it wasn't going to get better on its own, this was no longer an ordinary first-aid matter. When we weren't flying, I had to lie on my stomach. When we were, I had to sit on an array of homemade contraptions that resembled hemorrhoid helpers to keep it from touching the seat and causing intolerable pain. So I was putting myself, my buddies, and our missions in jeopardy.

The MASH unit at English sent me down to the MASH at Qui Nhon for what was supposed to be a quick operation, but they didn't have the time or expertise for something like this and sent me on to the MASH at Cam Ranh Bay, where they were inundated with war wounded and couldn't take the time, hands, or bed space for what was seen as serious but still noncritical surgery. On to Japan I was sent—and told that my recovery time from the surgery was going to be three to four months.

"Months or weeks?" I asked.

"Months—on your stomach."

Well, because my tour of duty would be over in weeks anyway, they decided to send me back to "the world." I didn't want to go and argued that I should stay, but the cost of taking care of me in Japan and then sending me back to Vietnam for only a month, if that, was too high. They gave me a choice of any military hospital in America. I chose the naval hospital in San Diego, to be near my mother and sister, and left Japan on a C-141, lying facedown for eighteen hours on a gurney. The whole way there I couldn't stop thinking about how I'd never gotten to say good-bye to McCullough or Somers or Cleveland or any of the others. We'd always thought that we'd come together, would survive together, and then leave together—but now I was just another soldier going home alone. These men had been my brothers, and I'd wanted to tell them in words when it was safe what I hope my actions had been proving to them for all that time.

A doctor looked at my fistula as soon as I got to San Diego. He said, "Oh, shit," and ordered his team to prepare for immediate surgery. The anesthesiologist came in to administer an epidural and noticed a relatively fresh scar on my lower back. I explained that at night we often had to run for the bunkers and shelters on a base's perimeter, when mortar shells started flying. One night I'd taken some shrapnel in the back and asked the guys in the bunker to dig out as much of it as they could with their fingers, and then forgot about it after the soreness went away in a week or so.

Suspicious, the doctors sent me for X-rays and decided that the remaining shrapnel had to come out. They said there was too much of it lodged too close to the spine. "It might cause problems later."

Now they administered the epidural and took care of both surgeries at once, then advised me that the deep epidural shot itself "might cause problems for your back later." At that point I didn't even ask why.

For the first time in my life I was depressed. The idea of lying in a hospital for months on my stomach on account of a wound that hadn't even been caused by the enemy, while the war was still raging and my friends were still fighting it, almost drove me to tears.

A couple of days later I called my mother. She cried when she heard my voice. I asked why.

"The Army sent me a telegram saying you were missing in action."

Typical Army. My paperwork in all the transfers had gotten fouled up, which of course meant I was MIA, missing in action.

I stood and began walking around in thirty days, and talked the doctors into letting me out of the hospital on convalescent leave, meaning I had to check in with them every week. I moved into my mother's house and twice a week called the Department of the Army. I said, "I feel good. I heal fast. And I wanna go back. You have a trained pilot here. I listen to the news. I read the papers. I know what's going on there. You need me there."

"Let us know when the doctors say you're ready."

"Any day," I always said. And I always believed it.

"We'll get back to you."

Administratively, they assigned me to Fort MacArthur a hundred miles north in San Pedro. I had to drive up there once a month to pick up my paycheck; that's all. But because my records still hadn't shown up—typical Army—the check was for only about a hundred bucks or so. That's not what upset me; I knew that would get straightened out, and then I'd get one huge check for back pay plus interest.

No, what bothered me was that this was late 1968, around the time the Pentagon had begun planning the first draft lottery intended to even out the inequalities of the system. That it didn't is another story. My frustration here was that, with so many young men trying to buck the system, the Pentagon had at its disposal a decorated war veteran who'd applied for a commission and possessed a skill very much in demand and very much needed, and I couldn't get anyone to pay attention—not even after the doctors gave me a clean bill of health three months later. I had to pound Ma Bell's long-distance lines and threaten to call my senators and congressmen to get an assignment. Clearly, I'd fallen through the cracks. This had nothing to do with race. I knew other guys, though not pilots, who'd fallen through the cracks the same way—and they were only too happy to live in nice apartments and drive nice cars paid for by the wages they were picking up at various bases while working full-time at other jobs. I could've done that, too; I could've gone on for another year or two, maybe more, with no assignment and full benefits. But I wanted to go back, and finally I got my assignment. It was to go to Germany—a way station, I believe, to Vietnam. The orders said that in fifteen days I had to be at McGuire Air Force Base in Wrightstown, New Jersey.

I rode a Greyhound two and a half days to McAlester for two reasons. One was to pick up my car, the new Ford I'd left with Joanna. The other was to sign the divorce papers that a lawyer I'd called ahead of time had already prepared for me. My mother and

Dorothy had reluctantly told me that Joanna was eight months pregnant. I'd been gone a lot longer than that. Her official address was her parents' house, but she spent most of her time at the gas station guy's place. I still couldn't understand how she could choose him over me but I decided not to make myself crazy trying to figure it out.

From the bus depot I took a taxi to Joanna's parents' house. The cabbie let me out next to what had been my new car. Damn. It looked like I'd ridden it into battle—dinged and dented and dirty; the only thing missing was bullet holes. I knocked on the door, expecting to see Joanna, but her father answered and for half an hour apologized for his daughter. When the time came, he handed me the car keys and wished me luck.

I filled up the car, emptied Joanna's trash from the interior, checked the clutch to make sure it would hold, and drove to the lawyer's, where I signed the papers and paid him in cash.

Two and a half hours after I got to McAlester, I was on my way to New Jersey. Two and a half hours was all I needed to stay to know that I didn't need to stay any longer.

★★★ **55** ★★★

The chopper comes from the east, as usual. I snatch both transmitters, surprised that they're still dry. Maybe they even work.

Yes! The helicopter homes in on the signal and flies straight over us—but this time it pulls a one-eighty and passes directly over us again before turning northeast. Northeast is the direction of the opening I spotted on the map.

"Jesus Christ," Burdett says, "I think it's happening. I think it's really happening."

"Look," I say, "you stay here and I'll run on ahead to scout and then be back."

"Not a chance," he says. "We're going together. I'll keep up."

I can see in his eyes that he will—and he does, even though we can't keep to the trail. No doubt the behavior of the chopper, making that one-eighty, alerted any enemy units in the area that there's about to be a pickup somewhere. They'd all be on the move in that direction. And for sure they know where every possible LZ is.

What worries me as we make our way is that the enemy in fact knows where we are and is letting us get to where we're going, so they can have us tap out the rescue code on the ETR and get that chopper to set down before attacking. What a devastating blow that would be to our side—psychologically and physically—to have a pickup foiled and lose more men and another chopper. And what a lift that would be to them. Maybe that's been their plan all along. Maybe they've let us live so that we could lead them to a bigger prize than just two worn-out pilots.

No, that doesn't make any sense. Or does it?

Like a paranoid, I spin my head at the slightest noise, or turn suddenly to try to catch men in the shadows. But I see nothing and no one.

Burdett pays no attention to me. He knows what I'm thinking. But for him, this is do or die—we make it or he dies; he'll accept nothing in between. I wonder if I can. I wonder if I'd survive the shock and heartbreak of seeing our rescue chopper overrun. I'm really not sure.

★ ★ ★ 56 ★ ★ ★

I had almost ten days to get to Jersey but didn't stop in Magee. With Pa dead, the only person I'd have wanted to see now was Aunt Lee, but in the mood I was in, I would've felt like an intruder. I stopped to say hello to some friends in Fort Campbell, Kentucky, and while I was there I bought a new car, trading in the one-year-old junker for a black-and-gray 1969 Olds Cutlass Supreme with a Rocket V-8 engine. So it could be shipped to Germany, I dropped it off at Port Elizabeth, then rode a bus to McGuire, getting there two days early.

The Air Force C-141 was filled with soldiers and their families, most of them going to spend two years in Germany. We landed at Rhein-Main. The temperature was about ten degrees, and I was dressed in a tropical uniform. Officers were directed to one place, enlisted another, to pick up our assignments and train tickets that would take us to wherever the assignments were. The scene at the airbase was like something out of Ellis Island, 1900. And the Frankfurt train station was like JFK airport, 2000. There must've been forty tracks, which is why they had a USO information booth in the center of the station, to direct Americans to where they needed to go. But the booth was closed when I got there, and

I apparently asked the wrong person for directions, showing him my ticket. I don't know if it had anything to do with my skin color or my citizenship or my military uniform, or whether he was just mistaken, but I would've ended up at the Polish border instead of Nuremberg if a porter hadn't redirected me. He came running at the last minute. No wonder. In those days, American soldiers didn't enter Communist Poland.

As it turned out, I was the only military man on the train to Nuremberg, too. Hungry, I took a spot in the club car but couldn't read the menu and the waiter didn't speak any English. Every time he came I ordered the only thing I knew how to say in German: *"Coca-Cola, bitte."*

A man sat beside me and struck up a conversation, asking me where in the States I was from. I told him as much as he wanted to hear, then saw no reason, when he asked, not to tell him that I'd been assigned to an air cavalry regiment. Germany was now, after all, thanks to America, a free country—and the American military presence was everywhere. Besides, American to American, I didn't mind telling him anything.

The waiter came to the table and asked the man what he wanted. I was astonished to hear him order something in what sounded like perfect German. He asked me what I wanted and then made a suggestion, which I took. Sauerbraten.

"Where'd you learn to speak German like that?" I asked.

"Here," he said.

"Really? How long have you been here?"

He laughed. "All my life. I'm German."

"But—"

He explained that most younger Germans, those who came of age after the war, learned English in school. He'd taken it a little more seriously than others, practicing whenever he could by speaking to Americans, whom he could easily identify by their uniforms.

It was a fast and enlightening four-hour ride to Nuremberg—for both of us, I hope.

My air troop was part of the 2ⁿᵈ Armored Cavalry Regiment, which was part of the 2ⁿᵈ Armored Division. In Nuremberg, we didn't have a proper base with barracks and its own airfield. Unmarried pilots were given a housing allowance and a list of modest hotels to live in. I ended up at the same one as John Brady, who, unlike most of the pilots, hadn't yet been to Vietnam. He was a warrant officer one, I a warrant officer two. We hit it off fast.

The airfield was a few blocks away, on the enormous old field where Hitler had made some of his most famous speeches to rally the troops and his people before World War II.

Our duty was to patrol the Czech border in our Huey gunships. It wasn't Vietnam, but it wasn't Fort Rucker, either. This was barely six months after Soviet tanks had rolled into Czechoslovakia on that late August night to crush what had come to be known as the Prague Spring—the naïve hope that there would be freedom from Soviet tyranny. Dozens died, and spring became winter when Brezhnev decided he'd seen more than enough young Czechs treat Russian troops the way American antiwar protesters were treating police and National Guardsmen—sometimes by putting flowers in the barrels of their rifles. By then it was known that he'd decided to put down the Czech movement even at the cost of starting World War III. If President Johnson had responded to the invasion with force, that's what would've happened. The stakes were still high—as high as the tension—and the Czech-German border crackled with the possibility of war being only a misstep away; anything could've become an international incident—anything like a helicopter on patrol drifting even a few feet into the Czech airspace.

Actually, it seemed like the Soviets were trying to instigate war. They'd set up beacons that operated on our frequencies, to lure our helicopters, so if you weren't careful with the instruments, especially with the constant clouds and overcast skies, you'd end up as a flying target for Russian artillery—and President Nixon, in office now barely a month, would have to decide whether to respond. Nixon being Nixon, so we thought, it would've been the war to end all wars—and life on the planet. So, yes, we paid attention to our work. It was tense enough so that we each flew only four hours a day, four days a week.

For reasons never explained, our airfield was changed from blocks away to miles away—on the other side of town, a half-hour drive. Good thing John had bought a used car; my Cutlass hadn't come yet, and hitchhiking wasn't very reliable. John and I flew together, ate together, drove together. We even joined the same international friendship club, which was a weekly get-together of young people from several countries sharing nuggets about their home country. That's where we met Tanya, a pretty blonde who spoke excellent English. One night the three of us were out to dinner at a restaurant. At the next table three drunken German men kept laughing uproariously and talking to us. I smiled and nodded and John smiled and nodded, both of us trying to be polite, but Tanya didn't smile or nod. She stood up and confronted them. They were surprised to find out she was German, and more surprised to find they'd each been ripped a new one for their rudeness and racism. Apparently they'd been making nigger jokes—whatever the word is in German—about me.

That was the only overt racism I experienced in Germany—at least that I knew of. The rest was subtle, like my not being asked first in a restaurant if I wanted to be seated, or being asked last to order at a table with others. Of course, that was the rule in America, too—and in France, and in Austria, and in all the other countries I visited on leave in Europe, except for Denmark, where they seemed to treat me better than whites I met there.

Major Thad Hughes was the commander of our air troop. He looked older than he was and that upset him—not for vanity's sake, but because it meant his superiors might think of him as old, too, and keep him from battlefields where he felt more at home than in his wife's living room. We told each other a lot of war stories. He'd served two tours in Vietnam as a gunship pilot and kept trying to go back again, though he knew it wasn't in the cards; this assignment would be at least three years. He and I felt that old warrior's bond, and when I wondered aloud why my commission was taking so long, he said he'd make gentle inquiries but that I shouldn't worry. The Army, he said, would be lucky to have an officer like me.

I made my need to be sent back to Vietnam abundantly clear to him. More than abundantly. Once a month I dropped my written request on his desk and strongly suggested that he hand-carry it to regiment headquarters on the other side of town, in a compound that had been established as barracks for Nazi SS troops.

"I'll miss you if you go," Hughes said. "But I'll envy you more."

I'd caught a ride up to Bremerhaven when my car finally arrived, about six weeks after I did. I couldn't wait to get her out on the autobahn, which didn't have a speed limit. You drove in the right lane unless you needed to pass, then crossed to the left lane just long enough to do it. The Cutlass turned a lot of heads, since it was much larger than most European cars and didn't look like any of them. Going ninety on the way back to Nuremberg, I'd just passed two cars and was about to move over into the left lane to pass a third when I heard a brief honk and watched a Mercedes zip by doing at least 130. If I hadn't checked, I would've checked out.

A few weeks later I drove off the airfield and tried turning left onto the icy road used mostly by military vehicles. The Cutlass made it halfway before its wheels started spinning without traction on the ice. I was trapped, facing laterally across the road. To the right, no cars were coming. To the left was a two-and-a-half-ton Army truck. If he'd seen me before, he would've already slowed down. But even if he saw me now, he wouldn't have time to brake that heavy thing on the ice. He was going to hit me broadside. If he did, I'd be buried without my commission. My only chance was to somehow maneuver the car in the next few seconds, so that he'd whack me head-on, which would at least give me the protection of the engine compartment instead of just the driver's door. It was the kind of decision-making and thinking that you learn in war, when every thought and decision separates life and death. Giving it just a little gas, I managed to turn the car just in time—just as he noticed me and tried to slow. As the Cutlass spun, I saw his face. We looked into each other's eyes as he barreled near, trying desperately to brake, the truck skidding now on the ice. He was a young black guy, probably a corporal. And he looked terrified—and not just because he was about to kill an officer. The only black officer around. What were the chances?

I came to with my head lodged in the windshield, then came back in and out of awareness often enough to see varying amounts of people and rescue vehicles hovering over me and at the site. I could see enough to know that, all things considered, I was actually in better shape than my car. At some point I realized I was in a Huey, and I struggled to stay awake for that. "Can I fly?" I said.

I don't remember anything that happened for a couple of hours after we landed at the hospital. But when I woke I only had a headache from the concussion and some stitches. It was, without question, a miracle. Not the first of my life—and not the last.

I'd been summoned to HQ. "Your ten-seventy-nine has been approved," the adjutant said, handing me an envelope. My orders indicated I was to leave Germany and report to Fort Sill in Oklahoma, to become a standardization instructor pilot, teaching pilots to become instructors. SIP was a step up from IP.

Anyone could read between the lines. My orders didn't say on them that I'd be headed to Vietnam, but in my mind that was the only reason to pull me out of my Europe tour early for an SIP course. There'd be way stations on the road back, but unless the war ended in the next few months or year—and that wasn't likely, not with half a million men stationed there and victory no closer under eight months of Commie-hating Nixon than under four years of LBJ—I was going back. Definitely, I was going back.

Before getting to Fort Sill, I was sent to the Sikorsky helicopter plant in Connecticut to learn to fly the CH-54. Comparing one of these giant Skycranes to Huey gunships and the new sleeker Cobras was like the difference between driving a Corvette and an eighteen-wheeler. Everything about the way it handled was different, from how fast you could turn, to how low you could hover, even where you could land. The rotors were so big and powerful, their downdraft would blow away staked tents if you got too close.

At Fort Sill, I wasn't very happy. The senior leadership assumed that every officer worth being saluted, especially if he was a pilot, could drink his weight in booze. It was their culture. I didn't fit in and probably wasn't trusted anywhere except in the air. Of course, being black didn't help their impressions of me, either. I heard "uppity" whispered now and then. Once again, they thought I thought I was better than they were. I'd dodge the pleas to have one itsy-bitsy teeny-weeny drink, and ignore the taunts when I held my ground. Why that wasn't considered a sign of character, I don't know. Sure, I'd go to the Friday get-togethers in the officers' club, and I'd sit and sip Cokes, and I'd laugh with everyone else at the dumb jokes and military humor—and then I'd excuse myself quietly and invisibly when the booze made the room a little too stupid.

It had been more than a year since I'd applied for my commission, and I couldn't help feeling that there was some invisible, nefarious hand at work. Race may or may not have been part of it, same with timing and bureaucracy and a dozen other factors. I didn't care what the reason was. I just wanted my damn commission. And I wanted to get back to the war.

☆   ☆   ☆

October something, 1969. You'd think I'd remember the exact date, but I don't. I only remember Major Coker, my company commander, grabbing me one day as I walked across the base.

"Congratulations, Ware," he said. "Your commission's come through." He wasn't likely to be elated for me. This was all business, and whatever happiness there was would be all mine—unless some of the others got pleasure in knowing I'd be leaving for ten weeks of mandatory officer's school at Fort Benning.

Coker said, "We'll have a ceremony to give you your silver bar on Friday at the formation. Congratulations," he said, saluting me.

Silver bar. That meant I was going straight to first lieutenant.

"Lieutenant Ezell Ware, Jr.," I said, rolling the words in my mouth till they came out easily. I liked the sound and loved the feel. Nothing had felt this good since my first combat run. Imagine how it would be when I was Captain Ware, then Major Ware and Colonel Ware. Then: General Ware.

Fort Benning was ten long, uneventful weeks of relearning stuff I'd either already learned in the precommission correspondence courses I'd taken or by being in the military for seven years now. I paid attention, though, as if I were hearing everything for the first time. You never knew when they'd sneak in a piece of invaluable info—something that might save your life or the lives of your men. Knowledge was ammunition, and you didn't want to get caught without it.

There were three hundred new officers in this course, three of them black. For the usual reasons, we didn't go out of our way to befriend each other. This was the tightrope walk, and the fact that we'd all three managed to come this far meant that we'd more or less mastered the art of balance.

I returned to Fort Sill just long enough to get my SIP authorization and then began hoping every day that my new orders would come through. They did. I soon found myself stationed for twelve weeks at the Alameda Naval Air Station on San Francisco Bay, at a school that was so classified, the classrooms changed every day and officers had to be escorted from room to room by MPs. My feeling was, they wouldn't have been teaching me secrets I was sworn never to reveal for some kind of ordinary stateside duty. Finding out how to survive in the jungle or communicate with friendly forces when you're captured isn't a necessary skill at, say, Fort Rucker—where I was sent next to learn to fly the OH-58, known as the Kiowa. It's a one-pilot aircraft made by Bell and used for visual recon, command and control, and target acquisition.

My sense was that this was all some kind of smokescreen, that I was being groomed and tested for something that even the people sending me here and there didn't know; only the brass in Washington would, and they were supposed to be thinking two and three steps ahead. Whatever my new duties were going to be, they weren't going to be ordinary. There'd be no reason to spend all this time and money on me just to put me back on a regular Army base flying combat missions in a daisy chain as part of a fire team.

Some days at Rucker I saw everyone else in black and white; only I was in Technicolor. Worse than usual, even, I felt apart from things and people—even other soldiers—and I wondered if anything would seem real until I got back out there and began doing again what I'd come to believe I was born to do. I didn't need more friends—more guys to worry about when the bullets flew.

Even the news I saw on television and read in the newspapers seemed distant. The coverage was of the war and the protests against it. I could see the correspondents twisting their coverage, because I'd been there, and I could see how they were making heroes of the antiwar protestors when they were actually costing more lives. I could see that, too, because I'd been there and knew how closely the enemy paid attention to and drew strength from the protests, which they knew about from Western newspapers and their own diplomats in Western countries. But this was America, and people had the right to protest. I didn't just disagree with them. I knew they were wrong. I knew what would happen if we lost—both to the Southeast Asians and to America.

✯ ✯ ✯

My orders arrived: South Korea.

Officially, I was to introduce the Kiowa to the Korean theater. These were tense days in the cold war, with a raft of incidents in and near the DMZ. Like the Russians trying to taunt us at the Czech border, the North Koreans were constantly intruding, probing for weaknesses in our perimeter defense and testing our resolve and readiness. My feeling was that our failure to protect the Czechs had emboldened them, as did the antiwar protests in America's streets, which after the killings of four Kent State students by National Guardsmen earlier that year (May 1970) were ratcheted up several notches. Kim Il Sung would've had sufficient reason to believe that the United States might not respond militarily to a concerted invasion of the south.

Unofficially—well, I wouldn't know till I got there. I strongly suspected that Korea was just a ruse for something else.

I took a commercial flight from San Francisco to Seoul, via Tokyo, and was assigned to 2nd Aviation Battalion, 2nd Infantry Division, up on the DMZ. My first day out there, I knew my suspicions had been right. They hadn't brought me all the way out here, covering my tracks at each step, just so that I could teach a couple of younger pilots how to fly the OH-58. For that, they could've gotten a zillion guys—guys who weren't battle-tested and gung ho, pleading to get back out there.

Sure enough, my services were soon given over to the Joint United States Military Advisory Group (JUSMAG) for Korea. It's a shadowy organization with octopus arms that belongs to a worldwide intelligence-gathering network—both aboveboard and below. And it was the kind of organization in which you knew you were supposed to listen, not talk, not even to the other people sharing your duties. We who'd gotten that far had gotten that far because we knew how to keep secrets without having to be told to keep them. We knew how to look at the other men we were working and dealing with without really looking at them—on a need-to-remember basis, our experiences and conversations akin to the *Mission: Impossible* tape-recorded message that self-destructed after delivery.

These were not finely honed units of young men who'd trained together and come to think of each other as a band of brothers, willing to die to save a brother's life. There would be no hanging out with your unit in the officers' club after a mission, no taking R&R together, no sharing news from home following mail call. No, these were unemotional, nothing-but-business, here's-your-assignment-hope-you-make-it-back missions whose military objective couldn't be easily discerned from the cockpit of the unmarked Cobra gunships we flew while dressed in jeans and T-shirts and vests instead of military flight suits. We weren't sent out specifically to engage enemy platoons and regiments. We were sent out to protect slicks either dropping off or picking up LRRP squads of Green Berets deep in the jungle, and if we'd ended up in a firefight, it meant things had gone horribly wrong. Nor could we ask permission to assist ground troops if we happened to fly by and see them being slaughtered in an ambush; that would've compromised the mission. The whole idea was to come and go unseen, and get the men in those slicks safely to their destination. One mission led to the next, which led to the next, all of them originating in Thailand.

Eight of us—pilots and copilots, crew chiefs, and gunners—would fly from Seoul to Bangkok on civilian airliners, because we didn't want that many military flights landing in Bangkok; and we'd wear civilian clothes for the same reason—so as not to attract attention. From Bangkok we'd get on a C-130 and fly east to an air base at either Utapau or Korat. Then other planes would carry us to an airfield in Vietnam, usually in the Pleiku area, where our Cobras would be waiting. The crew chiefs and gunners checked the gunships' airworthiness and weapons while the pilots got a last-minute briefing from the ops officer, who was no doubt the only person on the compound who knew more about our mission than we did. Every other soldier or pilot there would look at us suspiciously, knowing we were fighting the same war but by different rules. At dusk, only the four pilots in two Cobras took off—no crew chiefs or gunners necessary—and headed for prearranged coordinates in the jungles of the Central Highlands, holding to just above treetop level at 130 knots, using time and distance flown in the dark as our guide. Sometimes we'd be ordered to fly for fifteen minutes at a particular heading, then make a 150-degree turn, then turn again 330 degrees for exactly twenty-two minutes—to throw off any enemy forces watching us from the ground. Arrival time had to be just so. Within seconds after we got there, we'd see the slick ship and accompany it on its mission. When we returned to camp from the mission, the crew chief and gunner would check the Cobra while we sacked out in the hangar. Contact with anyone else outside of the team, except the ops officer, was impossible. Soon after first light, an Air Force C-130—no doubt flown by a pilot who knew only that he had to stop in Pleiku and pick up some guys and fly them to Thailand—would do just that. There was something very James Bond about the whole thing, but that didn't add to the excitement. Didn't take away from it, either.

I can't tell you who I was working for—I mean, *really* working for. I can't tell you not because I can't tell you but because I don't really know. Nor did I need to know, because it didn't matter. Following orders was what mattered. If you believed that each mission was part of a mosaic that wouldn't be complete until the war ended—and that the cockpit of a Cobra gunship was no place to pass judgment on overall strategy—then you believed that where orders came from was irrelevant. The Army? Maybe. The CIA? More likely. Everybody had heard of the Phoenix program (also

called Operation Phoenix), the Agency's plot to destroy the Vietcong by using small Special Forces teams to root out its infra-
structure through targeted assassinations—thousands of them.
Everyone on a fire base or LZ in 'Nam had seen unmarked choppers flown by pilots wearing civvies refuel and get the hell out of
there without talking to anyone, and we'd all assumed that these
shadowy guys were part of this shadowy plan—so we wished
them well. We were all on the same side.

$\star\star\star$ **57** $\star\star\star$

We reach the edge of a small LZ by about noon—or at least I assume this is where they want us. From our hiding place in the thick foliage it appears to be a clearing about thirty yards across and forty in length—the smallest of the possible LZs we've come across. I don't hear the chopper.

"Shit," Burdett says, "they wouldn't leave us out here another night, would they?"

They might, I say, because that would throw off the enemy, if he's around. Of course, if he's not around yet, waiting till the morning would give him time to get here. We're back to playing scissors-paper-rock—except that this time we don't have a say in the strategy. All we can do is wait. And hide.

For the first time, I'm nervous.

Both of us sit, Burdett with his eyes closed, listening hard. We figure that if the chopper doesn't show up by two, three at the latest, it won't come back—assuming it does, and we can't assume anything—till the morning.

"I want to get out of here," Burdett says.

"Me, too, Ron," I say.

But soon comes the *thwack-thwack* of the chopper. I grab both transmitters and press frantically, hoping that one or the other is still working. I stand and help Burdett to his feet. We stare across the LZ to the tops of the trees, waiting.

And there it is, like some beautiful bird. It's the first full view we've had of a chopper in the whole three weeks. It's a slick—but there's no gunship accompanying it to provide cover. There are probably a lot of reasons for that, the most important being that they didn't want the enemy to think they had any precious cargo, like Green Berets.

The chopper has locked on to our directional signal and is aiming straight for us. I have to stop myself from shrieking with joy and running out into the LZ and waving my vest. It passes and then pulls a one-eighty, passes again overhead—and begins to descend into the LZ.

"I can't believe what I'm seeing," Burdett says. "I thought it would never happen."

"We're going back to the world," I say. "Are you gonna be able to run? Where he's coming down, looks like we have about twenty-five yards to go."

"I'll try."

"Whatever happens, just keep moving."

I step around to his left and put my arm across his back, under his right armpit, and lift. He reaches his left arm across my back, resting it on my left shoulder.

"I'm a lot lighter now," he says, managing a smile.

"Nothing a couple Hershey bars and Paydays won't put back on."

Something occurs to me. I take Burdett's holster and, while he watches, strap it back on his arm, then put the revolver in it.

He whispers a thank-you.

It's time. The chopper's reached twenty feet.

We go, moving as fast as we can—which isn't fast enough. Burdett's leg isn't made for anything other than dragging, so that's what I let him do; I use all my strength to lift him, essentially making my right leg his left leg. His right leg hops to the rhythm.

Now comes a volley of rifle fire from the left edge of the meadow, probably an NVA squad that saw the helicopter's descent. I look over and see muzzle flashes and the smoke. I can't tell, but I think they're shooting at the chopper, not us—at least right now. That makes sense.

The chopper wouldn't dare pull up and leave, not with us out in the open. It reaches four feet and hovers, and a four-man squad with automatic weapons jumps out to return fire. One of the guys holds an M-60 and blasts the perimeter.

Fifteen yards to go.

"Come on, come on, come on," two of our guys yell. They come rushing toward us, firing at the NVA troops, while the other two stay just outside the chopper and don't let up the pressure.

Ten yards to go—a first down.

This is the most dangerous part for us. We're now in the line of fire.

Eight yards. One of our guys, about six-five, moves me away and throws Burdett over his shoulder, fireman-style, and pivots to run toward the helicopter.

"Come on, come on, come on," the other yells. He runs alongside me, between me and the perimeter, steadily firing his M-16 into the bush.

Five yards, four, three.

The soldiers crouch and keep firing. Burdett's guy gets him to the chopper door and launches him in. Then he turns and grabs for me just as I dive. He yanks me inside, making sure I get all the way. I roll over away from the door and lie next to Burdett. One by one the other three jump in, with firing from inside covering the last guy. He jumps in and off we go.

I grab Burdett's hand. He squeezes mine—and both of us start to cry.

"Gentlemen," the copilot says, turning around, "welcome back to the world. What kept you?"

By Duty Bound
Epilogue

The soldiers in the helicopter handed us canteens of water and kept throwing candy bars at us, one after another as we devoured them whole—the most delicious food we'd ever tasted. When we'd finally cleaned out their stash, we lay back and, holding hands, fell asleep; rather, we drifted in and out of consciousness, more out than in for the two-hour ride. One time I opened my eyes and caught the crew chief staring in horror at Burdett's leg, then fell back into oblivion. I came to as we landed at the MASH unit in Cam Ranh Bay, still holding Burdett's hand.

I squeezed it and said, "We made it, Captain. We did it."

He nodded, tears in his eyes, and tried to say something, but the emotion choked it off. All he could do was weep.

A moment later they came for us with stretchers and I let go. If I'd known that they were going to separate us, I'd have spent my last morsel of energy to lift my head from the stretcher and commit that moment to a photograph in my mind, so that I could pull it out whenever I wanted. Instead, it's now only an ordinary, fuzzy-edged recollection of bobbing on the stretcher. Nor do I remember being put to bed.

I apparently slept for two days and awoke with an IV in my

arm. A doctor told me I'd come through in pretty good shape. Aside from needing dental surgery, to correct the problems caused by malnourishment (I'd lost over thirty pounds), and maybe needing back surgery (it was too early to tell), I looked to be in remarkably good shape. Considering.

When the doc left, I got up and took my IV with me as I went to find Burdett, only to find that he'd been airlifted to Japan, where the hospitals were better equipped for the kind of major surgery he needed. And no, they told me, they didn't have any word on his condition. Nor would they.

I stopped and leaned against a nurse's desk and remembered everything—every moment of the three weeks and how it had or hadn't changed me and how it had or hadn't changed him. Funny, but the only really clear emotion I could manage was to feel sorry about his leg. I wondered if maybe we'd put the tourniquet on too soon; if maybe the leg could've been saved. Poor guy, I thought, he's going to have to relearn his whole life.

Soon after I got back to my bed the civvies-wearing intelligence officers, who were probably CIA, came in for the first time and began asking me questions about the jungle. I tried telling them the whole story, but they kept interrupting, asking me to clarify this and that, so I didn't get far. Then they came back the next day, and the day after that and the one after that, for nearly a week in all, to finish the debriefing. Actually, it was less a debriefing than an interrogation. All that was missing from the cliché was the bare lightbulb hanging above me. These guys were relentless, and relentlessly nasty. They weren't playing good cop/bad cop, either; they all but accused me of being an NVA or VC collaborator. How else could we have survived three weeks out there? they wanted to know. I realized they were only doing their jobs, but I couldn't help wondering what the purpose was. I tried telling myself that they were concerned I might be some sort of Manchurian Candidate, returned to the Army after a bout of enemy brainwashing, primed to wreak havoc at the appropriate moment. Burdett, I was certain, was going through the same thing—or would be when he regained his wits and energy.

In a few weeks I was sent back to Korea, my theoretical home base. I couldn't wait to climb into a helicopter cockpit, but it seemed the Army had little use for me now. They let me fly some meaningless missions near the DMZ, but compared to what I'd been through these had all the importance of Saturday afternoon errands. No wonder guys called them "ash and trash."

The brass let me know that my tour was up. Time to go back to the world. Didn't matter that I didn't want to go back. Didn't matter that I volunteered for a third tour, eager for another shot at the jungle. All that mattered was numbers. This was the end of 1971, and though the guys wearing the green uniforms and pulling the triggers didn't know it yet, the war had only another year to go. The big brass knew it, of course, and they were cutting back in preparation for bringing everyone home. In their eyes, I was obsolete—deadweight and expensive. First they promoted me to captain, which startled me a little. I hadn't expected it but I sure appreciated it (and believed, without confirmation, that Burdett might've had some hand in the matter). All that was left now on my climb up the general officer ladder was major, then lieutenant colonel, then colonel, then the prize. But my excitement was short-lived.

The Army let me—and thousands of other pilots and officers—know that they wouldn't mind terribly if we found new professions. The only officers they wanted to keep were those with college degrees. If I insisted on staying, I'd have to revert back to being a warrant officer. Revert? Not me. It meant getting further away from my dreams. After all this time, I didn't have any choice but to dream new ones. Crying about the old ones being broken would get me nowhere—at least nowhere I wanted to be.

It was February 1972 and I was thirty-one years old. I left Fort Campbell feeling more than a little anxious and uncertain, and drove straight to San Diego to visit my mother and sister for a few days. They hadn't even known that I'd gone missing for three weeks. Thank God for that.

Now what? For no other reason than instinct, I drove north— to where, I didn't know—to find a civilian job of some kind, something I hadn't done since joining the San Diego PD eight years before. I sped up old Route 99, through California's interior— desolate, barren landscapes that couldn't have looked more different from Vietnam. The contrast startled me, and it was hard not to attach some kind of cosmic significance to the images that life would never be the same. Still, I wouldn't let myself dwell on what I'd lost or what might have been. I'd met too many people who'd spent their todays lost in yesterdays.

After about eight hours of driving, I stopped for the night in Sacramento. In the morning, I exited the motel and spotted a Crocker Bank branch. Again, just on a whim, I walked in and inquired of the manager whether they were hiring. He asked what kind of experience I had. I told him, and the guy almost jumped out of his seat. He'd been charged with finding recruits for a management trainee program—especially "minorities." They hired me on to learn banking at a not very lucrative salary of $750 a month.

The job was interesting only because I was learning, and as always I enjoyed learning anything. But in reality, I was bored by the ordinariness of it—the lack of danger and intrigue; not having a specific mission. So I was in a receptive mood when a vet I knew encouraged me to join the California National Guard. He said I could make more money. More importantly, he said I could fly helicopters again. Most importantly, he said I could get my rank back—and from there, well, who knows?

"And they'll work around you," he said, "so you can still keep your bank job."

I checked out what he'd told me. He was right on all counts. I joined, got my old rank back, and put on a uniform again. It had only been a few months, but until I stood in front of the mirror, I didn't realize how much I'd missed being a military man. Actually, until then I hadn't *let* myself realize it.

Then I got back in the left seat of a helicopter and rose in the air. Ahhh! It was like one of those sharp intakes of breath that your body forces on you involuntarily when you've forgotten to breathe for some reason. I flew every mission I could, including some across the country.

Soon enough, my National Guard duties, including infantry officers' advanced training courses at Fort Benning in Georgia, began interfering with my Crocker Bank duties. I was asked by the bank to choose between the bank and the military, and I didn't have to think before answering. The Guard would now be my career.

Too bad nobody ever became a general just on airtime alone. Rising on the military ladder required that I move on to other military occupational specialties. For me, the rungs included being an equal opportunity officer; working to reintegrate guys who'd fled to Canada and been pardoned by President Carter; working with disadvantaged youth; and acting as a liaison counselor to gangs in Los Angeles. Right on schedule I made major, lieutenant colonel, and colonel.

A lot of guys—most, in fact—who reach colonel never make general officer. The distance between the two rungs is wider than the sum of all the ones before it. Your promotion packet has to be just so, with no room for anyone in the Department of the Army to send it back. It doesn't hurt to be part of the old boys' club, either. Actually, you almost have to be selected from a certain pool, and one of the ways you know you're in that pool is by being sent to attend the War College. Which I was. That didn't guarantee I'd make it, but I held out reasonable hope. My specialty had become military police, for which the highest position attainable in the California National Guard was brigadier general—a one-star. That was all right with me. I enjoyed my work and considered it an indispensable component of our national security. Many of my guys were sent to Iraq and Kuwait during the first Gulf War, in 1991. I tried to get myself assigned to combat duty, but the brass laughed at me; I'd just turned fifty.

In late April 1992, a Simi Valley jury acquitted four Los Angeles police officers of having beaten motorist Rodney King, and soon South-Central Los Angeles was going up in flames, with people beaten and killed and stores looted and destroyed. For a while it seemed that the violence would never end, and would eventually spill out of South-Central into the more affluent areas of the city. Among the LAPD and in the mayor's office, there was much talk about the riots possibly being engineered and controlled by L.A. street gangs. That's why I was sent from Sacramento to Los Angeles at the request of Mayor Tom Bradley, who'd become like a father to me during my years in Los Angeles leading a program intended to turn gang members into productive citizens. At the time, gangs were at the height of their viciousness and notoriety, with the vast majority of city murders committed by and against gangsters.

It was on the riot's last day of ultra-violence that a TV reporter pigeonholed me to ask my opinion on the gangs' role. Officially, I had no comment, but that didn't stop the pictures from ending up on national television.

Sometime that evening my adjutant told me I had an important call. A civilian. I said I was too busy; the only civilian I intended to speak with was Mayor Bradley or someone on his staff. He said that he himself had talked to the man and was convinced that I'd want to talk to him, too. Annoyed, I picked up the phone.

"Well, well," said the voice, which I recognized immediately. "You've done goddamn well for a poor boy on the other side of the tracks. I'm proud of you."

"Burdett?"

"Yeah."

"How'd you find me?"

"Wasn't easy, that's for sure"—pause—"Colonel."

"I'm glad you did, Captain."

"Colonel Ezell Ware, Jr. Damn, I like the sound of it. Good for you. Good for you."

I could feel myself choking up, and thought I could hear him do the same. He explained how he'd seen me on the tube back in West Virginia.

"I'm proud of you, EZ," he said. "Real proud. You know, I feel like a part of it."

"I've thought about you a million times over the years," I said. "How are you doing?"

"Oh," he said in a way that told me a lot. He didn't explain, though, so I didn't press him. We talked in generalities for a few minutes, but not about Vietnam. He mentioned his family, and I mentioned that I'd had a son, though we didn't live together. None of it seemed to be what either of us needed or wanted to talk about, and we both knew it. In fact, maybe there was nothing left to say about anything that we hadn't already said more than twenty years before. Small talk could only damage the intimacy we'd achieved then in circumstances entirely different than our present ones. Realizing that and hearing his voice made me strangely nostalgic for the miseries and privations we'd endured together—if only because that was the time in which I was most emotionally connected to another human being.

Then he said: "You gonna make general? No, never mind. Absolutely you are. They'd have to kill you to stop you. I know that."

"Thank you, Captain."

"I'd like to be there to see you get those stars on your shoulders."

"I'd like that, too," I said.

But Burdett wasn't there that day in 1998 when California's adjutant general promoted me to chief assistant adjutant general. He'd long since died of cancer. Still, in the euphoria of the day for which I'd waited nearly sixty years, thoughts of him kept sneaking in and out of my brain, always with gratitude. It was clear to me that I might not have been standing there were it not for our time together and the lessons we both learned in the jungle. Then, too, much of the country had taken its own path to learning most of those same lessons.

In the summer of 2004, having at last retired from the military life at the age of sixty-three, I decided to attend a reunion of the 61st. The guys in charge hold them annually during the Vietnam Helicopter Pilots Association convention. But this was, you may not be surprised to learn, the first one I'd ever been to. As soon as I walked into that Dallas hotel, I felt I was among old friends. Real friends. Friends who'd shared something powerful that could never be broken, not by time or distance. We laughed and joked and talked about the past and the future, recalling combat and remembering guys who hadn't made it back and those who'd later died of wounds or natural causes. I ended up speaking to most everyone, except for a couple of Southerners I remember not liking much because they'd already decided not to like me and my skin color.

As I was leaving to get my car, one of those guys timed it so that he could walk with me out of the hotel. I didn't know why and was wary until he said in his strong Georgia drawl, "I have to tell you something."

I stopped, and he stopped, and as he did tears filled his eyes, and then he wrapped his arms around me in a tight embrace, whispering in my ear, "I love you, EZ. I love you."

My own voice was trembling as I hugged him back and told him the truth: "I love you, too, buddy."

That'll be a hell of a story to tell Burdett when I finally see him again. Whether it's in heaven or hell, I know we'll end up on the same side.

ACKNOWLEDGMENTS

This book could not have been written without the generosity of relatives, military buddies, mentors, and friends. Their keen memory, timely photographs, and quick corrections greatly enhanced my recall of a magnificent journey. My many thanks to all of them. But first, I would like to acknowledge and thank my God for his many blessings and for allowing me to grow closer to Him with each passing day.

I am eternally thankful to Ma (Letha Kitchen), for being my inspiration and for her walks along those rocky roads in the country to acquire my necessary daily requirement of goat's milk; to Pa (John Kitchen), for teaching me that any work is honorable if it takes you where you desire to go; to my mother (Lorena) and father (Ezell Sr.), who never stopped loving me; to Aunt Lee (Leola McKinnis) and Uncle John McKinnis, who were my surrogate parents during the early years and who always told me that I was "smart enough to be anything" I wanted to be; to cousin Kaye McKinnis Lofton, who provided many of the childhood photos and who encouraged me to tell our Mississippi story; to my sister Dorothy and niece Adrena, who urged me to excel; to coach

Roscoe S. Pickett—my father figure, my mentor, and my friend; to the late Mr. Jake P. Magee, who saw my potential and encouraged me to reach for it; to the late James "Lolly" Brown, my dearest childhood friend, who challenged me to be as good academically as he was—though I never made it; to Johnny L. Lewis, who was the first high school classmate to recognize my athletic potential; to Walter McDonald, who was the first to teach me what *braver* looks like; to Sandi Hamilton, who always reminds me that God's on my side; to Annette Andrews McLaurin and my other high school classmates, for never giving up on me.

I would also like to acknowledge my flight school friends who helped me to make it through the challenging course, my 61ˢᵗ Assault Helicopter Company slick and gunship pilot, crew chief, and gunner friends . . . especially John McElhose, Charlie Hays, and Corky. They made Vietnam tolerable, if not fun.

Of course, it's my pleasure to acknowledge my wonderful editor, Doug Grad, for showing me what excellence and dedication look like in the literary world; and to my agent, John Talbot, for believing in me and my story from the beginning, and then doing what it took to make sure the story got out there.

I'd also like to acknowledge my friend Harve Bennett for encouraging me and insisting that my story be told.

Finally, I would like to acknowledge the one man without whom there would be no story—the man who endured the jungle with me. He, maybe more than any other, helped me realize exactly who I am.

ABOUT THE AUTHORS

Ezell Ware, Jr.

Ezell Ware, Jr., was born on February 6, 1941, and was raised by his mother's parents in Magee, Mississippi. Although Ezell spent four years as a Marine, he enlisted in the U.S. Army under the flight training program in 1966. He served with distinction as a pilot flying Hueys for the 61st Assault Helicopter Company; Skycranes with the 291st Aviation Company at Fort Sill, Oklahoma; Kiowas with the 2nd Aviation Battalion, 2nd Infantry Division in Korea, and Cobras on special assignment with JUSMAG (Joint United States Military Advisory Group). One year after leaving the active army in 1972, Ezell joined the California National Guard, where he remained for 30 years, and rose to the rank of Chief Assistant Adjutant General. Ezell is a graduate of the prestigious U.S. Air Force War College, the U.S. Army Command and General Staff College, and the U.S. Army Flight School, among many other military schools and courses. His military decorations include the Legion of Merit, thirteen Air Medals, three Meritorious Service medals, and an Army Commendation Medal with valor. An acknowledged fighter in all arenas of life, Ezell's

motto is: "Keep going until you get there, then keep on going."
Ezell is divorced and resides in Austin, Texas.

Joel Engel
A former journalist who wrote for both the *New York Times* and
Los Angles Times, Joel Engel is the author of more than a dozen
books. He lives with his wife and daughter in California.